THE SECRET LIFE OF THEATER

What is the secret DNA of theater? What makes it unique from its sister arts? Why was it invented? Why does it persist? And now, in such an advanced technological age, why do we still feel compelled to return to a mode of expression that was invented more than 2,000 years ago? These are some of the foundational questions that are asked in this study of theater from its inception to today.

The Secret Life of Theater begins with a look at theater's origins in Ancient Greece. Next, it moves on to examine the history and nature of theater, from *Agamemnon* to *Angels in America*, through theater's use of stage directions, revealing the many unspoken languages that are employed to communicate with its audiences. Finally, it looks at theater's ever-shifting strategies of engendering fellow-feeling through the use of emotion, allowing the form to become a rare space where one can feel a thought and think a feeling.

In an age when many studies are concerned with the "how" of theater, this work returns us to theater's essential "why." *The Secret Life of Theater* suggests that by reframing the question we can re-enchant this unique and ever-vital medium of expression.

Brian Kulick was the Artistic Director of Classic Stage Company and former Artistic Associate at the Public Theatre. He has staged the works of Shakespeare, Brecht, and Tony Kushner. He teaches theater directing at Columbia University's School of the Arts with Anne Bogart.

THE SECRET LIFE OF THEATER

On the Nature and Function
of Theatrical Representation

Brian Kulick

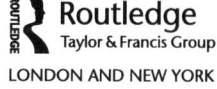

Routledge
Taylor & Francis Group

LONDON AND NEW YORK

First published 2019
by Routledge
2 Park Square, Milton Park, Abingdon, Oxon OX14 4RN

and by Routledge
52 Vanderbilt Avenue, New York, NY 10017

Routledge is an imprint of the Taylor & Francis Group, an informa business

© 2019 Brian Kulick

British Library Cataloguing-in-Publication Data
A catalogue record for this book is available from the British Library

Library of Congress Cataloging-in-Publication Data
Names: Kulick, Brian, author.
Title: The secret life of theater : on the nature and function
of theatrical representation / Brian Kulick.
Description: Abingdon, Oxon ; New York, NY : Routledge, 2019.
Identifiers: LCCN 2018036684 (print) | LCCN 2018049987 (ebook) |
ISBN 9780429445255 (Master) | ISBN 9780429817557 (Adobe Reader) |
ISBN 9780429817540 (ePub3) | ISBN 9780429817533 (Mobipocket Unencrypted) |
ISBN 9781138334588 (hardback :alk. paper) |
ISBN 9781138334601 (paperback :alk. paper) |
ISBN 9780429445255 (ebook) Subjects: LCSH: Theater.
Classification: LCC PN2037 (ebook) |
LCC PN2037 .K76 2019 (print) | DDC 792–dc23
LC record available at https://lccn.loc.gov/2018036684

ISBN: 978-1-138-33458-8 (hbk)
ISBN: 978-1-138-33460-1 (pbk)
ISBN: 978-0-429-44525-5 (ebk)

Typeset in Bembo
by Newgen Publishing UK

This book is dedicated to Anne Bogart who saved my aesthetic soul by inviting me to come teach at Columbia University's School of the Arts. What you hold in your hands is the fruit of a 16-year conversation with her remarkable students.

CONTENTS

ACKNOWLEDGMENTS

Writing this book, contrary to my naive understanding of such things, was far from a solitary affair. The work you hold in your hands is the beneficiary of a kind and gentle community of colleagues whose collective insights were invaluable to its slow and awkward development.

These guardian angels include Arnold Aronson, Anne Bogart, Nancy Keystone, Marike Splint, and Jonathan Vandenberg; all of whom braved early drafts of this book and lived to give me much-needed constructive feedback.

I am particularly indebted to Anna Brenner who came on board to wrangle my ever-wandering sentences and disappearing prepositions. Anna was also immensely helpful in her feedback on how to bring this book to its proper conclusion. I can't thank her enough for helping me find a way to put an end to this work.

I am also indebted to my editor Ben Piggott who has the great gift of saying that one simple thing that changes everything. This book would simply not be this book without three of those effortless epiphanies from Ben. I would also like to thank Laura Soppelsa, who kept everything on track and provided a continuity of encouragement when Ben was busy with other authors.

Finally, I would like to thank my wife Naomi and my son Noah who put up with countless dinners and family affairs where, by all accounts, I was there but not fully there due to the siren call of this book. I can't thank them enough for generously loaning me out to my fancies.

It is nice, now, to be fully back with them. Dorothy was right. There's no place like home.

In praise of not knowing

An introduction

1

WHAT WE CAN KNOW ABOUT THE ORIGINS OF THEATER, WHICH IS ALWAYS LESS THAN WE WOULD LIKE, AND YET NOT GROUNDS FOR DESPAIR

It just took one step and a shift in pronouns for drama to be invented. Or so legend would have us believe. Thespis, the world's first actor, stepped forth from the Greek Chorus, addressed himself as "I" instead of "he," and tragedy was born. Or, as Aristotle more prosaically tells us:

> After originating in the improvisations of the leaders of the dithyrambs, as comedy did in those days, tragedy gradually grew to maturity, as people developed the capacities they kept discovering in it, and after many changes it stopped altering since it had attained full growth.[1]

According to the Book of Yu, the origin of Chinese theater begins with an impulse by King Yu Shun of the Xia Dynasty. It was he who felt the need to help children grow to be "upright and gentle, generous and respectful, resolute but not abusive, succinct but not arrogant." The solution to such an education was *Yue*, which includes not only the performance of music, poetry, and dance but also incorporates "painting, engraving, architecture, rituals, hunting, expeditions, and feasts." Upon hearing this, his minister exclaimed, "Quick, let us play the instruments, and get the dance of a hundred animals started." This new found artistic expression kept the world in *dadang*, a harmonious state of affairs, free of famine, plague, and other natural disasters. Soon, according to the Book of Rites, other modes of expression arose. There was Zheng the disorderly; Song the licentious; Wei the reckless; and Qi the haughty. Such festive performances were initially frowned upon by the court for obvious reasons. It took Confucius to properly justify these new forms of expression. According to China's greatest sage, it is important to understand the significance of having one day of festivity after a whole year of hard work.

> String the bow and never release it, the sage kings Wen and Wu could not;
> release the bow and never string it, the sage kings Wen and Wu would not.
> String and release the bow in turn, that is the Way of sage kings Wen and Wu.[2]

Perhaps the most fantastical origin story of theater hails from India. It is found in *Natya Sastra* of Bharata. This is India's very own, unique and prodigious manual of poetics.

Bharata tells us the great god Brahma composed the fifth Veda, which incorporated all the arts and sciences. At first, he believed that it could only be carried out by the gods, but Indra convinced Brahma that the gods did not have the qualifications necessary to carry out the rigors of this new form of expression. Indra suggested that the theater should fall to the sages since they grasped the Vedic knowledge and had self-control. This lead Brahma to approach the sage Bharata, telling him:

> I have created Natyaveda to show you good and bad actions and feelings of both the gods and yourselves. It is the representation of (the ways of) the entire three worlds. Now dharma, now Aretha, now Kana, humor or fights, greed or killing, right for the people going wrong; enjoyment for those who are pleasure seekers; restraint of the ill behaved or tolerance for the well behaved.[3]

Having outlined the purposes of this new form of expression, Brahma informs Bharata that since, "You have a large number of sons, so take up the practice of Natyaveda." And with that simple injunction Bharata turns his full attentions to all things theatrical, telling us, "So I practiced it with my sons, assigning to each a fitting role, telling them where to stand and how to move and training them in words, emotions, movements."

In many ways these theatrical anecdotes tell us more about each culture than the actual origin of theater. We can already see the West's unwavering belief in the future perfectibility of things through Aristotle's account of tragedy's unhindered development; just as we can see the East's innate sense of balance found in Confucius' sublime allegory of the bow; and India's penchant for the prodigious proliferation of gods, Vedas, and philosophical categories. But in terms of giving us an accurate genealogy of theater, the actual origins of theater remain cloaked in mystery. We must make do, especially in terms of the West, with the fact that theater is a broken tradition. The East learns, rather quickly, the necessity of preserving its aesthetic traditions. The West, on the other hand, is much more negligent, absent-minded, losing traditions almost as quickly as they are forged, leaving great swaths of historical time between their invention, dereliction, and attempted resurrection. The mixing of certain pigments, or the understanding of particular musical notation are forever lost to the West. This is our legacy, a history of lost traditions, of ruins, of fragments. For many this is the cause of deep sadness. Who cannot think of the burning of the Library of Alexandria without a vestigial twinge of regret? And yet these losses that have resulted in our not-knowing have also been the secret catalyst to Western art, contributing to its fundamental difference with the grand traditions of the East. The West, in its pursuit to resurrect the long lost past, is constantly, inadvertently, creating a new future.

We see this dynamic at work with the West's first attempt in the sixteenth century to recreate what Greek theater might have been. It is intriguing to note such artists as Angelo Poliziano, Claudio Monteverdi, Jacopo Peri, and Giulio Caccini all chose the story of Orpheus as the subject matter of their first respective works. Like Orpheus, they were compelled to brave the underworld of oblivion to bring back a Eurydice whose very name became a symbol for the vanished art of the Greeks. What was supposed to be a recreation became a splendid new invention: Italian opera. One could argue that many of our greatest theater movements began as attempts at such recreation. For the West, the Ancient Greeks have become the perfect prompt, ever-tempting us to rediscover them, but ultimately allowing us to inadvertently discover ourselves in the process.

What is true of the Greeks is also true of Shakespeare. Of course, we know much more about Shakespeare's time, but still not enough for a truly faithful rendition. We know the actual scale of the Globe, but not the scale of the acting that filled it. Did it hold a mirror up to nature? Or were actors inclined to tear a passion that out-Herods Herod? How did they speak a line of verse? Trippingly on the tongue or taking a half breath between each verse line? These are things that we will never know, no matter how hard we try. For it is another broken tradition. Gone. Vanished forever. Leaving each generation with a challenge to return to Shakespeare and his theatrical world and to try to reimagine it; each generation has to figure this out for themselves; rediscover what Shakespeare is to them. This means, with each new generation, we get a new Shakespeare. It is foolish to think that we can know exactly how Shakespeare was actually performed. We'll never really know, but that not knowing keeps us searching. It keeps our understanding dynamic rather than static. Classics remain classics when they are in conversation with futures they never anticipated. Such works shed and accrue meaning as they continue to move through time.

Notes

1 Aristotle, *On Poetics*, translated by M.E. Hubbard, in *Ancient Literary Criticism The Principle Texts in New Translations*, edited by D.A. Russell and M. Winterbottom (Oxford University Press, 1972), 95.
2 Faye Chunfang Fei, *Chinese Theories of Theatre and Performance: From Confucius to the Present* (University of Michigan Press, 2002), 3–5.
3 Adya Ranacharya, *The Natya Sastra* (Munshiram Manoharlal Publishers, 1996), 4.

2

HOW GREAT WORKS WORK AGAINST OUR DESIRE TO KNOW, AND WHY THE QUESTION SHOULD ALWAYS EXCEED THE ANSWER

What makes one work timely and another timeless? Here we are at the heart of mystery of great works: why this strange need for us to return to certain key plays over and over, and not others? Perhaps part of the reason lies in the questions that these works ask of us. Questions that are impossible to fully answer. Questions like the one that begins Shakespeare's *Hamlet*: "Who's there?" This simple interrogative haunts every scene of Shakespeare's play. Who is the ghost? Who is Claudius? Who is my mother? My friend? My lover? And perhaps the biggest mystery of all: Who is Hamlet? How can we ultimately know him? He and his play remain a secret, like the cause behind the smile of the Mona Lisa. There is something fundamentally unknowable about both. Hamlet guards his mystery tenaciously, look at the moment deep in Act III where he taunts his friend Guildenstern, encouraging him to make music from a simple pipe. Guildenstern demurs, he does not "know the stops." This elicits the following famous attack from Hamlet:

> Why look you now how unworthy a thing you make of me: you would play upon me! You would seem to know my stops, you would pluck out the heart of my mystery, you would sound me from my lowest note to my compass; and there is much music, excellent voice, in this little organ. Yet cannot you make it speak. 'Sblood! Do you think I am easier to be played on than a pipe? Call me what instrument you will, though you fret me, you cannot play upon me.[1]

This reprimand of Hamlet, could be the credo of every great work. The greater the work, the greater its mystery. These enormous unanswered questions—as sounded by Shakespeare, or the Greeks, or Chekhov—strike at the very unknowability of being, provoking each generation to return to these works anew, confronting them on their own terms, from their own historical vantage point. The question circles back to us, like Nietzsche's curse of the eternal return. The play's essential query remains the same, but the answer shifts with the passage of time. In this respect, it reminds us of that other infamous philosophic metaphor: Heraclitus' river. The question of a given play may be eternal, but our answer is always changing, subject to the flow of time. As a result, theater and the questions it poses exist at the intersection between Nietzsche's curse and Heraclitus' river.

Note

1 William Shakespeare, *Hamlet*, edited by Anne Thompson and Neil Taylor (Arden Shakespeare, Third Edition, 2006), 322–323 (III.3).

3

THE PROBLEM WITH THINKING WE KNOW A THING OR TWO: OR THE RISE OF THE ANSWER AT THE EXPENSE OF THE QUESTION

Recently, as a theatrical culture, we have grown quite comfortable with a certain set of answers. This, it seems, has been at the expense of many of the great questions that provoked past generations to keep searching. These days the only questions that remain vital for us are ones of utility. We have book after book on the "how" or "when" of theater, rather than on the "why" or "what." We think that if we know how to deploy an action or that *Hamlet* was written in 1599, this will somehow be enough. Gone are the questions like: what is theater, how does it work, why did we create it and why, in this advanced technological age, do we still need it? These are the questions we, as theater practitioners, may ask when we are young; but, often the demands of just "making" theater override these larger philosophical concerns and we find ourselves very quickly turning our full attention toward something a little more manageable, like a better understanding of craft. The wonderful thing about craft is that it is tangible and, when properly tended to, it can yield immediate, discernible results. And so, our theatrical "product" may indeed be better wrought, but at the expense of a certain depth and majesty. The "gift" of our contemporary theater is exquisitely wrapped, *but often empty*.

The beauty of theater is that when you begin to really think about it, it is a rather odd human endeavor. Why do we feel compelled to gather as a group, all facing in the same direction to watch another group of people enacting a fiction? And how is this experiencing different from the experiencing of real people doing real things? Why do we need to view things that pretend to be like real things? Why aren't we content with just the real? And why do we need to *see* these stories? Why wasn't hearing about them, around a fire, enough? Is this transformation in representation merely illustrative? Or does something else happen to us when we shift and reprioritize our senses from listening to looking? Why does such a practice become more real than our reality, even when certain attempts at the illusion of reality are so terribly flimsy? What does it mean that we are so easily captivated?

And why, in these moments of captivation, do we sometimes find water coming from our eyes, or a loud, sharp sound emanating from our mouths? And even more mysteriously, why is this happening to the eyes and mouths of the people sitting next to us? And, perhaps most mysterious of all, why do we like being with all these fellow wet-eyed, barking people?

The tragedy of tragedy is that we now take this strange and complex phenomenon for granted. We are incurious as to what might be happening to our consciousness as we move from our real world to the world of theatrical illusion. Gone is a hunger for the theories behind theater, replaced by recipes for realism. And yet, we wonder why our theater feels somewhat anemic when placed alongside the work of previous generations. We think it is an issue of the kinds of stories we are telling or not telling, the loss of a certain degree of craft, or the lack of true talent. Perhaps what is really at issue is our lack of understanding when it comes to how theater goes about its secret work. Maybe an attempt to return to questioning the mysterious dynamics of theatrical expression might help pave the way for a more robust form of theatrical representation. That is the wager of this little book.

4

THE SPECIAL PROVIDENCE
OF CERTAIN QUESTIONS:
OR THE NECESSITY FOR THE
RE-ENCHANTMENT OF THEATER

I find that these questions, which so preoccupied my youthful dreams about theater, have returned as I now near the tail-end of my theater-making days. The answers are no closer than when I started out, but the sudden need to address them has somehow become louder and more insistent.

This project was written in fits and starts over the past several years between productions and teaching. Part I, deals with what I call "The invention of the outside." The "outside" being a metaphor for theater and the experience it engenders at certain key moments in the unfolding of a performance. It is an attempt to understand how theater goes about its secret business of engaging and changing us by creating a hyper-intentional space where the audience can move from its default position of passive looking/listening to the more active engagement of seeing/hearing. It uses Borges' extraordinary story, *Averroes' Search*, as its point of departure. In this marvelous tale, we spend a day with the great Islamic philosopher Averroes as he attempts to translate Aristotle's *Poetics*, a task made all the more difficult since Averroes' world has not yet discovered theater as a form of expression. This conundrum leads to an intriguing question: how would one attempt to explain the practice of theater to a person who has no concept or experience whatsoever with this unique medium? What would one say? How would one go about describing its function and meaning? In doing so, Borges, the master of fiction, has some intriguing things to tell us about the nature of the theatrical endeavor.

Having discussed the basic working components of the "theatrical machine," Part II ("Nine and a half tableaux") examines how theater makes certain phenomena manifest in a way that is unique when compared to its sister arts. It uses the history of stage directions, moving chronologically from Aeschylus' *Agamemnon* all the way to Tony Kushner's *Angels in America*, to tell us about theater's unique ability to bring forth certain ineffables like a person's secret motivations, time, space, being, nothingness, the secret life of objects, the symbolic tendencies of the world at large, other minds, the uncanny, and reality's proclivity toward duality. These subjects are usually thought of as the singular domain of philosophy, but they are also very much the special province of theater. Perhaps philosophy's longstanding ambivalence toward theater stems from this intriguing overlap of concerns. Be that as it may, the focus here is on theater's power to bring certain unseen workings of existence to the very foreground of our perception.

The third and final part of the book, "From Sophocles' urn to Wittgenstein's box," turns its attention to the other key component and endpoint of the theatrical equation: the audience. It looks at how the machine of theater and its manifestation of certain ineffables are all geared toward moving the hearts and minds of the audience toward a crucial sense of "fellow-feeling." Here we move from its origins in the Greek concept of pity, through the long reign of sympathy, to our current penchant for empathy. Such an investigation reminds us that these words are not necessarily synonyms for one another; but rather very specific, historically constructed responses to the necessity of feeling for others. In this genealogy, we are also reminded that the tears a twenty-first-century New Yorker sheds for Antigone are not necessarily the same as the ones that initially streamed down the face of a fifth-century Athenian. Both cry, but for rather different reasons. The focus here is on elucidating these fundamental, historically determined differences. Finally, the chapter questions what type of fellow-feeling might be best suited to this already bewildering twenty-first century, a question that is tied to the very future of theater itself.

Having worked on these questions over the past several years, I have grown to respect their fundamental mystery. As I said earlier, the greatest tragedy of tragedy, or theater in general, is that we now take its very process for granted. My hope, in writing the following, has been not so much to answer these questions of theater in a definitive fashion (an impossibility if ever there was one), but rather to present answers that might also restore some the mystery that engendered these quandaries in the first place.

As I come to the end of this introduction I find myself once again thinking of theater's favorite son, Hamlet. He, and the play that bears his name, have become synonymous with theater. And why not? What better figure to represent the theater? Is there another dramatic personage who loved the medium more? And so Hamlet and theater fuse in my imagination. His mystery becomes emblematic of theater's mystery. Both are ultimately impenetrable. We try to make sense of Hamlet and what he has ultimately learned. All Hamlet will tell us of his end is, "the rest is silence"—a sentiment that the philosopher Wittgenstein echoes in his *Tractatus Logico-Philosophicus*, warning: "Whereof one cannot speak, thereof, one must remain silent."[1] But following such pronouncements, even when they come from the likes of Hamlet or Wittgenstein, is just not possible for many of us lesser mortals. We refuse to listen and cannot help but attempt an answer to certain elusive questions. We do this with the full knowledge that our answer, like the ones that proceeded us, are provisional; a subject of our time, and therefore, all are bound to fall short.

But each attempt adds another layer of resonance to the question, beckoning future generations to follow suit, expanding the question's potential to mean even more. Explication becomes a kind of reincarnation, allowing certain questions to live many lives.

Note

1 Ludwig Wittgenstein, *Tractatus Logico-Philosophicus*, translated by C.K. Ogden (Routledge, 1990), 189.

PART I
The invention of the outside
On the nature and functions of theater

5

BORGES AND THEATER

What the great Argentine poet can tell us about the secret life of theater

I realize that to associate Borges with theater might strike both those who know Borges and those who know theater as something of a misnomer, since neither the poet or the medium seem to have had very much to do with one another. The great twentieth-century Argentine author is known for his poetry, short stories, and essays, rather than any overt interest in the theatrical. During his youth, you would have been more likely to find him at his local cinema than attending a performance at some threadbare theater. We can read a treasure trove of insightful and enthusiastic critiques that Borges wrote on the movies of his day; but with the exception of a handful of random musings on Shakespeare and one intriguing short story, Borges seems to display little passion or even passing interest in the stage. And yet, it is this one story, often translated as *Averroes' Search*,[1] where in seven short pages he is able to get to the very heart of the strange nature and functions of the theatrical enterprise. For this reason we will use Borges and his amazing story for our guides as we attempt to understand the inner dynamics of this ancient practice we call theater.

Averroes' Search has its roots in actual history and concerns the great medieval Islamic philosopher Abulgualid Mohammed Ibn-Ahmed Ibn-Mohammed Ibn-Rushed (who the West, with its impatience for the grandeur of Islamic patronymics, has hastily dubbed Averroes). Borges' story finds Averroes in his library composing his famous translation of Aristotle's *Poetics*. All had been going splendidly, until he comes to two dubious little words that are beyond his comprehension: tragedy and comedy. The reason behind Averroes' quandary is due to the simple fact that Islam has not yet discovered the art of theater-making. This will not happen for several more centuries; long after Averroes' initial wrestling with the meaning of tragedy and comedy. The first stirrings of Islamic dramatic imagination will arrive with the advent of Ta'ziyeh—a kind of passion play first performed by Shiite Muslims in Iran. Ta'ziyeh literally means "to mourn" or "to console" and grew out of the ritual observances that surrounded the historic sacrifice of Hussein, the grandson of the Prophet Muhammad.

But, as we said, the advent of such theatrical practice is still centuries away and Borges' Averroes is at his wits' end to make sense of these impenetrable terms. We will follow Averroes over the course of the day as he struggles to define these two simple words. Throughout the next 24 hours, fate (or rather, Borges in the guise of our omnipotent narrator) will place before Averroes a sequence of clues that, were the philosopher to take note of them, would help him to unlock the mystery of Aristotle's nomenclature. The painful irony of our story is, given Averroes' historic circumstances, he is incapable of comprehending what we can so clearly see. This forms part of Borges' larger epistemological argument, which we will politely bypass to focus specifically on his clues and what they can tell us about the nature and functions of theatrical expression.

Note

1 Jorges Luis Borges, *Collected Fiction*, translated by Andrew Hurley (Viking Press, 1998), 235–242.

6

BENEATH AVERROES' WINDOW

Borges' first clue; the family resemblance of play, ritual, and theater

As Averroes is hard at work trying to decipher the meaning of tragedy and comedy, his mind and eye wander toward the window of his library where he sees in the courtyard several children at play. One is pretending to be a muezzin and chanting, "There is no God but the God." The second, unfortunate, child is hard at work playing the minaret, which is responsible for holding the muezzin aloft in the air. The final player kneels in the dust like a faithful worshipper. The entire affair does not last long since all want to play the muezzin and none the tower or the congregation.

Here we have one of the most popular assumptions about the origin of theater, that it somehow grows out of the human impulse to play. It is intriguing that of all the games these young children could choose to partake in, they gravitate toward a rather esoteric activity for their collective flight of fancy. It is not exactly what one would expect to be among the top scenarios in their imaginative arsenal. One might think of other more popular moments of make-believe, beginning with, let's say, a fight to the death with sticks as scimitars, or perhaps the releasing of a jinn from a neglected lamp, or even that age old favorite, the abduction of a girl from the Sultan's seraglio. No, wonderfully, these youths want to re-enact a variation of the Islamic call to prayer.

The choice of game points to an essential part of Borges' art. Like dreams, Borges enjoys trafficking in a kind of literary condensation, the nesting of images one inside another. It is this nesting that leads to Borges' often vertigo-inducing meaning. Think of this as the narrative equivalent of the game of Russian dolls: here we have the doll of children's play, which contains the doll of ritual, which contains the intimation of the doll of theater. Each concept/image is housed neatly within the other. It is not such a huge leap to move from the idea of children at play, to a community enacting a rite, to an audience assembled before a proscenium arch in anticipation of an impending show. The nesting of images quietly provokes us to ask what similarities, if any, bring these three human activities under the same tent of signification. Let us begin then, with the first "doll."

Play: a fundamental form of human expenditure

Johan Huizinga, one of the first historians to focus on play and the author of the seminal *Homo Ludens*, wryly notes that the one common denominator that runs throughout all theories of play is that "play must serve something that is not play."[1] Roger Caillois, another major thinker on the subject and author of the equally influential *Man, Play and Games* agrees but points out:

> A characteristic of play, in fact, is that it creates no wealth or goods, thus differing from the work of art. At the end of the game, all can start over again at the same point. Nothing has been harvested or manufactured, no masterpiece has been created, no capital has been secured.[2]

He provocatively concludes that play is pure waste—a waste of time, energy, ingenuity, skill. But it would seem that there is something sublime and necessary about this particular form of human expenditure that can be found in all cultures around the world. Play seems to address the excess or surplus energy that is bound up in the human condition, as well as its desire for release. Huizinga gives play the following working definition:

> Summing up the formal characteristics of play we might call it a free activity standing quite outside "ordinary" life as being "not serious", but at the same time absorbing the player intensely and utterly. It is an activity connected with no material interest, and no profit can be gained from it. It proceeds within its own proper boundaries of time and space according to fixed rules and an orderly manner.[3]

The first element to note in Huizinga's concept of play is that it is outside of ordinary life. Play begins with a re-restructuring of time and space; removing us from our familiar quotidian moorings, marking out a territory that separates us from the everyday. This new space can be a chess board, a field, an abandoned lot, or any old patch of pavement marked out by chalk; there is an infinite variety of ways to delineate the space of play. Having done so, the world of immediate wants and appetites recedes, becoming "the outside" of our experience. We are now left to our own imaginary impulses and interests. This shift in space allows for a shift in focus that impacts on our sense of time. The regular flow of time is altered, creating an interlude or intermezzo of sorts. "Clock time" dissolves into "felt time." Now any given moment can expand or contract in ways that defy our ordinary sense of duration. Time itself can become timeless.

Play flourishes within these new spatial-temporal boundaries. Caillois tells us that there are four fundamental categories of human play: agon (which pits one players strength/skill against another); alea, (where chance is a major factor in the outcome of the game); illynix (when the player is rendered unbalanced or incapacitated and then expected to accomplish a given task); and finally mimesis (which is what Borges' children are engaged in beneath Averroes' window). All other types of games, according to Caillois, are re-combinations of these four elemental building blocks of play. For example, when we combine agon with alea we have the dynamics of many card and board games, which require both skill and luck to succeed. Our immediate interest is in the category of mimesis, which, as Borges intimates, feels like the great progenitor of things theatrical. Here the subject makes believe or makes others believe that he is someone other than himself. He forgets, disguises, or temporarily sheds his personality in order to experience the world from another vantage point.

Let us return momentarily to the courtyard beneath Averroes' window where Borges' children are still deep in play. Let's take the child who fancies himself the muezzin. What is happening to him in this moment of mimesis? He always wanted to be a muezzin. To become the one who stops everything with his powerful voice, calling the faithful to prayer. As a child, no one ever listens to him but at this moment, in his imagination, the entire world hears and obeys him. He's memorized all the words, the inflections, the almost sung/almost spoken melodies, it is all there on display in his impeccable performance. He sings out, full voice, the sound filling the courtyard and ascending toward the heavens. As his voice ascends, so does he. For this brief instant, the boy that no one listens to, the boy who is always shushed, the boy who must always wait his turn—that boy has vanished and he has become the muezzin! But then his fellow playmate, who is impersonating the minaret, loses his footing and our momentary muezzin falls tumbling back into that neglected little boy again.

Huizinga calls this, "The 'extra-ordinary' nature of play as it reaches perfection. The disguised or masked individual 'plays' another part, another being. He IS another being."[4] And so, in the play of mimesis, we find not only time and space shifting, but our very selves as well. Dormant aspects of ourselves or entire new selves can be realized within these new found boundaries. This also has an important social component, for as the self changes, so do the others around it, giving each player a sense of a new horizon of social interaction and potential collaboration. Such interaction engenders the possibility for a new and more cohesive sense of communitas. What Caillois provocatively calls "waste" might actually be the space for the ever-incremental reinvention of the self and re-enchantment of the world. Not that the child or world are instantaneously and irrevocably refigured by play, but some residue of the play-self and play-world follow the child back into real world. The child, according to Huizinga, returns with an image of something different from the known world, "something more beautiful, or more sublime, or more dangerous than what actually is."[5] This brings us to the border between play and ritual.

Ritual: that uniquely human endeavor

We will designate ritual as that which encompasses all the circumstances necessary for an encounter with the "numinous" or "sacred." The mysterious reality that is of a wholly different order than our everyday world. Here the religiously inclined person finds certain key intervals of the day, week, month, and year to leave the profane world aside and return to an alternative sacred reality. This is accomplished through a series of stylized and symbolic repetitions of body (kneeling, dancing, etc.), voice (song/chant) and mind (internalized prayer and meditation). For instance, the children playing in Borges' first clue are attempting to enact Salat, the Muslim ritual for daily prayer. This act not only depends on an exact sense of timing and directional orientation, but also an equally structured repetition of body actions that includes standing, kneeling, prostrating, and standing again while reciting an intricately inflected prayer from memory.

All of this begins, like play, with the marking off of a consecrated spot that separates the now sacred space from the otherwise profane world. Huizinga notes that from an objective point of view, it is difficult to distinguish the formal differences from playground to sacred ground. Both, according to Huizinga, are temporary worlds dedicated to the performance of an act apart.

With this shift in space comes another shift in time. But the nature of this temporal shift is different from the one experienced during play. Play celebrates the infinity of next; ritual, the forever of now. What we have here are two forms of timelessness with a significantly different emphasis. Thanks to ritual's formalized use of repetition we are able to reverse Heraclitus' famous dictum and feel as though we can always step back into the same flowing river of the spirit. Ritual practice creates a cathedral made out of time—one that the believer can return to over and over again with a simple set of symbolically endowed repetitions of his or her body, voice and mind.

Within this consecrated spatial-temporal world we find a multitude of ritual activities. Anthropologist Antony F.C. Wallace[6] attempts to break these seemingly infinite activities into five basic categories: technological rituals aimed at controlling non-human nature (food supply, rain); therapy rites (curing the injured, exorcizing the possessed); ideology rituals used to shape a group and its values (rites of passage, or even "Sunday Services" that renew social solidarity); salvation rituals to help people cope with personal adversity (shamanic rites, mystic rites, and expiation rites); and last, and perhaps most intriguingly, revitalization rituals created to aide a crisis in society, such as millenarian movements. The ritual participants must submit themselves to these deeper understandings that were discovered by their ancestors. In the process of doing so, they "re-center" themselves, allowing their personal will to be absorbed by divine will. Such a process reconnects the ritual participant with the transcendent, a way of experiencing the reality that is otherwise occluded by the hustle and bustle of the everyday profane world.

Let us imagine for a moment that the boy who has been playing beneath Averroes' window, the one who wants to be a muezzin, has indeed grown up to obtain such a prestigious post. Now he sits atop a real minaret and calls the city to prayer. Today he has been fighting a cold, his voice is not what it should be, but what can he do? A part of him wishes he were still in bed. He kneels down, just as he has knelt ever since he was a child. He places his head to the tip of the prayer mat, just as his father and his father's father had done. He intones the words, "Allah Akbar," just as his son has just learnt and will someday teach his sons. Suddenly he feels the strange sensation of being part of an unending continuum, the thought of which brings sudden tears to his unprepared eyes. He continues the prayer, the words are so simple and yet when placed in this particular order they seem to mean more, to reverberate deep within his chest, as though a long extinguished lamp was suddenly relit, its illumination spreading throughout his body.

Huizinga explains this dynamic in the following fashion:

> Something invisible, an in-actual takes beautiful actual, holy form. The participants of these rites are convinced that their action actualizes and effects this definite beautification. It brings about an order of things higher than that in which they customarily live.[7]

He calls this "actualization by representation" and believes that this phenomenon retains the formal characteristics of play. Caillois almost agrees with Huizinga, taking pains to point out: "The sacred and play resemble each other to the degree that they are both opposed to the practical life, but they occupy symmetrical situations in regards to it." He goes onto explain:

> Through the sacred, the source of omnipotence, the worshiper is fulfilled. Confronted by the sacred, he is defenseless, completely at its mercy. In play, the opposite is the case. All is human, invented by man the creator. For this reason, play rests, relaxes, distracts, and causes the dangers, cares, and travails of life to be forgotten. The sacred, on the contrary, is the domain of internal tension, from which it is precisely profane existence that relaxes, rests and distracts.[8]

In other words, the situation is reversed. For Caillois, the nature of ritual and play are not so much the same as they are symmetrically opposite. So to, to a certain extent is theater.

Theater: the invention of the outside

Theater, like ritual and play, also stakes out its own spatial-temporal boundary; within this boundary, the player or ritualist becomes an actor who embodies a character within a story. This "embodiment" has many of the aspects found in mimetic play and the dramatic story that unfolds often borrows its form and content from ritual practices.

These stories, like ritual, rely on a repertory of structural repetitions that shape the nature of the event; informing how it will begin, develop, and resolve itself.

Within these often highly regimented performative arcs, we find the return of certain set devices. We can see this tendency toward formalization in early Greek theater, which deploys the same set of performative tactics from play to play and author to author. Every play must have a prologue, followed by a chorus, followed by five episodes (scenes) with each episode separated by another chorus. Each of the five episodes are built around one of a set of established modes of expression, such as: an *agon logon* (a battle of wits), a *rhesis* (an intricate story that has happened offstage), a *kommos* (an extended solo lamentation), and so on. All of these recognizable set elements are arranged, like a rite or ceremony, to bring the story to a very specific conclusion that these authors designate as tragic.

Not only are there structural similarities between a theater piece and a rite but both often overlap in thematic concerns. We can see, for example, that many of the ritualized themes found in early pagan rites migrate into the medieval conception of carnival and ultimately find their way into the repertory of the commedia dell'arte during the Renaissance. And so, the tangled courtship of two young lovers mirrors earlier initiation rites; the cuckolding of an older authority figure by a younger man recalls the trajectory of certain fertility rituals where the corn-king is supplanted by a younger surrogate; and perhaps most famously, the servant becoming master and the master becoming servant harkens back to carnival's penchant for the topsy-turvy, where all hierarchies are overturned for a day and the fool becomes king.

What we are experiencing in these developments from play to rite to theater is what Caillois calls the movement from Paidia to Ludus. Caillois imagines a continuum where on one side there is Paidia, a term he uses to designate the primary power of imagination and joy that is at the beginning of all play. It is a spontaneous eruption of the play-instinct in all its carefree and uncontrolled exuberance. At the opposite extreme is Ludus, which Caillois sees as the refinement of Paidia. Ludus will discipline and enrich the impulse of Paidia. It will provide training and lead to the acquisition and mastery of special skills. And so, the free form game becomes a specialized sport. Or, as we have seen in the above examples, the early choral festivals of Greece or the carnivals of Europe give way to the more structured expressions of Greek theater and commedia.

This incremental development happens within these spaces that were first marked out for play and ritual. Thanks to these initial demarcations and this movement from Paidia to Ludus, we can begin to imagine how theater could, ever so slowly, emerge. But perhaps, in many ways, the most important foundational gesture was in that original spatial-temporal differentiation that divided the world into a space for play and a space that was forever outside of it. What is being discovered here is an imaginal interior/exterior of experience as a opposed to the concrete inside/outside dialectic of actual space. Play and ritual begin with what happens inside this demarcated imaginal space. But what about those on the other side of this newly delineated outside? Those who are too young, or old, or unfit, or simply "other" and therefore kept from the immediacy of the game or rite? As games and rituals become more and more complex, those who were once "inside" the event now find themselves joining these others who have been "cast out." What once was open to all, becomes the domain of a select few. It is they who remain "inside" the event while the rest are exiled from the Eden-like garden of immediate experience. It is at this point that we see the rise of athletes, priests, and actors. The rest become a new entity called the spectator. Theater begins with the advent of being thrust outside, when one shifts from actor to audience. The distance between the two opens up a new relation.

Play and ritual will always remain inside the realm of immediate experience, they will always be about the first-ness of an experience, what happens directly to and through the "I" of the player or ritualist as they play or pray. Theater (when it moves beyond the world of the actor) begins from the experience of being outside the event, the "I" is experiencing things once removed, through the watching of a "you." It is what we could call a second-degree experience. What exactly does this feel like?

Let us return, one last time, to the children playing in the courtyard beneath Averroes' window. Let's put that courtyard on stage. The children are now actors and we are their audience. At first we might watch them with a degree of detachment, they seem well-intentioned but what they are doing is of little interest to us. There are so many other pressing things on our minds, there's the laundry to do and the dinner to make and don't forget to pick up that cake from the bakery. It is hard to free your mind of these things but you begin to warm to the children on stage, they are actually rather endearing. There is something about the one that wants to be a muezzin that wins you over, something in his zealousness that brings a smile to your face and his song, well, it is actually quite beautiful in its slightly off-pitch, childlike way. The melody enters you and suddenly the boy's yearning rhymes with some vestige of your own forgotten aspirations. But wait, what's this? The other boy, who is playing the minaret, has lost his footing and now the boy who fancies himself a muezzin is falling. Suddenly we find our heart is in our throat as the boy tumbles to the floor. Our body contracts just like his as he hits the ground with a humbling thud. We wonder if the child is all right. Was this part of the story or simply an accident? No, it seems to be part of the story. Now the other children want to be the muezzin, it seems no one likes being the minaret or even worse, one of the faithful …

What has happened here is rather miraculous, even when we are relegated to the outside of an event, we can still find our way back into it through imaginative projection. We can do this with an infinite variety of experiences. In fact, when we begin to examine our everyday life we find that we spend much of our time "inside" events, experiences, and states of being. Take our hero, Averroes—there he sits in his library, toiling away, trying to translate those alien words "tragedy" and "comedy." He is deeply inside his work, the hours pass, but suddenly he is thrown "outside" by the sound of children playing in the courtyard beneath his window. He wonders to himself, "where has all the time gone? Have I actually been here all morning, lost in this futile attempt to unlock the meaning of these two impossible words?" The moment he asks such a question he has resolutely moved from the inside to the outside of an experience. And if he were to compare this day, with all his days, he would discover that this being-inside-of-things seems to be a basic human predisposition. We seem specifically wired to function in such a way. And so, we can go through a day, moving from the "inside" of our work, to the "inside" of a ritual, to the "inside" of a good meal. All of this can transpire with very little sense of an "outside" to these experiences.

Theater reverses this pattern of being, we find ourselves outside the event from the beginning and experience this sensation repeatedly over the course of the theatrical unfolding. In our above example, the children's fall also threw us momentarily "outside" of the event. This is not exclusive to the domain of theater, for we can find such oscillation in moments of play, and ritual and a myriad of other artistic mediums. But, for reasons we will discuss later, the impact and frequency of being potentially "outside" an event seems more pronounced in the theater. In these moments we can become conscious of ourselves experiencing experience. Theorists like Viktor Shklovsky and practitioners like Bertolt Brecht were fascinated with such moments where, through a series of theatrical strategies, the spell of mimesis is broken and the spectator is put into a heighten state of critical attention (the "experiencing of experience"). We can find numerous examples of ancient authors deploying such techniques that move us back and forth, between being inside the story and then being thrust outside of it. One of the most common examples being the theatrical "aside," where an actor "breaks character" and speaks directly to the audience, thereby momentarily throwing everyone back outside of the theatrical event. This simple act can be found from Aristophanes to Chekhov and beyond. Even without the intervention of such authors, theater seems to inherently harbor a basic perceptual instability, where the whole theatrical enterprise is on the constant verge of collapse, as though this were part of theater's very DNA. We can be thrown out of our engagement with a play by the simple movement of an audience member's head. One moment we were in Renaissance Italy and then, thanks to this ever-so-slight obstruction to our field of vision, we are yanked back to the twenty-first century, to an overly air-conditioned theater.

Ironically, many audiences judge the success of a theater piece by how deeply inside the work they find themselves, but as we will come to see, theatrical consciousness is a subtle game of imaginatively moving inside and outside of theatrical event. Play and ritual are attempts to erase all vestiges of an outside. They rouse us to plumb the depths of our imagination, finding meaning in the interior of play or a prayer. It is taking our ability to move inside of things to its furthest extremes. Theater also plays with this impulse, but cannot sustain the same success of mining the interior. This is due, in part, to what we have designated as its second-degree relationship to experience, which is, by its very nature, fragile and therefore keeps collapsing back to the outside of the event. This, at first, may be viewed as a failing of the theatrical enterprise, but it is actually part of what makes theater unique among imaginative endeavors. What theater begins to understand is that there are particular benefits to returning, every now and again, to an exilic vantage point. But we are getting ahead of ourselves and Borges has a second clue for our ever-patient Averroes.

Notes

1 Johan Huizinga, *Homo Ludens: A Study of the Play Element in Culture* (Beacon Press, 1955), 2.
2 Roger Caillois, *Man, Play and Games*, translated by Meyer Barash (University of Illinois Press, 2001), 5.
3 Huzinga, *Homo Ludens*, 13.
4 Ibid.
5 Ibid.
6 See Antony F.C. Wallace, *Religion: An Anthropological View* (Random House, 1996).
7 Huzinga, *Homo Ludens*, 14.
8 Caillois, *Man, Play and Games*, 4.

7

THE STORY OF ABU-AL-HASAN AND THE HOUSE OF PAINTED WOOD

Or Borges' second clue, the ascension of the ocular

Sadly, the children at play beneath Averroes' window remain more a distraction than an epiphany. Our translator returns to Aristotle's text, scouring page after page for any hints that might lead to a further elucidation of those strange and ever-elusive words: "tragedy" and "comedy." Dusk arrives and with it a reprieve from such study. Averroes has been invited to his friend Faraj's house where the great merchant/explorer Abu-al-Hasan is the guest of honor. Abu-al-Hasan has the singular distinction of returning from the far-off kingdom of the Sin (China) and Averroes is eager to hear of his adventures. It is with this encounter that Averroes is, unknowingly, given his second clue into the potential meaning of Aristotle's elliptical theatrical nomenclature. Abu-al-Hasan tells the following story to Averroes and the other assembled guests of the party. He speaks of having been invited to a strange "house of painted wood" where many people seemed to live. It is difficult for Abu-al-Hasan to describe the house, which was more like a single expansive room with row after row of cabinet-like contrivances that resembled balconies, one atop another. In these strange cabinets one discovered people eating, drinking, and looking down at a strangely suspended terrace.

As we can see, Caillois' Ludic enterprise has been hard at work refining the free spirited Paidia of the theatrical impulse. It is quite a leap from our three children at play beneath Averroes' window. Yet this is the lacunae we face when we move from our anthropological musings on play and ritual to the creation of the first theaters that miraculously rose up throughout antiquity. Somehow play and ritual give way to the formation of such theatrical edifices. At present, we are bereft of any actual genealogy of early theater. This is one of antiquity's many tantalizing secrets. Who knows, perhaps one day the Egyptian desert will cough up a lost papyrus text that connects all the theatrical dots; but until such time we must make do with the gap that exists between the play of those children beneath Averroes' window and Abu-al-Hasan seated in the resplendent house of painted wood awaiting the start of a theatrical performance.

Let us begin by examining the space itself. Borges gives us a sense of how an alien intelligence might look at what we take for granted. Box seats become "cabinet like contrivances" and the stage, "a suspended terrace." Thanks to the marriage of the slightly surreal and the vaguely recognizable, we are able to sense the profound bifurcation of space that creates two worlds in one room. There is the world of the actors and the world of the audience. What may have begun as an informal distance between the spectator and the participant has now been made all the more definitive with the architectural layout of this new space. What was once an experiential dialectic is now a highly formalized spatial dichotomy. We have become an audience of Adam and Eves, forever exiled from the Eden of immediate experience. And so, having been cast out, let us take our seats in the uppermost tier of these "cabinet-like contrivances" and see what this new vantage point might tell us about our paradise lost.

Abu-al-Hasan has no name for this space other than the "house of painted wood," but we recognize it for what it is: a theater. What Aristotle would call a *theatron*, the word roughly translates as "a space in which to see." Hence, the tiered balconies that gives each spectator an optimum view of the stage before them. Although language and music are still at the center of the event, it is visibility that is the new focus. This is a space that not only privileges the ear, but now also makes way for the eye. The tale that is about to unfold is no longer just told, but now is also seen. With the construction of such spaces we are witnessing the ascent of the ocular. The ear gives way to the eye. The event, and our understanding of it, is forever altered by this reprioritizing of the senses. The separation of the tiered seats from the stage creates the proper distance for the eye to take in the whole of the space. This distance gives us our sense of the outside, our objectivity. There is us (the audience) and, at a certain remove, what lies before us (the stage). It is a porous boundary and we will find ourselves, over the course of the evening, magically moving back and forth between our awareness of being part of an audience (the outside of the event; the experiencing of our experience) and other moments where we can imaginatively project ourselves into a given character and their situation (what we designate as being inside the event). This is the moment when the self is forgotten and all that remains is what is before us. At that instant, the viewer is one with what s/he sees.

We cannot underestimate the significance of this moment for the Greeks who called such visual engagement *oida*. The word means both "seeing" and "knowing." The privileging of sight over the other senses runs deep in Ancient Greek thought. *Oida* is only one of a veritable arsenal of words that the Greeks deployed to capture the various aspects of seeing and understanding. There is *blepein* ("while seeing, they do not see"), *idein* ("to see and to comprehend"), *skeptesthai* ("to see distinctly"), and, perhaps, most intriguingly, *theasthai* ("to look with one's mouth open" or "to gape or stare in rapt attention"). *Theasthai* is etymologically linked to both *theoria* (theory) and *theoros* (the spectator in theater), as well as the verb *theorien*, which (like *oida* and *idein*) yokes sight and knowledge under the same name. Hans Thies Lehman observes that "the mode of seeing that underlies both *theoria* and *theoros* amounts, on a certain level, to marveling from a standpoint far from meaning, of gawking without understanding."[1] This is what Abu-al-Hasan seems to be doing as he views the stage before him where, we will learn, everyone wears crimson cloaks and outlandish masks. Faraj, the host who is honoring al-Hasan, thinks this is all the acts of madmen. Abu-al-Hasan corrects Faraj and attempts to explain that the people down below were more like storytellers who spoke, sang, and gave boring speeches. Faraj is curious as to how many storytellers the evening employed. Abu-al-Hasan tells him that these storytellers numbered about 20 in all. Faraj concludes that Islamic art is superior to the Chinese since it only requires one storyteller, no matter how complex the tale.

It would seem rather natural for both the Chinese and the Greeks to move from aural to ocular storytelling since both cultures give such precedence to the visual. The Chinese language, is by its very nature, ideogrammatic. We have also seen how the Greeks elevate sight above all other senses, yoking its power directly to our understanding. This is in opposition to the cultures of Islam and Judaism where the word, not the image, is central to the culture. One of Judaism's most cherished prayers begins, "Hear O Israel" and reflects the power of the word. For Judaism and Islam there is no distance between the word and the thing it is meant to represent, they are one. The word is "the thing-itself"; whereas, with a culture like the Greeks, there is always a fundamental distance between the phenomenon of a thing and the word that tries to represent it. The word, as far as the Greeks are concerned, is never "the thing-itself," but always a meagre stand-in and therefore subject to constant lexical doubt and reconsideration. Since Judaism and Islam believe there is no distance between words and things, there is little need for any further representation, such as the pictorial. The word and its hearing are enough. But with a culture like the Greeks, the opening up of a distance between words and things leads to new found objectivity; such an objectivity is only further enhanced when one moves from the phenomenon of the thing to its visual representation. This is part of the fundamental difference between aural and visual cultures. Let us try and look at this from a phenomenological point of view.

Our experiencing of sound is an intriguing phenomenon. It is activated in us as early as our time in our mother's womb, long before we are even aware of our ability for sight. Even after we are born, the recognition of family members happens first through sound, since our ocular capabilities are still slowly developing. Eventually, vision will catch up and seemingly dominate our aural predisposition; but, we should not underestimate the profound primal impact hearing has made on our relationship with the world at large. It remains almost magical. Sound, on a basic level, is a moving vibration that is both there and not there. And yet, it still has the ability to envelop us, it happens around us; but also includes us. It seems profoundly indifferent to the border between ourselves and its source and, as a result, we can easily become one with a siren, a melody, or the words of the storyteller. The sound resonates between our ears, within our head. The voice of the storyteller is registered inside us, just as our own voice is. The experience of a storyteller's voice is similar to the experiencing of our own mental stream of consciousness, both seem to be inside us. This is the subjective power of sound, it collapses distance.

Vision, on the other hand, has the tendency to enhance our sense of distance. In vision we are more aware of the space that separates us from another person or thing. We remain resolutely "here," inside ourselves, looking out at the other person—or world—both of which are resolutely over "there." Our "here" and the world's "there" remain distinctly delineated. With vision, there is always this sense of separation. It engenders a kind of de facto objectivity of "ourselves" and "the world." Thanks to this fundamental division, we find ourselves constantly considering the differences and similarities that bring us closer together or further apart. The two may fuse, momentarily, in an imaginary projection of our own making; but, inevitably, we return to our "proper" places; aware of ourselves, once again, outside of the world, looking in. Such an "awareness" can be existentially exhausting, which is why many of us fold ourselves into the interior of multiple activities, or prefer to inadvertently practice the Ancient Greek form of *blepein*, a kind of vision where "while seeing – one does not see." This can become something of a default setting; one we must dispense with when encountering the theater, since it is a medium that demands much from our eyes.

Although theater gives precedence to the visual that does not mean it has forgotten the primal power of the aural. Sound is still very much an essential part of the theatrical equation and Ancient Greek and Chinese theater are very quick to exploit the strengths of both senses to make for the most impactful event. The old aural mode of bardic tale-telling is still a central ingredient in all Ancient Greek drama. Such moments are known as the *messenger rhesis*. This is where a secondary figure steps forward and tells us of a significant event that has happened offstage. Often these stories relate the death of a main character and are expressed in a manner that clearly harkens back to the essential enjoyment found in listening to a great Homeric bard tell a tale. One would think that such moments would be anti-climactic in comparison with fully dramatized scenes and yet these well-placed stories are often the most memorable moments of entire productions (think of the messenger who tells of Pentheus' death in *The Bacchae*). They have the power to draw us even deeper into the theatrical experience. This is the primacy of the ear which maintains an almost hypnotic ability to fold us into stories. Greek theater may celebrate the ascension of the visual, but it still understands and honors the art of the aural. It will continue to explore the unique power of these two senses, putting them to work throughout the unfolding of a performance, to draw us in and out of the event. It will utilize a sound like the wail of a widow in mourning to pierce us to our very core, evaporating the distance between ourselves and this poor soul in grief. And it will use the spectacle of something like Agamemnon's defilement of precious red fabrics to show us the problematic nature of this tragic warrior, suddenly thrusting us into a critical state of mind. Greek theater reaches a level of sophistication where it is able to play to the eye in one moment and to the ear in the next; understanding how a shift from one sense to another brings about a profound shift in our experiencing of meaning.

Shakespeare is also awake to this theatrical dialectic of pitting the eye against the ear. It becomes a major theme throughout *Hamlet*, his most meta-theatrical of plays. Right from the play's opening we find both senses battling for pride of place. The night watchmen ask one another, obsessively, what they have *seen* and implore Horatio, the visiting scholar, to *speak* to the ghost. In the first scene alone there are 21 references relating to sight and 26 references to hearing. Hamlet will alternate between both senses throughout the entire play as he tries to arrive at some semblance of truth. He will learn of the vulnerabilities of the ear, which can be victim to falsehoods and poison. The ghost tells us that it was through the "porches of my ears" that Claudius poured "the leperous distilment" that killed him. Shakespeare, a master of words, knows how they can play games, cast spells, lie, and ultimately destroy us. This is the susceptibility of the ear; why it must, at times, be balanced by the eye. That is why Hamlet will resort to the ocular when he asks Horatio to use his eyes to see whether or not Claudius reveals his true self while watching the incriminating play within a play. In the end, Hamlet seems to have come to favor the ear over the eye, availing upon Horatio to *tell* his story once he is dead. This is in opposition to Fortinbras, Hamlet's princely rival, who seems more interested in showing the world Hamlet's dead body rather than staying to hear Horatio's tale of woe.

This same dialectic of eye and ear is at play in Shakespeare's *The Tempest*. Here we find Shakespeare pitting Elizabethan spectacle against good old-fashioned Tudor storytelling. The work opens with visual enactment of a storm. It was inspired, no doubt, by the designer Inigo Jones and his latest advances in special effects for indoor theaters. Such spectacle was all the rage in the early 1600s. This is immediately juxtaposed by Prospero's elaborate tale of how he and Miranda came to be shipwrecked. The tale itself, with interjections, spans a lengthy 165 lines; this is rather long, even by Shakespearean standards. It is as though our author was intent upon proving that his words could remain as compelling as any visual effects. This does not mean Shakespeare and his designated narrator aren't sensitive to their audiences, whose attentiveness may be somewhat compromised thanks to a new diet of "bells and whistles." Prospero, throughout his telling, will query Miranda (and, by extension, the audience) with a defensive, "Dost thou attend me?" Miranda, no doubt speaking for herself and the audience, wryly replies, "Your tale, sir, would cure deafness." But can it cure the future fears of Shakespeare? Of the triumph of the ocular? We moderns, who have become slaves to the visual can sympathize with Shakespeare's prophetic concern for balance. But let us return to Abu-al-Hasan who is about to relate the strange and wondrous things he saw from his elevated perch.

Note

1 Hans-Thies Lehman, *Tragedy and Dramatic Theatre*, translated by Erik Butler (Routledge, 2016), 27.

8

FROM THE MIMETIC TO THE META-THEATRIC

The four modalities of theatrical expression

Abu-al-Hasan continues his tale where some below play the tambour and the pipe while others wear masks and engage in prayer, song, and speaking among themselves. Several of these masked figures will be imprisoned in jails with no bars, others will ride horses that cannot be seen by the naked eye, while a select few will wage battles with sticks of bamboo rather than swords. But perhaps the most miraculous occurrence of all was that the dead, in the end, would rise and walk again.

It is worth noting that what Abu-al-Hasan is viewing would be completely incomprehensible to Aristotle or Plato. In their theater they would expect to see what they called mimesis. This, as we know, is the mirror-like manner of presentation which reflects back to us our world and our behavior. According to these Greek masters, theater's power, for better or for worse (better in Aristotle and worse in Plato) is in its propensity for a stringent reproduction of our reality. What al-Hasan shows us is not, by any means, an image that could be found in a mirror; rather, it is a series of seemingly incomplete pictures. Pictures which, in these specific instances, invite an imaginative collaboration, asking us to visualize the missing bars for the cell and horses for their riders. Without such creative intervention on the part of our imaginations, these actions would indeed belong to the world of the asylum rather than the theater. What we are experiencing here is another kind of seeing, one that has been favored more in the East than the West. Such images, as a cell without bars or riders without horses, belong to the realm of the symbolic. It is one of the four modalities of theatrical expression, the others being the mimetic, the metaphoric, and the meta-theatric. These modalities of expression could be defined as follows:

1. The mimetic: the world as we see it.
2. The symbolic: the world when it mysteriously means more.
3. The metaphoric: the world as we remake it.
4. The meta-theatric: the world that hides behind the illusion.

The above ordering reflects each modality's increased representational complexity. Taken together, they make up four basic ways we tend to experience the theatrical. A theatrical event can be made up of one or, in the case of truly great works, all four. In such cases, we shift from one modality to the other throughout the course of the play's unfolding. In order to understand theater's full expressive possibility we must better understand each of these modalities individually. We will start with perhaps the most popular and straightforward.

The mimetic: or what Borges forgot to mention

Mimesis, like many seminal Greek words, has a long and intricate etymological history. Its lexical relatives include: *mimeisthai*, *mimetes*, and *mimos*. Its earliest usage was in relationship to mime, dance, and music. In this initial incarnation, it designated humankind's attempts to capture the inner reality of things through movement or sounds. Only in the fifth century, with the rise of theater and the visual arts, was mimesis used to describe imitations of outward reality. By the time Plato and Aristotle got their hands on the word it was almost solely interested in the relation between an image (eidolon) and its original model. Mimesis in this new manifestation becomes synonymous with the concepts of resemblance, likeness, and reproduction. Early on in *The Poetics*, Aristotle tells us:

> We enjoy looking at the most exact portraits of things we do not like to see
> in real life, the lowest animals, for instance, or corpses. This is because not only
> philosophers, but all men, enjoy getting to understand something.[1]

The operative phrase in the above observation is "exact portrait." The power of mimesis, according to Aristotle and his subsequent followers, is in our innate human ability to capture nature, recreate it, and in that recreation discover more than might be found in the actual flow of real life. The mimetic act wrenches a moment from our world, wrestles it to the canvas or stage, and in that transformation ensures that the moment, in its newly reconstituted form, has lost none of its vividness. Here, exactitude is all. The more detail that is found, the more pleasure it seems to give.

Plato is, notoriously, on the other side of the "mimetic fence" when it comes to giving mimesis such priority in human affairs, regardless of how brilliantly it might manifest itself in the realm of painting, poetry, theater, or any other artistic endeavors. In his tenth book of the *Republic*, Plato dismisses such activity as "secondary representation" (*mimesis mimeseos* or imitation of imitations) and gives precedent to the "primary representation" found in human thought (Plato's theory of pre-existing forms, the "nous" or idea of an object that allows us to recognize it in life).

It is at this juncture that Plato equates mimesis with the mirror. He is not the first to use this image as an analog to mimesis (we have Pindar and Alcidamas before him), although Plato has the singular distinction of being the first to use this metaphor in a negative light. Whether he actually dismisses all art as nothing more impressive than the reflection of a mirror, or whether he is being his usual philosophically provocative self, he has kept commentators guessing for centuries. Stephen Halliwell, one of our generation's great interpreters of ancient aesthetics, wonders if this is actually a thinly veiled challenge by Plato, addressed to all who value art, prodding them to find something more significant in the act of making than simply counterfeiting the look of the real.[2]

Regardless of this unique condemnation by Plato, mimesis flourishes in the West. It remains the dominate mode of expression in art and theater. Aristotle seems content to attribute the success of mimesis to an innate aspect of our species that is drawn to following the patterns of nature (*mimeisthai ten phusien*).

The theatrical state of affairs that made up Plato and Aristotle's understanding of mimesis is a far cry from our own modern-day understanding and usage of the term. In this early manifestation, stories from the heroic past are presented in a highly structured theatrical event that alternates between choral sequences and dramatic scenes. All the actors wore oversized masks and footwear to enable an audience of 5,000-plus to see them better. No wonder the first spectators of this new form were held in a state of *theasthai* ("looking with one's mouth open").

How, you may ask, is any of this even remotely mimetic? Well, Aristotle tells us that theatrical mimesis is the imitation of human actions and how these actions unfold through plot. Here the theatrical world follows the same universal laws of cause and effect that we find in the real world. Characters should act as we do in life, reflecting our needs, desires, fears, and cares. How these characters fight, love, laugh, and mourn should, according to Aristotle, rhyme with our experiences, thereby allowing us to easily identify with them.

Let us take a look at Aeschylus' *Agamemnon*, the reunion scene between our titular hero and his wife Clytemnestra. It is a beautiful working out of mimetic action. The last time they saw one another was the day that Agamemnon sacrificed their daughter Iphigenia to appease the gods and gain a wind to take his thousand ships to destroy Troy. That was ten long years ago. Now he has returned, victorious, and Clytemnestra, has placed before his tired feet a bolt of precious red fabric that leads all the way to the entrance of their palace. She asks him, before the entire populace of Mycenae, to unloose his sandals and enjoy the feel of these fine silks beneath his feet. He demurs, such an action is a defilement of their worth and a show of hubris to the gods. Clytemnestra counters that after Agamemnon's labors he deserves such an honor. Agamemnon suspects, as does the audience, that there is something not quite right about all this. His suspicion will prove true. Clytemnestra, despite her protestations of love, has never forgiven him for the sacrifice of their daughter; luring him onto these fine fabrics is a trap. Their defilement will indeed be punishable by the gods. All Clytemnestra needs is for his foot to tread across that fabric and her husband's fate is sealed. It is highly unlikely that anyone reading this paragraph has ever experienced such a situation and yet we all have found ourselves, at one time or another, tempted like Agamemnon to do something we know we should not do. Aeschylus' dramatic genius is to show, through an exacting use of actional mimesis, how Clytemnestra lures Agamemnon onto those fine red silks.

The sequence is a perfect piece of mimetic argumentation. Such attentiveness to how scenes humanly unfold is at the very heart of *The Poetics*.

Aristotle believes there must be an internal logic that propels a plot forward to its natural and inevitable end. That in theater, like life, there is a basic causality at work that links action to action, allowing each to grow naturally out of the other, unfolding toward a conclusion that is inevitable. What we see in Aristotle is plot behaving like a rigorous mathematical equation. Here a string of actions functions like a series of integers, eventually adding up over time; coalescing into a given meaning for the character and, by extension, the audience as well. Drama, in Aristotle's eyes, is as rigorous as the working out of a problem in logic.

Again, it is important to remember that Plato refuses to grant mimesis such status. For Plato, painting, poetry, and theater remain a mirror that merely reflects back to us what we already know. This is certainly true of mimesis in the nineteenth-century naturalism, which becomes so intent on accurately capturing our reality that it goes to extraordinary pains to bring every single detail of the world onstage. Here, not only is the stove present but the very gas that allows the stove to go about its daily business. The interesting byproduct of such an approach is that it actually dulls our ability to see. When everything is so present, nothing can stand out. Such an approach takes us from the *oida* (seeing/comprehending) of the Greek stage and returns us to our real world default-stance of *blepien* (seeing while not seeing). We could argue that the function of Greek theater was to move us from passive "looking" (*blepien*) to active "seeing" (*oida*).

We, in the West, have still not quite recovered from the advent of naturalism. We, have through the twentieth century, softened naturalism's voracious hunger for hyper-representation by creating its cousin, realism. The pursuits of realism are much more modest, preferring to be far more selective about the amount of reality that it feels necessary to show. The sober aims of realism attempt to take from our reality only what is essential for our understanding of the story. It does not need the constant pressure to represent, but is perfectly content with what it can evoke. In such a world, the kitchen can be conjured just by a stove alone. Realism is confident that we, the audience, can "fill" in the rest with our imagination since that is what we have been doing from the Greeks, through Shakespeare, all the way to the neo-classicists. In those worlds, language itself would suffice, doing what it does best, standing in for reality. The idea of a simple object or language evoking an entire world leads us from the realm of the mimetic to its sibling, the symbolic.

The symbolic: "jails without bars; riders without horses"—between the mimetic and the metaphoric

Let us return to al-Hasan who, when we last left him, was patiently seated in one of those tiered cabinet-like contrivances watching a group of masked figures on a suspended terrace as they escaped from a jail without bars and rode away without horses. Such actions break the mimetic spell and bring us to the realm of symbolic representation in theater.

Aristotle has little to say about the symbolic in his *Poetics*; we must turn to his *Interpretation* to begin to get a clear understanding of his relationship with symbols. There he tells us that spoken words are symbols of affections in the soul, written words are symbols of spoken words. We can say that Aristotle thinks of symbols primarily as we think about signifiers in semiotics: A name that stands in for a thing. A "token" of sorts. In the classical period of Aristotle, the word "symbol" was generally thought of in such straightforward terms. It will not be until the Hellenistic period that the concept of a symbol will slowly transform into the word as we understand it today.

For us moderns, a symbol has become a sign that maintains a certain mystery, not quite at home with its signifier, and thereby demurring from a simple, straightforward signification. In the theater a symbol can be an object, person, or situation. In all these manifestations, the common denominator is the symbol's refusal to make immediate/ total sense on its own. Unlike a mimetic representation, it resists stabilizing into a single graspable meaning. It suggests there is something in its current constitution that is missing, that there is a more-ness that escapes us. Find whatever that might be, bring that back to the symbol, and it will settle down and behave itself, finally making sense. Without that discovery, it will continue to radiate, taunting our consciousness to make sense of it. Meaning happens when we find the symbol's missing half or context. The symbolic process is the imaginative "putting it all together," that period between the sign's ambiguity and its resolution into complete meaning.

This understanding still has a relationship with the symbol's etymological roots in the word *symbolon*, an Ancient Greek custom of identification where a coin would be broken in two, one half would belong to one's family and the other half would be sent to a far off family member or friend of the family. This would insure that when a future relative met up with her distant family or friends of the family s/he could prove her identity by placing her half of the coin with the other missing half, thereby making the coin complete again. Both aspects, the fragmentation and its reconstitution, are central to the meaning of *symbolon* which comes from *symbollein* (to coincide). Another example of symbolon can be found in Plato's *Symposium*, where Aristophanes holds forth on the origins of love. In this famous recounting, we learn that a human being, before taking up terrestrial residence on earth, is cut in two equal halves by the gods. These halves are then brought into the world as "man" and "woman" where they subsequently spend the rest of their lives in search of the other. Man and woman are fragments/*symbola*, when they are joined, they become whole again, thus completing the symbolic process.

One of the simplest forms of this sort of process would be the incomplete images that al-Hasan encounters in Borges' story. These images provoke the viewer into a symbolic engagement. The man who is trying to escape a space where there seems to be no visible restraint, is symbolizing being imprisoned. In such an instance we are asked, with the aid of our imaginations, to complete the picture and add bars for the cell. Or, in al-Hasan's other example, create imaginary horses for their riders. In doing this, we give back to these fragmented images their sense of the whole. To complete such a process is to have engaged in a form of symbolic representation.

Eugen Fink, the student of both Husserl and Heidegger and a distinguished phenomenologist in his own right, observes that being, by its very nature is "fragmentary, splintered, rent apart, and cleaved asunder" into a multiplicity of finite things so that it is difficult to maintain a sense of the whole, what Fink (following Heidegger) calls "the world."[3] This "world", according to Fink, has a tendency to keep receding from our view and is in constant threat of being forgotten thanks to our engagement with the immediate, seemingly infinite field of finite things. And yet each of these fragmented things has the potential to become symbola, reaching beyond itself and thereby connecting up to the larger whole that would otherwise slip away from us. It is at such moments, that a thing turns into a symbol. It becomes, in Fink's vocabulary, "world profound", allowing us to experience how the whole resonates through the symbolic potential of any one thing. In such moments "thing and universe" are miraculously rejoined in our consciousness. Fink calls this, "the most primordial enchantment." The last vestiges of this process remains in certain superstitions, rituals, children's play and in the theater, particularly the theater as practiced by the East. At such moments, our ability for symbolic engagement is reawakened and we are granted access to the ever allusive whole of being. We can say of such moments that we enter into a heightened state of awareness, where things suddenly have the ability to mean more. Unlike the mimetic, which simply shows us one thing after the next with an unquestioning regularity that lulls us into a passive state of reception, the symbolic provokes us to engage with what is before us. The symbol is there, like other things around it, and yet it means more, points to more, and will not stop radiating until that more-ness is fully understood.

As we noted earlier, Aristotle has very little to say about the symbolic nature of Greek theater in his *Poetics*. Greek theater itself does not overtly traffic in symbolic undertakings, but this does not mean that such manifestations are not present throughout the Greek drama. The symbolic is there, but revealed in a rather subtle manner. This happens, almost secretly, just underneath the captivating spell of mimesis. One could say it is an inadvertent by-product of the Greek theater's proclivity for an empty theatrical space to tell its stories. Unlike nineteenth-century naturalism's penchant to display everything on stage, Ancient Greek theater is highly selective with what it represents. The tales of Theseus, the trials of Hercules, the fall of Atreus, and the revelations of Oedipus all play out in the neutral space of the Greek theater. There might be a painted skene that represented a palace or the nearby sea; but, short of this, the drama unfolds on a bare stage with actors and a handful of select objects. These few items, wrenched from their quotidian moorings, find themselves transplanted to a stage where they stand virtually alone under the newfound scrutiny of some 5,000-plus spectators. Simple everyday objects like a letter, or urn, or knife that might, in life, have gone virtually unnoticed now seem to shimmer with a new status. All thanks to this simple shift from our densely populated world of things to the selective nature of the Greek stage. It is at such a point that mere things have the potential to transform themselves into potent symbols, some of which have the potential to over-mean, suggesting a multiplicity of significations that stretches to infinity. It is at such moments when the object from the stage seems to operate like an object in a dream, refusing to give forth its immediate meaning and requiring further, deeper interpretation. Freud would call such symbols "overdetermined," suggesting that there were too many variables at work within them for us to settle on one simple meaning.

Let us return to Aeschylus' *Agamemnon* where we can find perhaps one of Greek drama's most "overdetermined" symbols. We are back before the palace where Agamemnon and Clytemnestra have been reunited after ten long years. She has convinced him, as the victor of Troy, to walk upon that bolt of fine red fabric that extends from his tired feet all the way to the entrance to the palace. He lifts his foot, looks at the bolt of red fabric beneath him and pauses. A brief eternity opens up, time itself seems to stop and in that stoppage the red of the fabric seems even more vibrant. The entire pathway, from his suspended foot all the way to the palace door, seems to shimmer in his and our consciousness, as if the very molecules of that red fabric might be loosed, strand by strand until it transmogrifies into something entirely other. Only moments ago it was a mere ground cloth for dignitaries to walk upon and now—well now, it seems to mean more. But what? What does it mean? Suddenly there seems to be as many meanings as there are strands of silk that make up the fabric itself. Now it seems like—dare we say it—a river of blood. But is it the blood of his daughter, or the blood of all the men he lost at Troy, or a premonition of his own soon-to-be-spilt blood, or all those bloods indiscriminately mixed together? Or is it the path to Hades, where Agamemnon suspects he is headed? Or is the red his shame for what he has done? Or Clytemnestra's hate made manifest? All we know for certain is that this image of a red bolt of fabric refuses to mean one thing anymore and instead has the audacity to insinuate an infinity of new meanings. At this juncture, we are no longer in the world of things, but rather find ourselves transported into the realm of symbols. A space where objects over-mean. Our minds race to complete the meaning of this image of the red carpet and in that very moment we are engaged in perhaps the most complex form of symbolic representation.

We could say such objects stand out. And in this standing out they reveal how they can mean more than the mere name they were initially given by our progenitors. They show us that their existence will always exceed our capacity to name. They are not just things, or signs. They all have the capability of returning to their inherent mystery. When they do so, they become symbolic, patiently waiting for us to grant them new names so that we might once again domesticate their unnerving, overflowing mystery. But until we do, they radiate. This is particularly true in the theater where the combination of being wrenched from the everyday, divorced from brother and sister objects and subjected to the pressure of a collective gaze confers a hyper-intentional potential onto each remaining object. One could say that the empty theatrical space is a space made for hyper-intentionality, allowing everything the possibility of meaning more. We can see this tradition beginning with Clytemnestra's bolt of red fabric and running through Othello's handkerchief, and Treplev's seagull, all the way to Willy Loman's two suitcases. Each of these objects has their own transformation from thing to symbol, where they signify more, demanding our active engagement to complete their full meaning.

As Fink tells us, the symbolic impulse is a world-building impulse, it connects things back to a larger picture that often escapes us. This is what happens when al-Hasan imaginatively adds the bars to the invisible cell that he sees before him on stage, or how the image of the bolt of red fabric leads us to try to understand the larger world of fate in the story of Clytemnestra and Agamemnon. In both instances a seemingly mysterious object provokes us to create a world around it. Such a process returns us to an almost childlike state where everything is once again mysterious, in need of a name and a context. Our early formative years are spent engaged in slowly, deciphering each mysterious object, which is connected to an infinite chain of other mysterious objects that, when all put together, conjure a world for us. This is what Fink calls the intraworldly nature of things and symbols, which we learn at a very early age. Each thing is not only itself but also the pathway to an entire world; say, for example, the world of the kitchen. This is why, in realism, all we need is the stove and we can imaginatively recreate the rest of the kitchen ourselves. There is something joyful about returning to this childlike state of rediscovery and perhaps one of the reasons why, even though we have the ability to create complete and total mimesis, thanks to technology, there still is space and enjoyment in the selective nature of theatrical realism and its subtle play of symbolic thinking.

As we have noted, such symbolic representation requires a more active stance from the viewer than that of basic mimesis. For Aristotle, theatrical mimesis is a kind of ordering of a chain of action/events that, like integers in a math equation, add up, in the end, to mean something that we did not see at the beginning. The tension of the mimetic rests in meaning slowly coming into sight with each additional action/event until what seemed perplexing becomes clear. This is how our engagement with the mimetic works. The symbolic process demands more. In theatrical mimesis we can sit back and the story will do its work for us, reveal what needs to be revealed, all we have to do is be patient and watch. Symbolic processing (which often happens within a mimetic unfolding), demands our intervention in the making of meaning, it asks us to fill in what is missing, becoming something of a collaborator in the event. This demand for collaboration reaches its zenith when theater asks us to think metaphorically; where the interpretive becomes fully creative and the spectator can become co-author.

The metaphoric: "bamboo sticks for swords," or when "this" magically becomes "that"

Where Aristotle is virtually silent on the working of the symbolic in his *Poetics*, he does have this to relate about the nature of metaphor: "Metaphor consists in giving the thing a name that belongs to something else, the transference being either from genius to species, or from species to species, or on the ground of analogy." In his *Rhetoric* we find him somewhat suspicious of metaphors, defining them as "strange" and likening them to "obsolete or foreign words … Or vowel lengthening and everything contrary to proper usage." He warns, "But if someone composes entirely these sorts of things, it will be either an enigma or babble. If composed from metaphors, an enigma, if from obsolete or foreign words, babble." It is hard to read this passage and not wonder what is so problematic about the metaphoric and why Aristotle would be so allergic to its usage. Perhaps, this is due to his penchant for a certain kind of mimesis that follows a logical unfolding. Metaphor works by leaps and sudden intuition. This is at the very heart of the metaphoric disposition: to see something and project an entirely other meaning or use on to it. This brings us close to the origin of the Greek *metaphora*, which comes from *metapherein* and means to "transfer," or "carry over." The *phora/phrerein* suggesting a movement, or a traversal of distance from "here" to a far off "there." This is the transporting of meaning from one object onto another, seemingly dissimilar object. What Sanskrit aesthetics calls *asav evayam*, when "this is that." It is the potential of free play in our meaning-bestowing capabilities; part of our prodigious ability to find connections between the most disparate of things.

And so, when al-Hasan sees those masked figures upon the stage using sticks as though they were swords, we are in the midst of the metaphoric. Vygotsky, the great twentieth-century Russian neurologist, was fascinated with the development of metaphoric thinking in children. He tells us in his seminal essay, "The Role of Play in Development," about this momentous transition that the child makes from the realm of the literal to the realm of the metaphoric. First, there is, as we know, the long struggle to name things, where all the child's cognitive energy goes into learning that "a stick is a stick." During this period of cognitive development the child is completely under the spell of "the thing" and the tyranny of its literal meaning. But then, much later in the child's development, there is the extraordinary moment when the "stick" can become "a horse" for a child to ride. At such a juncture, a child's imagination now rescripts the meaning of an object to his/her new needs. Vygotsky calls this a divergence between the fields of vision (seeing a stick as a stick) and meaning (the stick becomes a horse). This ability to shift fields usually occurs at the pre-school age where:

> In play, thought is separated from objects and action arises from ideas rather than from things: a piece of wood begins to be a doll and a stick becomes a horse. Action begins to be determined by ideas and not by objects themselves. This is such a reversal of the child's relation to the real, immediate, concrete situation that it is hard to underestimate its full significance. The child does not do this all at once because it is terribly difficult for a child to sever thought (the meaning of the word) from the object.
>
> Play provides a transitional stage in this direction whenever an object (for example, a stick) becomes a pivot for severing the meaning of horse from a real horse. The child cannot as yet detach thought from object. The child's weakness is that in order to imagine a horse, he needs to define his action by means of using "the-horse-in-the-stick" as the pivot. But all the same, the basic structure determining the child's relation to reality is radically changed at this crucial point, because the structure of perception changes.[4]

Vygotsky sees this as a liberation from the literal, "the first manifestation of the child's emancipation from situational constraints." In such moments a child can take a half-eaten muffin, hold it up and say, "it's a smile," then turn it and say, "it's a crescent moon," then turn it again and say, "it's a hat." Borges defines such a metaphor-maker as "someone who can perceive resemblances which aren't immediately apparent." It is important to note that the metaphoric is not a synonym for the symbolic, but is its own unique process of making sense. Although both symbol and metaphor, to a certain degree, traffic in resemblance, there are still important differences in how they both go about their imaginative work.

To understand this better, let us return, one last time, to Clytemnestra's red bolt of fabric to try and untangle the difference between symbol and metaphor in the theater. When that bolt of red fabric lays before Agamemnon's feet, we have said that this object can move from its mimetic moorings (i.e., a simple red carpet) to become a symbol. In such a transformation its meaning becomes open-ended: it could represent Agamemnon's bloody deeds, Clytemnestra's rage, Agamemnon's path to Hades, etc. The potential meanings are infinite. This is the domain of the symbol in its most extreme manifestation. But let us say, a scene later, we see Agamemnon brought onstage murdered, and the red bolt of fabric is no longer at his feet but now wrapped about his dead body. Does this image radiate the same potential meaning? Not quite. Here the image has shifted from the symbolic to the metaphoric. The red bolt of fabric can now be read as blood streaming from Agamemnon's wounds. In seeing the fabric this way, we have performed "Vygotsky's pivot": The bolt of red fabric becomes blood, like the stick becomes the horse. In both instances we transfer the meaning of one object onto another. This is the quintessence of the metaphoric. It is a slightly different experience from that of the symbol. The symbol seems to murmur to us, "I could be this, or this, or this …" The metaphor simply exclaims, "This is that!" The symbol unfolds like a mystery; the metaphor explodes like a magician's sleight of hand. Part of the magic of metaphor is how great the distance of resemblance can be between the "this" which is before us and the "that" of our mind's remaking. What we are teasing out is not just a shift in processing, but also emphasis. Most "overdetermined" symbols (like Clytemnestra's bolt of red fabric at the feet of Agamemnon) work on us, beckoning or enticing us into discovering their potential meaning; whereas with metaphor, it is we and our imagination that work on the object, projecting a new meaning onto it (the bolt of red fabric becomes blood). In this sense, we could say that in symbols, the world tends to "work" on us; in metaphor it is we that tend to "work" on the world. Theater creates moments for both symbols and metaphors to happen. Each, as we have said, have a different time signature of revelation and level of engagement. The symbol tends to take longer to unravel and requires a certain degree of reflection, while the metaphor happens more suddenly and engages us to move from reflection to projection; with metaphor we must make "Vygotsky's pivot" and turn the red fabric into blood. Such actions, as we've noted earlier, return us to that magical moment in childhood; here vision, object, and meaning detach from one another and can be re-shuffled like a deck of cards to create new combinations of signification. Much of the power of theater resides in our return to this charmed domain of childhood perception where we first experienced the magic of symbols and metaphors; at such moments, we are taking part in what Borges calls, "the secret connection of things."

The meta-theatric: "they died and then they walked again," raising the dead with a round of applause

Abu-al-Hasan's last example is a wonderful misunderstanding of the theatrical convention of actors taking a bow. He misreads this simple custom as a strange form of resurrection. But hasn't that thought momentarily flashed through all of our minds at one time or another? There we are: the tragedy ends, dead bodies strewn about the stage, the lights dim, then restore to reveal the same figures now standing and smiling before us. Haven't we all thought of those figures as both actors bowing *and* the characters resurrected? At such a juncture, we are granted a kind of double vision where the theatrical story and the reality of its making exist side by side; or put another way, the metaphoric peeps from behind the mimetic to give us the shiver of the meta-theatrical. Where moments ago we saw only one reality (characters in a story), we now are reminded of the second reality (actors playing characters). Suddenly two worlds exist simultaneously.

The same sort of double vision often happens when we see Shakespeare's Ariel take flight in a production of *The Tempest*. Often the actor playing the part is suspended in the air by wires that, no matter how discrete, remain perceptible to the eye. As a result we simultaneously see both the illusion of Ariel flying and the mechanism that enables this to happen. Both realities exist at the same time. At first we are aware of the actor suspended by the wires, but soon the wires recede from our consciousness. They do not miraculously disappear, they are still there, just not in the forefront of our consciousness, thereby allowing us to fold into the image of Ariel in flight. The wires will return, recede, and then return again to our consciousness as the scene continues. The two realities co-exist in our mind.

Here, we return to the dialectical movement of inside (illusion) to outside (reality)—a dynamic that Brecht brought to the forefront of our theatrical attention, highlighting the importance of when reality and illusion dance with one another before our eyes. In such moments, our seeing transforms into a kind of "seeing-through." We see through the illusion to the reality of its theatrical root. When the "dead" actors rise for a bow or when we see the wires that make Ariel fly, we are able to pierce through the thick veil of the mimetic back to its secret metaphoric core. We realize that underneath every mimetic moment is a suppressed or forgotten metaphor. Borges reminds us that all words began as metaphors. Thanks to their persistence over time, we've forgotten the linguistic alchemy that first brought these words into being. A similar sort of forgetting is at work in theater. Theater begins with the most fundamental metaphoric transaction: "this" actor becomes "that" character. A reality we forget, almost instantaneously, thanks the hypnotic power of mimesis. Metaphor, like its favorite subject, the moon, waxes and wanes throughout our consciousness as we experience a work of theater, but is ultimately upstaged by the relentless sun of mimesis.

Metaphor, seen in this light, is the secret power of theater, a power that has been somewhat neutered by Aristotle's privileging of mimesis. This, as we know, is less the case with the theater of the East. Many envious Western artists, as disparate as Brecht and Artaud, have longed to put an end to the stranglehold of Aristotelian mimesis and return theater to its full metaphoric roots. One of the inadvertent missteps in Aristotle's theory of mimesis is that it is not a completely accurate distillation or understanding of the dynamics of Greek tragic theater practices. It only focuses on one aspect of what Ancient Greek theater nets. In reality, the experience of seeing/understanding in the theater of the Greeks is much more complex and blended than what Aristotle describes. Aristotle sees the mimetic possibilities of Greek theater, but misses the symbolic, metaphoric, and meta-theatrical aspects that live alongside it. By missing this more holistic aspect of the actual experience, he inadvertently creates an unnecessary binary approach to theater, where mimesis is pitted against these other modalities of expression; giving it pride of place. This has been subsequently followed, with pockets of resistance, ever since Aristotle was rediscovered by the West during the Renaissance.

Aristotle is correct in understanding that the mimesis of action is a key component of the theatrical event. But his seeming inattentiveness to the symbolic and his suspicion of the metaphoric gives us something of a crippled theater. Yes, mimesis is important. It is what draws us in, but the key to Greek drama is in the movement from the mimetic, through the symbolic and metaphoric to the meta-theatrical. It is through the work of these other modalities that we momentarily move outside of the story to contemplate its larger signification. This is the way theater quietly goes about its secret work.

Mimesis draws us in, makes us feel, but the use of symbols and metaphors pushes us out, lets us think. Before we get too detached by thought, we are drawn back in by the mimetic action. This back and forth nature of the experience is what gives the unfolding of Greek theater its dimensionality. Brecht is right to criticize Aristotle for placing too high a premium on mimesis and feeling—but he makes a similar error when he tries, in his theoretical work, to reverse the polarity of the theatrical experience and give priority of place to metaphor/thought. These impulses, the mimetic and the metaphoric, are equal and give the theatrical experience its rounded-ness. Brecht may have missed this as a theorist, but intuitively understood it as a dramatist. We can see this understanding at work in his late masterpieces (*Mother Courage, Galileo, Good Person of Setzuan*, etc.). Each follows the same circuitry as Greek or Elizabethan theater, allowing us to move from one modality of expression to the next. Brecht (as theorist) and Aristotle pit mimesis and metaphor against one another when they actually work hand in hand. Great theater, whether it is the theater of Ancient Greece, China, India, Shakespeare, Chekhov, or late Brecht is a blended theater, a theater where you can feel a thought and think a feeling. This experiential synesthesia happens by the shift in modalities from the mimetic, to the symbolic, to the metaphoric, to the meta-theatric. The imperative for the artist is to understand how to deploy these dynamics throughout the unfolding of the theatrical event.

Look at the journey of Clytemnestra's red bolt of fabric: it is introduced in a scene of absolute mimesis, where it seems nothing more than a ground cloth for the feet of dignitaries; then it transforms before our eyes into an overdetermined symbol that refuses to stabilize into a single meaning; finally, it can be re-envisaged, meta-phorically, as the blood of the now dead Agamemnon. Such a process moves the spectator from what we could call a passive looking (*blepien*) to active seeing (*oida*), returning us to the etymological roots of *theatron*: a space in which to see. It employs the powers of the mimetic, symbolic, metaphoric, and meta-theatrical so that we might leave the theater, return to the world and, in the words of Shakespeare, "See better." This is the impulse behind building "the large painted house" where we left our ever-patient friend Abu-al-Hasan.

Notes

1 Aristotle, *On Poetics*, translated by M.E.Hubbard, in *Ancient Literary Criticism: The Principle Texts in New Translations*, edited by D.A. Russel and M.Winterbottom (Oxford University Press, 1972), 94.
2 See Stephen Halliwell, *Aristotle's Poetics* (University of Chicago Press, 1998).
3 See Eugine Fink, *Play as Symbol of the World, and Other Writings*, translated by Ian Alexander Moore and Christopher Turner (Indiana University Press, 2016), 160–169.
4 L.S. Vygotsky, *Mind in Society: The Development of Higher Psychological Processes*, edited by Michael Cole, Vera John-Steiner, Sylvia Scribner and Ellen Souberman (Harvard University Press, 1978), 97–98.

9

THE COMPANIONS OF THE CAVE

Borges' third clue, on the necessity
of thresholds

Sadly, Abu-al-Hasan's story fails to capture the imagination of those at the party who have gathered to hear him speak. None of the guests, Averroes included, seems to understand Abu-al-Hasan. This leads Abu-al-Hasan to a further elaboration that becomes Borges' third and most elliptical clue. Abu-al-Hasan, in search of a helpful analog, begs the assembled guests to imagine someone showing them a story instead of telling it. He uses, as an example, *The Companions of the Cave*, also known as *Ashab al Kahn*, a popular tale for the early Christian and Muslim faiths.

The first extent version (circa 450–521) is of Syrian origin (derived from a now-lost Greek source). It tells the tale of a group of young Christian men who take refuge in a cave to escape the persecution by the Roman Emperor Decius. It was subsequently made popular in the Middle Ages thanks to Gregory of Tours and his *Golden Legends*. In this version, the emperor grants these seven young Christians time to recant their faith. Instead of doing so, they choose to live out their last days hiding and praying in a mountain cave where they fall fast asleep. The emperor's men discover them still in this sleeping state and are ordered to seal the mouth of the cave so that no one escapes. A hundred years pass and the cave is reopened by an unsuspecting landowner in need of a place to keep his cattle. There he discovers the seven who subsequently awake and think that they have only been asleep for one night rather than for a hundred or so years. They send one of their companions into the city for food, warning him to be on his guard for the pagans who are looking for them. The companion is stunned to discover crosses now growing from the tops of so many buildings and, when he tries to buy food, the townspeople are equally stunned by the old coin he possesses with the ancient emperor's profile stamped on it. The truth is revealed to all, these seven have, indeed, been asleep for a century. A bishop is summoned to question the seven, who praise God for this miracle and die, content to know that the Almighty has watched over them. Although this tale is Greek in origin, it has achieved its greatest prominence in the Islamic culture, finding its own immortality in the Koran (Surrah, 18, verse 9–26).

In Abu-al-Hasan's telling he is particularly interested in just the showing of the key moments, using the constant refrain of "we see" to capture the highlights of the tale: the seven escaping, entering the cave, praying, falling asleep with their eyes open, growing old while they sleep, waking many years later, learning this, and finally being granted a place in paradise. In this respect, Borges' third clue continues to keep the ocular aspect of theater particularly explicit with the refrain of "we see" stated some seven times in quick succession. But other than foregrounding the visual nature of the theater, this final clue is by far the most ambitious and elliptical. Andrew Harley, one of Borges' translators of this story, confesses in his footnotes that, "it is difficult (at least for this translator) to see the relationship of this particular tale (unlike the other stories such as the children playing) to Averroes' quest."[1] It does seem as though Abu-al-Hasan has jumped centuries and is suddenly describing a symbolist play by the likes of Maurice Maeterlinck. No doubt, Borges is having some fun with us by finding the most anti-theatrical subject matter in the world for an example of the dramatic. We can almost hear his faint laughter as he constructs the above sentences. Is this nothing more than a grand joke? Perhaps the meaning of this clue simply resides in its repeated emphasis on the audience's ability to see. But what does it see? Repeated instances of people not seeing until the very end when all is finally revealed? Is this the crux of theater? A space that enables us to see others not seeing? Is theater, then, just a series of cautionary tales where we either laugh or cry at other people's inherent blindness? This certainly feels like part of Borges' argument. But as with his other clues, we sense a certain density within each example. They always seem to want to tell us more. It is hard to think about people and caves, without thinking of the one Plato creates in the seventh book of his *Republic*. Is that what Borges is alluding to? Is he using the famous Koranic tale of *The Companions of the Cave* as a kind of arcane rebuttal of Plato's cave? In order to attempt to understand what Borges is up to, it behooves us to take a brief look at the history of the cave in the imagination of our ancestors.

Cave as metaphor

The cave still has a strong hold on our collective imagination. It is, after all, where we find the first creative expressions of our primitive ancestors. In such spaces they adorned the walls with the first representations of the world around them and began to practice initiation rites that continued well into the Ancient Greek and Roman period. One of our first surviving works of literary criticism is *On the Cave of Nymphs* by Porphyry. This brief treatise attempts to untangle the symbolic meaning behind a few cryptic lines from Homer's *The Odyssey* where Odysseus journeys through a cave to reach the underworld. This becomes the basic template for many tales about encounters within the caves; they are a place of descent, enlightenment, and transformation. Caves become tied to the myth and rites of Orpheus; in these circumstances they represent death and rebirth. One's descent into the cave becomes either a return to the womb to be born again, or a decent into Hades where one dies a symbolic death and is then granted a return to the world of the living. Here it is not an image or sign but the very experiencing of the cave that becomes a metaphor. Each phase takes on a transformative meaning whether it is in the crossing of a threshold, the dwelling within this strange new world, or the return to society at large. Yulia Ustinov, in her *Caves and the Ancient Greek Mind*, reminds us that to sojourn in the cave was a means toward acquiring superhuman knowledge.[2] What Greek mystics called *epopteia*, which roughly translates as "the beholding" and suggests admittance into the highest mysteries. Legend has it that the playwright Euripides possessed his own cave and used the space to pen his vast corpus of plays.

Plato, famously, reverses this ancient reverence for caves and turns it into the realm of ignorance. Here we find the inhabitants of a cave who have been prisoners of this inhospitable abode since birth, shackled together and facing away from the cave's entrance. All they ever see is one of the cave's interior walls where shadows are projected. These shadows are produced by figures above and behind the captive inhabitants. These strange figures carry various objects back and forth in front of an ever-burning fire, which cast their shadows on the cave wall for all to see. These shadows are the only reality that our captive inhabitants know. It is only when one prisoner finds a way out of his shackles, turns around (*periagoge*), and heads for the light at the entrance of the cave that a new reality is discovered. This lone inhabitant ventures past the threshold and finds himself blinded by the intense light of the out-side, unable to make sense of anything before him. Eventually his eyes adjust and he sees the world of true forms. Emboldened by this vision he returns to the cave to share what he has seen with his fellow cave dwellers. As with all of Plato's parables, there have been numerous glosses on this famous passage. Perhaps the two most per-vasive readings tend toward the epistemological or political. In the epistemological reading, the cave stands for our representational thinking and the prisoner's venture out into the world is an encounter with Plato's notion of true forms. In the equally popular political reading, the cave and the outside become two different ways of ruling a populace; one through illusions (represented by the shadows manipulated in the cave) or by truth (represented by the encounter with the light of the sun).

The question now before us is how does Borges' use of the tale of *The Seven Sleepers* relate to this rich genealogy of cave as metaphor, particularly in its most famous variation by Plato, and what, if anything, does this tell us about the nature of theater?

Plato's prisoner vs. Borges' companions

Part of the meaning of both Plato's and Borges' parables are imbedded in this simple movement back and forth, across the threshold of the cave; a crossing that delineates one's sense of exterior and interior. We can say, that in both cases, it is this movement across this threshold that leads to a truth about each protagonist's reality. But before discussing this intriguing similarity, let us see how these two stories differ from one another.

In the case of Plato's prisoner, he begins inside the cave in ignorance, but when he crosses the cave's threshold, he becomes aware. The revelation of truth that follows is not immediate, it takes his eyes awhile to adjust to the bright light of the sun, but when he has done this, the truth of his reality is revealed. He returns to the cave to share this newfound knowledge with his fellow prisoners. Borges' story of the companions begins not in the cave but rather outside. It is an outside far from the sublime transcendental realm depicted by Plato. Borges' outside is a harsh, remorseless, and deadly place. Our endangered seven escape into the interior of the cave where they find solace, prayer, and rest. It is more womb than Platonic prison. Rather than enslave the seven, this cave protects them; placing them into a magic sleep that allows them to outlive their peril. When they finally wake, some hundred years later, they have no sense of the miracle that has transpired.

What we see at the outset, is both Plato and Borges assigning radically different valuations to the cave and world beyond it. For Plato, the interior of the cave is a form of incarceration that not only arrests the inhabitants' freedom but also their intellectual development; for Borges, the cave is a magical place of sanctuary, succor and survival. In short, one could not find two more radically different depictions of the same object. And yet, both parables begin to align when one of the inhabitants from each cave turns (*periagoge*) towards the entrance and makes their way past the threshold. The truth of the companions' miraculous survival is revealed when one of the seven, like Plato's prisoner, leaves the cave. At first the world outside does not make sense; not because of, as in Plato, the intense and unfamiliar light of the sun; but rather, because the world at large no longer conforms to the sleeper's memory. Here he finds Christian crosses displayed freely about the town he once knew. Such an occurrence makes no sense to him since any gesture toward Christianity was banned in his day. It is not until he shares a coin (a nod to our old friend *symbolon*) that the townspeople inform him that what he believed to be newly minted currency is no longer worth anything. It is at that moment that he realizes the truth: a great stretch of time has indeed passed. He, like Plato's prisoner, returns to the cave to share this momentous news with his fellow survivors.

And so, although Plato and Borges deploy many of same narrative integers (the cave, the outside, a journey from one to the other), their readings seem to be in polar opposition to one another. Not only are the narrative integers given different value, the very trajectory of the narrative is reversed. In Plato, it is important to note that the outside is discovered; in Borges, the outside is the place of origin that is rediscovered and radically transformed after the interim in the cave. Borges, step by step, seems to be countering each of Plato's moves; except, as we noted, in one crucial instance:

The turning: or *periagoge, peripeteia* and *paideia*

The key moment in Plato's parable and Borges' story within a story is when Plato's prisoner and Borges' sleeper perform a *periagoge* (turn). From that simple movement everything changes. It leads them across the threshold of the cave, from the inside to outside and outside to inside. The direction is not as important as the event of turning-toward and the knowledge that it reveals.

Aristotle is also interested in such turns in drama where the character undergoes a *peripeteia* (a turn of fortune, usually for the worst) that leads to *anagnorisis* (a re-cognition). The turn in Plato's cave (*periagoge*) and the turn of fortune in Aristotle's *Poetics* (*peripeteia*) both lead to a new understanding. This "reorientation" in Plato and Aristotle brings us back to the etymological roots of understanding and its original usage; to understand is to make sure one "stands in the midst of" or "stands between" what he or she is attempting to see. Where you stand, tells you what you can know. Here the key to knowledge comes from a change in our relation to our surroundings; re-cognition comes from a re-position.

This is also true of anamorphic painting, which Shakespeare likens to our understanding of tragedy. Anamorphosis is a distorted optical image. When viewed straight on, the given image can seem like nothing more than a jumble of chaotic lines; but, when we re-position ourselves to the left or the right of the image, it suddenly snaps into focus, revealing its true form. The most famous example of this phenomenon can be found in Holbein's painting of *The Ambassadors*. In this work we find two imposing sixteenth-century gentlemen of the world surrounded by all their significant possessions, including a strange fossil-like figure that lays before them on the ground. But, when we shift our position to the right of the image, the fossil transmogrifies into a human skull. Suddenly our whole understanding of the painting has been altered, what we thought was a celebration of these men's good fortune, becomes a sober reminder that all is vanity. Shakespeare suggests in *Richard II* that a similar sort of anamorphic transformation of meaning happens in the experiencing of tragedy. What first seems a chaos of contradictory lines of action can also suddenly coalesce into meaningful event. Prior to the arrival of meaning, the spectator is held in a constant state of *theasthai* ("to look with one's mouth open"). How does this meaning suddenly materialize? Shakespeare tells us in *Richard II*:

> Like perspectives, which rightly gaz'd upon,
> Show nothing but confusion, ey'd awry,
> Distinguish form ...[3]

To "eye something awry" is to experience the world from the vantage point of Richard's fall. Only when Richard falls from king to commoner does new meaning begin to reveal itself. It can only happen once Richard has been dislodged from his habitual point of view, once this repositioning happens he can begin to see himself and the world anew. As he falls, we fall with him, seeing what he sees. Such changes in position open up a new view, a new understanding. Again, to re-position oneself leads to re-cognition. Anamorphosis becomes anagnorisis.

A similar repositioning happens to us as audience. Every time we enter the theater and find ourselves no longer "inside" the world at large, but seated just "outside" of a representation of it. It is from this new vantage point that we are able to eye things awry, thereby distinguishing forms we might never see had we not taken this altered vantage point. We turned from the world toward the stage and, eventually, turn back to the world. In those turnings, when we cross the threshold between our reality and fiction and fiction and reality, we are able to compare the two, such juxtapositions (the crossing of liminal boundaries) activate thought.

Heidegger would devote an entire semester of his 1931 lectures to such *periagoges* (turnings). Particularly the turning in Plato's cave and how this leads to true *paideia* (learning). Late in the seminar he tells us:

> The essence of Paideia does not consist in merely pouring knowledge into the unprepared soul as though it were a container held out empty and wanting … Paideia means *turning* around the whole human being. It means removing human beings from the region where they first encounter things and transferring and accustoming them to another realm where beings appear. This transfer is possible only by the fact that everything that has heretofore manifest to human beings, as well as the way in which it has been manifest, gets transformed.[4]

For Heidegger, one is turned around in "the very ground of one's essence" and thereby attuned to the world at large in a new and deeper manner; person and world are revealed to one another in a new light.

Such a process can happen in either direction, whether entering or departing from our encounter with art or philosophy. In both traversals, we find, this transition from one world to the other often difficult since we must re-attune ourselves to their fundamental differences. There is an uncomfortable moment as we try to settle into a philosophical text, or sit down to watch a theatrical work. Both encounters require time for us to readapt ourselves to the new demands of the given medium; but having done so, these difficulties quickly vanish. The same is true upon our return (especially if our encounter has been truly profound) and can require us to take a moment to reorient ourselves. In such a reorientation, a new relation to the world can open up. For Plato it is the status of being outside that represents the power and importance of philosophy; whereas for Borges it is the interiority of art that can help transform ourselves and our world. Regardless of which might be superior, it is only when we move from one to the other that true understanding begins. Both are necessary. Both outside and inside must be traversed in order for new relations/meaning to happen, allowing each to inform the other. We could call this the movement between truth and illusion, or subjectivity and objectivity; whatever names we want to give to these two different ways of relating to our world at large, we need both in order to truly navigate and enrich our lives.

Be that as it may, Abu-al-Hasan's story does little to win over its audience. The party gives way from Abu-al Hasan's description of theater (which no one seems to understand) to Averroes holding forth on the nature of metaphor. By the time he is finished, dawn is threatening and the partygoers disperse. Averroes returns home. None of the clues that he has encountered over the course of the day have pierced his consciousness. Sleep beckons, but so too does his desk where he has left his work. The desk, momentarily wins his attention. He sits down before the two obscure words that have eluded him all day and writes that the great Aristu (Aristotle) gives the name "tragedy" to panegyrics and the name "comedy" to satires.[5] Sleep finally overtakes our hero. He unwinds his turban while looking in the mirror, but there is no reflection of his face for he, the house, the court-yard below, his books, manuscripts, Abu-al-Hasan, and his friend Faraj have all vanished. The imaginary world that Borges has worked so hard to sustain, over seven dense pages, collapses back into nothingness; like a dream, or the memory of a play.

Notes

1   Jorge Louis Borges, *Borges Collected Fictions*, translated by Andrew Hurley (Penguin Books, 1999), 541.
2   See Yulia Ustinova, *Caves and the Ancient Greek Mind: Descending Underground in the Search for Ultimate Truth* (Oxford University Press, 2009), 177–209.
3   William Shakespeare, *Richard II*, edited by Charles R. Forker (Arden Shakespeare, Third Edition, 2002), 276 (II.2).
4   Martin Heidegger, *Plato's Doctrine of Truth*, translated by Thomas Sheehan, in *Pathmarks*, edited by William McNeill (Cambridge University Press, 1998), 167. For a full tran-scription of the original 1931–1932 lecture by Heidegger see Martin Heidegger, *The Essence of Truth: On Plato's Cave Allegory and Theaetetus,* translated by Ted Sadler (Continuum, 2002).
5   See Averroes, *Averroes' Middle Commentary on Aristotle's Poetics*, translated by Charles Butterworth (St. Augustine's Press South Bend, 2000).

10

ANATOMY OF FAILURE

Why the machine of theater breaks down

In the final paragraphs of *Averroes' Search*, Borges, the author, steps forth from behind the curtain of his prose and addresses his readers directly, telling us that his story mocked, foiled, and thwarted him at every turn, making him realize that trying to imagine Averroes was ultimately as difficult as Averroes attempting to imagine the meaning of comedy and tragedy without ever having seen a play. But failure is a crucial part of any artistic process. Art is never all-knowing, complete, or perfect. This is perhaps best summed up in Samuel Beckett's modest hope, at the start of each a new work, that he might, "fail better."

But part of theater's great success, as we have intimated earlier, is in its essential failure. Unlike its younger sibling, film, its ability to sustain an illusion is precarious at best. It is always just a moment a way from breaking down completely. In fact, it begins with the perceptual odds stacked against it. It takes a small eternity for an audience to enter into just about any theatrical construct; at first everything seems stilted, artificial, impossible to relate to in any significant manner. But then, ever so slowly, we find ourselves suddenly inside of the event. At that moment, like the dreams of our seven sleepers, we forget ourselves, our concerns, our very world. All this recedes into the background before what, just moments before, seemed so terribly artificial. Now it has become more real than our own reality. Then someone seated nearby coughs and, before the sound completely disappears into silence, we are thrust out of the world of the play and back in the auditorium with its well-worn carpet. Again, like the prisoner in Plato's cave, or one of Borges' seven companions, we have shuttled back and forth between two realities. We do not necessarily need Brechtian alienation techniques to cure us of the potential thrall of theater, theater by its very nature has its own built in alienation techniques. It is the very DNA of theater; as natural to theater as breathing is to us; becoming the very respiratory system of theatrical consciousness. This seeming insubstantial-ness of theater is its actual power; allowing us to move inside and, more importantly, outside of an event as it unfolds before us.

Ancient Greek theater understood and exploited this ongoing oscillation, it built an experience that guides audiences inside and outside of the theatrical event through a sophisticated alteration of dramatic episodes juxtaposed with choral interludes. The actual architectonics of Greek theater feels more like a strange Frankenstein's monster than one of our well-made contemporary plays. A Greek play is stitched together from a wide variety of contradictory forms of expression. It can move from an intricate *agon logon* (rhetorical argument), to a reflective choral ode, to a spellbinding *rhesis* (the telling of a bardic tale), to a heartfelt *kommos* (lament). Some of these approaches were designed to draw an audience into an event (*kommos* or *rhesis*) and others to specifically thrust an audience out (chorus or *agon logon*). Our modern theater seems fixated on drawing audiences inside and keeping them there to the final curtain call; Greek theater, on the other hand, was actively engaged in a series of impulses that pushed the audience outside of the event so that an audience would build up their objective muscles for when they returned to the world at large. Just as we find moments of resistance in the experiencing of theater, we can also cultivate similar moments of resistance against the spell that the world casts. It is a fundamental aspect of humanity that we find comfort in "being inside" the worlds we create, whether that is work, social relations, or belief systems. Theater shows us how we can develop moments of resistance to our propensity toward such total immersion; how we can step back, imaginatively thrusting ourselves outside of a given situation, to "see better."

Brecht, as we have noted, was equally afraid that an audience, left to their own devices, would fall under the spell of the dramatic and end up no more aware than a patron at an opium den. And so he put in a song, a joke, a placard, an aside, all to jolt the audience out of the event. Shakespeare was also profoundly aware of this interplay between illusion and the real. He would often use the first act or two to draw us in and the final acts to return us to the realm of the real (the ultimate outside). Such an approach reminds us that no matter how powerful an illusion can be, it cannot keep the real forever at bay. One can see this masterfully realized in *Antony and Cleopatra*. It is Cleopatra who is the queen of illusion-making. Toward the end of the play, after the death of Antony, she plans her own death with a zeal that would rival any theatrical showman. Death by sword is too commonplace for her. No, she must die by poisonous snakes biting each of her breasts. The history books will love such a death. And so a snake charmer is called to the palace. There is nothing magical about this poor soul, instead of imparting any final mystical advice, he resorts to a series of puns, replete with enough sexual innuendo to make in the stoutest of us blush. He is quickly brushed aside and Cleopatra is alone with her snakes, she makes her grand speech, but the snakes miss their cue and forget to bite. She has to smack each on the head to get them go about their venomous business. Finally she dies. But her chambermaid notices, too late, her poor queen's crown is terribly askew and she looks more like a fool than an empress. The real, in Shakespeare, always finds a way to humble whatever illusion has been spun. Even in *Midsummer Night's Dream*, the world of fairies gives way to images of brooms, dusty floors, and patiently awaiting marriage beds, all in need of a blessing or two. No matter how much one may try to sustain an illusion, the outside always returns.

This realization grows over the course of Shakespeare's late plays and reaches its apotheosis in *The Tempest*. Here we find the magician Prospero, who has spent his entire life devoted to illusions. We even get to see him weave one before our very eyes, a mythical pageant of sorts, with goddesses and a gaggle of other mythological characters, all for the delight of his daughter and her future husband. But a stray thought in the magician's mind brings the whole fantastical vision to a stop. He has forgotten about his servant Caliban, who is intent on usurping his power. The thought eclipses his vision and the illusion vanishes. Prospero apologizes to the newlyweds and to us, humbly explaining,

> Our revels now are ended. These our actors,
> As I foretold you, we're all spirits, and
> Are melted into air, into thin air,
> And like the baseless fabric of this vision,
> The cloud-capped towers, the gorgeous palaces,
> The solemn temples, the great globe itself, shall dissolve,
> And like this insubstantial pageant faded,
> Leave not a rack behind. We are such stuff
> As dreams are made on, and our little life
> Is rounded with a sleep.[1]

Prospero's daughter and her intended, like us, are not quite sure what has happened, why our master illusionist has let his vision collapse before us. Prospero explains that he is vexed and needs to walk a bit to "still my beating mind." Prospero's illusions, like those of all theater, are vulnerable, fragile, and impossible to sustain. One's ever-beating mind returns and the illusion crumbles. At such moments we feel the intimation of something larger at work. For our reality, like theater, is something we also construct. Our reality is an intricate network of relations that have been engendered by the creation of key social structures: family, religion, and the state. These constructions have had such longevity and been so all-pervasive that we confuse them with the real. But the real is quite separate from our human-made reality. The real is the ultimate outside, it is indifferent to the human. It has its own laws independent of our needs. The real is what science is still at pains to understand. In the meantime, reality is the re-scripting of the real, an attempt to mitigate its indifference which manifests itself most profoundly in our finitude. We create a reality, what we call a world, to try and explain and domesticate the real; but the real ultimately defies our quaint explanations and comes to us in all its incomprehensible catastrophe, destruction, and death. All of which can feel devoid of any meaning. But a world without meaning is intolerable to us. Hence our socially constructed reality that keeps the real and its potential meaninglessness at bay. If the real is the ultimate outside, then reality is a cunningly disguised inside posing as an outside. In short, reality traffics in illusion, the same as theater. This is why the church and the state have always been antagonistic toward the theater; its artificial nature mirrors their own. Just as the reality of theater can easily dissolve before us, revealing itself to be no more than mere illusion, so too can the meaning of such social constructs as church and state. No matter how robust or concrete they may seem to be, since they are constructions, they are susceptible to collapse. Just as we can see the "seams" in the construction of theatrical illusion, we can also return to reality and discover a similar "faulty workmanship." This is one of the lessons of theater, it teaches us to see the seams in reality.

The height of such an awareness occurs at the conclusion of a play, just as we are returning to the world at large. It is an intriguing and vulnerable state of being, similar to the liminal moment between sleep and waking, when we are most susceptible to questioning our own reality. Suddenly our world is not as stable as it seemed just moments ago. For a brief instance we sense its flimsy construction, how it suddenly seems as insubstantial as one of Prospero's illusions, nothing more than the stuff of dreams. This is about as close as most Westerners will ever get to the sensation of *maya*, the Sanskrit concept for doubting reality. Such moments lead to a kind of double vision, where one can pierce through our world to catch a glimpse of its illusionary nature. This, for Brecht, was the first step toward remaking reality; knowing that our world is indeed a human construct can embolden us to go out and build a better one. Or, as Shakespeare seems to intimate, knowing our reality is as fragile as our illusions demands that we be vigilant in our protection and preservation of what is meaningful to us. This is theater's ongoing project, to bring to the fore that which needs to be critiqued and that which needs to be cherished. How the machinery of theater brings these things momentarily to light will be the subject of our next chapter.

Note

1 William Shakespeare, *The Tempest*, edited by Frank Kermode (Arden Shakespeare, Second Edition, 1958), 103–104 (IV.1).

11

RECAPITULATION #1: OR TOWARD THE WHAT OF THEATER

It should come as no surprise, having read any Borges story, that the concept of a labyrinth is a favorite symbol for this most playful of authors. The density of his stories have a deep affinity with the maze-like complexity that both literature and reality can elicit. It is more than understandable that a reader might easily get lost between the tale's already twisting narrative and its tangle of potential meanings. Such a result is only compounded when one adds the gloss of a commentator; who, even with the best of intentions, often ends up adding to the maze, as opposed to elucidating the path toward liberation or understanding. It is this vestigial fear that leads to this last chapter, whose goal is to retrieve any reader that might still feel lost in the inadvertent labyrinth of Part I of this book. In this spirit, let us review Borges' essential clues so that we can create a kind a thread to lead us out of this labyrinth of potential meanings and toward a clearer understanding of the "what of theater."

1. Theater's family resemblance to play and ritual

We agree with Borges' basic taxonomy of these three human activities (play, ritual, theater) and understand how each might grow organically, one out of the other. What we find intriguing is how play and ritual cultivate a rich interior space for participants to occupy; while theater, in opposition to this, begins with being outside of the event of play or ritual. What interests us is how, even from this exilic vantage point, we can return to a sense of the interior of such things, through a form of imaginative projection. It is this repositioning of the participant and the ways in which we project ourselves back into the event that becomes the foundational aspect of theater. The result of this shift in perspective develops a kind of mental respiratory system where we can move back and forth from being imaginatively pulled into an event and, at key moments, find ourselves thrust out of it. This return to the outside can be inadvertent, a head obstructs our view and we are reminded that we are watching a play; or highly controlled, as in the theater of the Greeks, Shakespeare, or Brecht. Such authors want to create moments in which we are momentarily thrust back to the outside where we can reflect upon a certain key aspects of what is unfolding before us. Aspects that if we remained inside the event might otherwise go unnoticed. This return to the outside is part of the gift of theater, since we, as humans seem to be hardwired to place ourselves inside of things like work, play, or ritual. Theater gives us access to another, more objective stance.

2. Theater's play between the ocular and the aural

With this repositioning of the participant, we move from being within the midst, to being at a distance. This shift places a new demand on visibility, forcing the creation of the *theatron* (spaces in which to see) like the Ancient Greek amphitheaters or Borges' house of painted wood with its tiered seating and performative platform. The emphasis is no longer on just what we are hearing, as in the epic poems of Homeric bards or Chinese balladeers; but, in what we now also see before us. Just as theater encourages a dialectic between interiority and exteriority of a given event, it also depends upon a dialectic between what the eye sees and the ear hears. Theater reminds us how differently these two senses go to work on us. How the nature of hearing is more porous and subjective, where the sound from outside seems to still register within us; whereas vision, by its very nature, maintains a more rigid distinction/objectivity between our sense of self and the world around us. Put another way: inner and outer are kept distinct through sight and have a tendency to collapse in sound. Theater plays on this fundamental dichotomy. It often pits the eye and the ear against one another to ask which sense can get closer to the truth of the matter. Such an agon between the eye and the ear ultimately reminds us how much we can never depend on one sense to give us full access to truth. It is ultimately a negotiation between the two that guides us to any balanced conclusion. Theater, at its core, is fascinated with negotiation between the senses of sight and sound.

3. Hyper-intentionality: when things mean too much

Perhaps one of the most significant aspects of theater's shift to the outside is that it becomes a "limit field," which engenders a kind of hyper-intentionality. This profound shift in perception occurs when the collective gaze of the audience is directed toward the stage's limited field of representation. When such a condensation in representation meets an increase in collective attention, we find the audience moving from looking to seeing; or, put less poetically, from a passive reception to an active interpretation of the world before them. If we were to create a basic axiom for this heightening of perception we could say: the less placed within the space, the more it has the ability to resonate with potential meaning (i.e., stand out and warrant further investigation). These meanings can also possess profoundly different registers of signification. From Borges' examples of Asian theater we can designate four basic modalities of meaning in theater: the mimetic (which mirrors the way things are represented in the real world), the symbolic (where the object seems to transcend its quotidian designation and point to beyond itself to a surplus of further, often unknown, meanings), the metaphoric (where we transform an object into something other than itself; i.e., Vygotsky's stick becoming a horse), and finally the meta-theatrical (the moments when we are reminded that we are in a theater and how this sudden remembering strikes at our suspicion of an unseen metaphysics that operates just behind the "curtain" of our own reality). One of the challenges of Western theater has been an ongoing attempt to free itself from its relentless reliance on the mimetic as the only modality of expression and meaning.

4. Liminality: or the necessity of thresholds

The hope of every theater-maker is that the heightened modalities of meaning that can transpire during an audience's encounter with the theater can be brought back to the world at large. If theater is the movement from looking to seeing, the great question becomes how long an audience can take theater's perceptual gift and use it on the real world before the demon of habit dulls us back into our ocular complacency.

This acuity is perhaps most powerful at the beginning and the end of a theatrical encounter; when the audience first crosses the threshold from the world to the theater and then, two hours later, when the audience returns from the theater and back into the world. It is this liminal crossing of thresholds, between the real and the imagined, where we are reminded how easy it actually is to move from reality to illusion. The ease of such a transformation calls into question the very substance of the real. Just as it did for Borges and his *Companions of the Cave*.

It is, in this moment, that what we call "the world" or "the real" is at its most vulnerable, most open to questioning. All thanks to our time conversing with illusions. In this juncture, when we return to the world, it can actually feel more illusory than what transpired on stage. This is part of the secret critique that theater engenders. Here in this liminal moment between reality and illusion, when we turn from the stage and cross that threshold back into the world, the world, as we know it, is most open to interrogation.

5. The triumph of theater lies in its inherent failure

In the end of Borges' story, he bemoans the inability of the artist to sustain an illusion. His lamentations on this subject are very close to that of Shakespeare's rumination in *The Tempest*. It is there that Prospero reminds us that theater is ultimately the "stuff of dreams," and therefore something of a fragile affair. It takes tremendous effort to create and yet is so easily dispelled. The mere movement of an audience member's head can undo an entire evening's enchantment. But it is this very porous aspect of theater that is its ultimate gift. We can see the seams in some ill-crafted set and still fall under the spell of the story, believing that what stands before us is a room rather than a series of haphazardly assembled flats. The fact that theater can engender such imaginative leaps and yet is incapable of sustaining them is part of its secret metaphysical resonance.

Shakespeare uses the instability of theater as a metaphor for the instability of the world itself. He reminds us, over and over, how hard it is to sustain anything human, whether it is a play, a belief, or an entire civilization. Things fall apart. Why? Because things like the theater and our world are both man-made constructions. Brecht is also interested in this fundamental rhyme between the theater and the world. He believed that if you could show the seams in theatrical reality to an audience, they could go back out into the world and see its shoddy workmanship. Brecht's wager was that if the audience can be trained to see the construction of theater, then they can take this knowledge and apply it to the world itself, thereby seeing through to its own makeshift nature. This, for Brecht was not a cause of despair, but rather a means toward liberation. If the world was not an *a priori* given, if it were indeed man-made, than it stands to reason, that it can be *remade* for the better.

These are the foundational elements that make for "the what of theater." With these in mind, we can turn our attention toward how theater goes about making its myriad meanings manifest. Let us see, if in the next chapter, we can catalogue some of these unique manifestations.

PART II

Nine and a half tableaux

Theater's ek-static ability to bring what
is hidden into view

12

WELCOME TO THE MUSEUM OF EK-STASIS

Or when things "stand out" in theater

Let us direct your gaze to a random sampling of moments drawn from our everyday experiences:

A man walks on a red carpet.
A father and son reach their destination.
A young girl is watched by a boy from the street below.
A woman stands absolutely still.
A husband hides from his wife.
A man wants to leave while his lover wants to stay.
A soldier shaves his superior.
A family and their friends pose for a photograph.
An elderly man gets dressed.
A young man wakes in the middle of the night, having heard a sound.

In life, such a catalogue of quotidian deeds might very well, thanks to their collective banality, recede from our memory. But in the theater these seemingly uneventful incidents become the stuff of *Agamemnon, Abraham and Isaac, Romeo and Juliet, The Winter's Tale, Tartuffe, Faust, Woyzeck, The Three Sisters, Galileo,* and *Angels in America.* We will endeavor to understand how these simple moments from life, once placed on stage and put in their proper dramatic context, become so iconic for us. How, through this basic transposition, they begin to resonate in a manner that is unique to the medium of theater and seem to suddenly *mean more.*

This returns us to the Greeks who first created this mode of expression and gave it the name *theatron,* a space where seeing becomes a kind of knowing. It is a knowledge born out theater's very limits; since theater is not capable of showing everything, as in film or television, it must be selective in what it represents. This selectivity is further heightened through the relentless pressure of the audience's collective gaze. The result is a space that becomes hyper-intentional. This brings us to the doorstep of the ek-static. We turn to this word, in its earliest etymological meaning, to address those moments where certain presences literally "stand out" from their surroundings and come to occupy our complete attention (*ek* = out and *stasis* = standing). Not too long after the Greeks coin this word, it begins to take on a mystical cast that is further developed in the works of Plotinus and the early Christian theologians. Hence ek-stasis will ultimately evolve into ecstasy and this new etymological offspring will be thought of in terms of trance states. For our purposes, we will think of ek-stasis in its earliest, non-mystical usage.

The repurposing of this word overlaps with James Joyce's reappropriation of the Greek *epiphanien* (*epi* = upon and *phaino* = to shine/appear), which ultimately becomes epiphany. Joyce uses this word to help explain those moments where "the soul of the commonest object, its structure, is so adjusted, it seems to us radiant." To apprehend such moments, Joyce tells us, we must "lift [the object] from everything else; and then you perceive that it is one integral thing. That it is a thing. You recognize its integrity."[1] This "lifting of the object from everything else" would be, for us, the moment of ek-stasis which enables the object to "stand out" so that it can obtain Joyce's epiphanic realization (i.e., shine forth with meaning). Theater, by its very architectural nature, moves us from being in the midst of the world to standing apart from it; thereby engendering an atmosphere for a variety of potential epiphanies to manifest themselves. Joyce thinks of such endeavors as the groping of a spiritual eye that seeks to adjust its vision to an exact focus. The moment the focus is reached, the object is epiphanized. Theater supports Joyce's "spiritual eye," becoming the very vehicle for such an ocular adjustment, leading to that more exacting focus. The end result of the *theatron* is that it moves us from our passive way of looking to a more active form of seeing.

This unique ek-static vantage point also enables theater to see what often hides in plain sight. What we will call, for lack of a better word, the ineffables of existence. These can be thought of as: certain actions, time, space, being, nothingness, the secret life of objects, the symbolic tendencies of the world at large, other minds, the uncanny, and the duality of things in general. Unlike literature, it does not *tell* us this, but rather *shows* it. Theater reintroduces us to those languages beyond words, to another kind of reading, what we might call the reading of being. This can be the language of the body, tone of voice, or even certain silences. It makes the ineffable tangible for all to comprehend.

So, imagine if you will, a museum of sorts. The Museum of Ek-Stasis. It houses a series of living tableaux rather than paintings, statues, or antiques. Here we have gathered nine and a half representative moments taken from the stage directions of plays that move us from the days of theater's inception to its most recent iteration. Watch each carefully, for embedded within these semi-silent unfoldings is part of the secret power of theater. Let us start at the beginning with the Greeks, as Aeschylus' Agamemnon is about to make his way, yet again, across those precious red fabrics Clytemnestra has strewn before his feet. You may have thought that, thanks to our previous discussion, we have thoroughly investigated all there is to know about this extraordinary moment. But we have still not exhausted this iconic tableau for all that it can tell us about the ek–static nature of theater.

Shall we begin again? Agamemnon awaits.

Note

1 James Joyce, *Stephen Hero* (A New Directions Book, 1963), 211–213.

13

EXHIBIT ONE: *AGAMEMNON* REDUX

The optics of the tragic

He stands there, foot suspended in midair, about to step on this precious red fabric laid before him by his wife. Who is this man who knows he is about to tempt fate by walking on this rich red pathway? Is he the cold-blooded murderer of his daughter that his wife will, only moments from now, accuse him of being? Or is he the misunderstood leader of a thousand ships that were set to destroy Troy and made immobile by the absence of a wind? The gods, as usual, promised to rectify this, but it came at a price; a sacrifice, to be exact. The terms were relatively straightforward: the life of his daughter for the return of the wind. An impossible demand, but one he ultimately obeyed. It brought him victory and with it, a question that forms in the minds of all who now encounter him. What kind of man could do such a thing? Sacrifice a daughter for a wind? Is it possible, in such a moment, to be both a father and a general? Or must one choose? And if so, which one plunged the knife into the young girl's breast? The father who had no other choice? Or the general who was impatient for a place in history? Who, indeed, stands before us now, about to step on those resplendent fabrics laid out for him in honor of his victory.

All that happened some ten years prior to this fatal step on the red carpet. Agamemnon was on the island of Aulis, a decade away from that longed-for victory, waiting for that wind. It is said that Timanthes of Kythnos, the great fourth-century artist, captured this moment in his painting of the sacrifice of Iphigenia. This work has not survived the vagaries of time, but we do have a carved relief now on display in the Florence Archaeological Museum that is believed to be based on Timanthes' painting. The figure of Agamemnon with his head covered also reappears in a later version of the same scene discovered in the House of the Tragic Poet in Pompeii. This mural shows Menelaus and Odysseus carrying a disoriented Iphigenia toward her father. They are framed by Calchas, the seer, on the right-hand side of the painting and Agamemnon, who is found on the extreme left, as though he were trying to flee the very borders of this tragic scene. His back is turned from the whole affair. He is veiled. His face eclipsed by his hand and his cloak. An apt depiction of Agamemnon whose motives and agony are incomprehensible to us. What is he thinking? We do not know. His motivations, like his face in this painting, seem forever veiled to us.

But his wife, Clytemnestra, knows. To her, he is guilty of hubris. When faced with the choice between glory or his daughter's life, he chose glory. She has waited ten years for this very moment, for his return. Now she can exact her revenge for the murder of her daughter. She has set a trap to show the world Agamemnon's true intentions. The trap is now before his feet. It is that bolt of precious red fabric that lays before him. A strange and enigmatic trap. What does it signify?

The red of the fabric seems to bifurcate Clytemnestra's potential meaning into two basic symbolic paths: one of ostentation and the other of blood. Both Agamemnon and Clytemnestra speak only of the first potential meaning: rich fabrics worthy for the foot that toppled Troy. But the second meaning is also always present, lurking on the cusp of consciousness, patiently waiting for its recognition as a secret sign for the blood of Iphigenia, or perhaps the blood of all the men lost at Troy, or the soon-to-be-spilled blood of Agamemnon and his reluctant Trojan concubine, Cassandra. Regardless of which meaning, it is not something Agamemnon wants to step upon. He tells his wife, "Such things are for the gods, not mere mortals." But Clytemnestra must get him to walk on these precious fabrics; for such an action, in her eyes and the eyes of the Ancient Greeks, will make it clear to all that Agamemnon can never resist the call of glory. It is the only thing that matters, more dear to him than his own daughter. Clytemnestra believes, on a cellular level, that this is the sad and simple through-line of Agamemnon's irredeemable life. If he steps on the carpet then everyone will know the terrible secret of his insatiable vanity, and his subsequent "dispatch" by Clytemnestra to Hades will therefore be justified for all, including the gods above.

"Would Priam walk on such silks?" She asks.

"Priam would love to walk on such fine fabrics, he is a barbarian. I am a Greek," he replies.

"Yet a victor must acknowledge his victory," she says with a smile.[1]

This is a beautiful rhetorical move on Clytemnestra's part, leaving Agamemnon with very little room left to maneuver. And so, Agamemnon finds himself once again, faced with what fascinated fifth-century Athenian audiences more than anything: *hairesis*. A new word for an old dilemma known as choice. In the ancient days, that were ancient even back then, the gods entered men and made them do the things the bards would subsequently sing about. But now, modern man must choose for himself and be held accountable for those choices. That is what it means to be part of a burgeoning democracy. Tragedy, being democracy's precocious cousin, grows up at the same time in Athens and chronicles the Athenian's newfound sense of agency. And so, tragedy loves nothing more than to place its heroes on the threshold of a decision and watch, with the greatest of attention, which course they will take.

Agamemnon has been at this threshold before with his daughter's life in his hands. Save her and be a father, or sacrifice her and become the general you were meant to be. Agamemnon, as we said, chose the latter. Now he must choose again, only this time it seems to be his fate, rather than his daughter's, that hangs in the balance. What to do? With every *hairesis* there is the risk of a subsequent *hamartia*. *Hamartia* has had a difficult time in translation. For centuries it had been misunderstood as a "tragic flaw," which was due to how the word was used in the Greek of the New Testament. Hamartia, for the Ancient Greeks, has far humbler lexical aspirations. In its oldest incarnation, it was related to the art of archery and simply meant "to miss the mark." The word subsequently enters the everyday vocabulary of a fifth-century Athenian as "a mistake." Something no one wants to make, particularly fifth-century Athenians. The ancient poets warn us that innocence is dangerous, it can attract wolves. In Greek tragedy, very few escape the attention of our canid friends, which means that the heroes who populate this genre seem congenitally predisposed to making the wrong choice. This sets in motion two final words in the machinery of Greek tragedy: the vaguely familiar sounding *peripeteia* and the much more elusive *anagnorisis*. *Peripeteia* is also known as a "reversal of fortune" (almost always for the worst) and the more elliptical anagnorisis is defined as the moment at the end of tragedy when ignorance crystallizes into a sharp and cutting knowledge. In this respect, tragedy's education is one of *via negativa*: the hairesis becomes a hamartia that leads to a *peripeteia* that ends in a sobering form of *anagnorisis*. This is tragedy's brutal equation and it is as exacting as physics' second law of thermodynamics.[2]

And so, Agamemnon is faced with a new *hairesis*. He must decide whether or not he is deserving to go against the decorum of mortals and trample fine fabrics reserved for the gods: an act that could very well bring about their displeasure and his end. Ah, but to feel that soft pathway beneath his tired feet. Hasn't he earned it? Who would begrudge him this, after all he has done? Will he succumb to the temptation? Does he have the gall to do so? And if he does, will it suggest the hubris Clytemnestra suspects? Before we can answer any of these mounting questions, we find, to our shock and horror, Agamemnon taking his first fatal step. His foot touches the fine fabrics and the gum stuck machinery of tragedy wakes, its metaphysical gears begin their relentless and irrevocable rotation toward Agamemnon's ultimate destruction. The choice was made. In the eyes of the gods it is indeed a terrible mistake, leading to a catastrophic reversal of fortune, and ending with the final recognition of Agamemnon's all-consuming hubris having gotten the better of him. It is all as simple as that, as simple as putting one foot in front of the other, of moving step by step, from *hairesis* to *hamartia* to *peripeteia* to *anagnorisis*. A crimson pathway to his death, just moments from now, courtesy of his wife Clytemnestra and a nearby ax.

Now what the Ancient Greeks called a *peripeteia*, Stanislavski would come to call an "event." An event not only changes the nature of a situation but also allows us a certain kind of visibility. It makes things that would have otherwise gone unnoticed suddenly legible. In the moment of an event we can see things that have heretofore remained latent, unseen. Events change situations and, in doing so, bring certain things to light. Let us look at the event of an earthquake. Such an event changes the situation: I had a home, now it is in ruins. But it also allows us to see things we would not see otherwise. For instance, one person, whom we may have never taken seriously, suddenly proves themselves, in the moment of the earthquake, to be courageous. This is the twofold power of events, they bring about change and visibility. At this juncture, we are more interested in what this can show us, what we could call "the optics of the tragic"; rather than how it changes Agamemnon's situation, or "the mechanics of tragedy." This is the moment the Greek's call *anagnorisis*, or recognition, when a revolution in plot leads to a revelation in character. Agamemnon, this man whose motives have been shrouded in mystery, whose true self even Timanthes, the greatest of Greek painters, could not capture on canvas, shows himself to us in this moment. So, what do we see?

The answer depends on what production you might have encountered. The moment remains uncommented on by its author Aeschylus. There is no stage direction explaining what the actor should show or what the audience should feel. This is one of the interesting paradoxes of theater. Every time Aeschylus' *Agamemnon* is performed, we know he must walk across that red carpet to his predetermined end but what this walk shows us and what that might mean is left in the hands of each actor and director. The results can vary greatly. Let us follow three potential Agamemnons as they make their way across this crimson path and see what their steps might reveal.

Our first Agamemnon, his foot suspended in midair, brings it down, ever so carefully, as skin and fabric meet. Stopping there, afraid for his foot to leave an imprint, it remains uncommitted to the ground beneath him. A brief eternity passes as he slowly puts his full weight on this one extended foot until he can sense the cold and indifferent ground that not even the gentle weave of these precious fabrics can entirely hide. Another pause, as if he were waiting for a thunderbolt from Zeus, but no such heavenly rebuke arrives and so he begins his ever-cautious journey across the carpet. Midway down this crimson path there is still no sign of displeasure from the gods above. All this is oddly freeing, empowering even. Not to mention the feel of the fabric under his bare feet, why it is nothing short of sublime. The pleasure it gives, courses through his entire body. It is a strange and wonderful kind of intoxication. Each of his ensuing foot falls become more and more assured, bold actually; as if to say, in those final steps that have become triumphant strides, "To hell with you all and whatever you might think, I deserve this."

Or …

Agamemnon's foot meets the fabric and a sensation of wrongness, almost like an electrical current, shoots upward through his body, warning him to proceed no further. But he must. All eyes are on him. He can't take back that initial first step. How would it look if he were to change course now? No. Such a thing is simply impossible. He must continue. After all, he is Agamemnon, the king of Mycenae. Kings don't retract their steps, they venture forth with royal resolution. He has no choice but to take the next step and so he does, with the full assuredness that befits a king. This is more like the conqueror of Troy. He is not about to let himself be undone by a bolt of fabric woven by barbarian women. The shock felt from the first step is gone, replaced by another low-grade sensation. Something is still not quite right. What is it? This feeling? What should he call it? Nausea? Vertigo? Whatever it is, it is becoming overwhelming, growing with each step, sapping whatever vigor he has left. Finally, he finds himself at the entranceway. It seems as though he has aged 50 years in 50 paces.

Or …

Agamemnon's foot meets the fabric and he feels nothing. Nothing at all. One foot follows the other in a slow and steady tread and still no feeling is felt. There is no discernible fear, or relief, or defiance, just profound indifference. The indifference of the dead. For it becomes clear to us that this man died long ago, on the Island of Aulis, at the precise moment his knife pierced his daughter's breast. Two deaths with one simple stroke: her sacrifice and his secret suicide. A living dead man, everything lost its meaning: Troy, home, these fabrics now beneath his feet, even the real death that he knows awaits him in the palace. Perhaps, this is why he has come home. To meet his end at the hands of his wife.

None of these interpretative options would have been available to us without the arrival of an event. Events make things manifest. What they reveal we could call the very core of the person or the situation: that Agamemnon is an egoist, or Agamemnon is already dead. Events exist to force such core moments of truth to the surface. It is worth noting that events are the domain of playwrights, they create them to clear the ground for a new vision to occur. But that vision and the core moments that they produce, are open for the actor and director to explore. Events (Agamemnon must walk on the carpet) are scripted; cores (*how* Agamemnon walks on the carpet) are interpreted. Let us say that an author tells us that Character X slaps Character Y. That is an event. How the actor responds (the core moment) will be different and individual to each actor. One might burst into immediate tears, another may hold his or her tears back until everyone leaves the room. This is one of the reasons why we can return again and again to watch a multitude of Agamemnons walk across a red carpet, or a parade of Hamlets attempt to kill Claudius. The event is always the same, but something on the other side of it, is uniquely understood and revealed in the performance of each new actor. Theater needs both the inviolable structure of events as laid out by playwrights *and* the interpretive freedom of actors and directors to delineate the core moments that the events engender.

Events jolt us from our complacency. They force us to shift from looking to seeing. This heightened acuity is crucial to the hermeneutics of theater. Events help us (as Kent enjoins a distracted King Lear) to "See better" and see more. Thanks to the pressure of events, a hidden truth of Agamemnon's character comes to light. The event of Agamemnon walking on the carpet opens him up to us. It is a moment where his actions, rather than his words, reveal something quintessential about him. "Tragedy," according to Heidegger is, "the movement from seeming to being."[3] Before Agamemnon walked on the carpet, he was a mystery to us, an inhabitant of the realm of seeming; after his walk on the carpet, he is known, we have grasp an essential part of his being. He is now understandable to us.

But before we leave Agamemnon to the fate that awaits him, let us return one last time to the moment that sets it all in motion, just to be certain we have exhausted its full range of potential meanings. It is important to note that the visibility that an event gives forth is not only reserved for what occurs in its aftermath. It can also shed light on what comes before. The closer we are to the actual happening of the event, the more it has the capacity to reveal what is essential on either side of its occurrence. And so we can learn as much about the event's cause as we can its consequence. In the slapping of Y by X, we focused on the aftermath of the slap, what it revealed about Y. But, the event also has the capacity to help us understand its root, what provoked X to slap Y in the first place. Again, the event has the possibility of shedding light on what is before or what is after. It is, in terms of theater, a matter of emphasis, which moment one decides to give more weight, or, perhaps more precisely, which moment has the capacity to reveal more to the audience. With this in mind, we can ask ourselves what can be learned about Agamemnon and Clytemnestra before the event of his stepping on the red carpet.

There he is, again, Agamemnon standing before the red carpet. Clytemnestra is in the midst of enticing him to take that first crucial step: You deserve this, Priam would do it had he won, the people expect it, it is unbecoming to ignore the desires of your people. None of these seem to do the trick. Agamemnon remains unconvinced. And then, almost as if out of nowhere, he asks:

"And truly, do you yourself desire (treasure) this victory?"

And Clytemnestra responds, "Prevail upon yourself fully, relax your strength entirely, willingly, for me."

And that is the clincher, those last two little words, "for me."

And Agamemnon relents, "Very well then, if these things seem good to you, may someone release me from these boots."[4]

And so, Agamemnon does not walk upon this bolt of red fabric out of pride, or under pressure, but simply for her. To appease his estranged wife. As if to say, "If this will satisfy you, after the wrong that I have done you, the daughter I have deprived you of—then, yes—I will, against my better judgment, walk upon these fine fabrics. I do this, *for you*." Not for him, but for her. He dies for her.

In this reading Agamemnon steps on the fine fabrics and it feels right, inevitable, as if everything he has done has actually been in preparation for this very moment, which he now gives himself over to: simply, soberly, completely. And, in the end, it is a kind of relief, an acquiescence of sorts, and for the first time in ten years his body relaxes. Tears fill his eyes, although he is not quite certain why. He hasn't cried since that day, all those years ago, on that dreaded island and now these tears return, reacquainting themselves with his parched cheeks. He wipes them away, but they refuse to relent. Let them fall, he thinks, what do I care. He reaches the end of the carpet and turns one last time to his wife. Her eyes are dry, her face implacable; nothing, not even his journey across this bright red expanse, will change the way she feels. But he knew this, just as he knew that these would be his last steps. And so he enters the house, to the death that patiently awaits him.[5]

Agamemnon has traversed this red carpet for some 2,500 years, each time revealing yet another aspect of his secret self. A kind of inadvertent theatrical variation of Nietzsche's "curse of the eternal return." But isn't that the calling card of all great works? That we must return to them and they to us. It is as if, with each purgatorial return there is also the potential of new understanding, of further revelation. And so, we commit to making that long and intricate journey one more time, from the realm of seeming into the mysterious workings of being. Each time asking ourselves, what more can we see, each time humbled by inexhaustible nature of what can be revealed.

You are more than welcome to linger here, with Agamemnon. He will return momentarily and once again begin his journey across Clytemnestra's carpet. A traversal that will, no doubt, bring forth further reflection. Or, you may join us for our next tableau; equally ancient, equally iconic, and equally revealing in what it can tell us about the nature of how theater makes things stand out.

Notes

1 My very literal translation of this passage.
2 For a truly in-depth understanding of how Ancient Greeks constructed their plays, see Malcolm Heath, *The Poetics of Greek Tragedy* (Duckworth, 1987) and for its social-historical implications of such dramatic architectonics, see Jean-Pierre Vernant and Pierre Vidal-Naquet, *Myth and Tragedy in Ancient Greece*, translated by Janet Lloyd (Zone Books, 1990).
3 Martin Heidegger, *Introduction to Metaphysics*, translated by Gregory Fried and Richard Polt (Yale, 2000), 112.
4 My second very literal translation of this passage.
5 I was heartened, during my research, to see that my preferred reading of this moment rhymes with the great Eduard Fraenkel who wrote perhaps the most in-depth commentary of *Agamemnon*, see his three volume: Aeschylus, *Agamemnon*, edited with commentary by Eduard Fraenkel (Oxford, 1979).

14

EXHIBIT TWO: *ABRAHAM AND ISAAC*

Difference, variance, and making time manifest

They have walked in silence for some time now. The walk is familiar, something they have done ever since he can remember. There has always been this path, that pack, his father's staff, and their slow and careful ascent up the mountain. But the silence between the two is new, extending beyond them and seeming to envelop the whole wide world. All is hushed, still, waiting. But for what? His father is beside him, but the old man's mind is somewhere else; far, far away. The boy, who is barely 12, develops a string of inconsequential questions, anything that comes to him, anything that will draw his once loquacious father back to his former self. But that father is gone, in his place is a man of monosyllables. There is a yes or a no and then silence again, only to be broken by the next tentative question from an increasingly distraught son. And so they go on like this, until they reach their destination and begin to set up for the sacrifice. It is at this point, some 125 lines into what is known as the medieval N-Town rendition of the story, that Isaac notes:

> Fadyr, fyre an wood here is plenty,
> But I kan se no sacryfice.[1]

This happens at a much brisker pace than the version found in the Chester Cycle, which has its Isaac question his father some 270 lines before realizing the absence of a sacrificial lamb. The Chester Cycle Abraham responds by inadvertently baring his knife toward his innocent son. The Chester Isaac (spelled Yssack), cries,

> Fadyr, I am full sore afrauyde
> To see you beare that drawn sworde.
> I hope for all myddy larde
> You will not slaye your chylde.[2]

The Abraham of the more economical York Cycle explains, around line 185, to his Isaac:

> Sertis, sone, I may no lengar layne
> Thyselfe shulde bide pat bitter brayde.[3]

The York Abraham leaves it for Isaac to intuit that it is indeed he, by God's decree, that must be sacrificed. This makes a certain psychological sense, a sensitivity that the York author is often known for displaying. Compare this to the more prosaic N-Town Abraham who goes to great and careful lengths to explain:

> Alas, dere sone, for nedys must be me
> Evyn here be Kylle, as God hath sent!
> Thyn owyn Fardyr bi death must be![4]

Many prefer the more straightforward anguish of the Chester Abraham who, in response to his son's query, sobs:

> Ah, Isuack, Isuack, I must thee kill.[5]

One of the things which we often forget about ancient plays is that their audience entered the theatrical space knowing the story they were about to re-encounter. This was an interesting prerequisite of Greek theater as well as the Medieval Mystery Cycles which recounted tales from the Old and New Testament. New or contemporary stories proved to be too painful for the Ancient Greeks. There is a famous anecdote regarding one of Aeschylus' contemporaries who mounted a play dealing with a recent military defeat. The audience, all of whom had lost relatives in this battle, were so overwhelmed with grief that the actors were unable to finish the performance. Legend has it that ever since that fateful event, the Greeks decided to place all their plays in the safe and distant past of Homer. For the early church, the stories of the Old and New Testament were simply the only stories that needed to be shared. There would be nothing new to be told till Judgment Day. So, until that time, a congregation would just have to make do with the timeless tales of the Bible. The special treat would be that that these stories were no longer conscripted to Latin or consigned to representation in stain glass windows. Now they could come to actual life and be performed by the congregation themselves, just outside the church, in their own earthy vernacular. That was new enough for them.

Although the privileging of pre-existing stories was not aesthetically driven by these cultures, its inadvertent impact formed a unique and essential part of the theatrical experience of Ancient Greek and medieval audiences. The key to such an experience was not *what* was going to happen; but rather *how* it would happen. This is somewhat different from our modern expectations of storytelling where what we look for in a story is that it should be "new." The major criterion for such an experience of "newness" is, to a certain extent, not knowing what will happen next.

The closest we come to the idea of telling a story that everyone knows is in our contemporary penchant for genres: westerns, thrillers, mysteries, etc. In such cases, the surface of the story feels new, but the deep structure is still built upon a series of familiar devices: heroes as outsiders, implacable foes, chases, and death-defying climaxes. In short: old stories in new packaging.

But what exactly is the difference between experiencing *what* will happen rather than *how* it will happen? The significant shift is in where we put our main focus. When the issue is what will happen, we tend to place much of our mental energy on issues of the plot, trying to anticipate its unfolding, predicting how one event will lead to the next, creating an inextricable chain that also chains our consciousness to the mechanics of the story. But, when we are relieved of the profound gravitational pull of what happens next, than our mind is allowed to dwell on details such as character, choices, outcomes. This is the *how* of the story and it can lead us to a deeper understanding of the story's *why*, of what it all might mean. In this respect, early drama is closer to the dynamics of mythology which also has a penchant to have its tales told and retold over and over again. The lifeblood of a myth is in its subtle variations, its *difference from* one telling to the next. Where there is difference, there is meaning waiting to be discovered. We can trace such a methodology of implied meanings as it passes from Greek myth to Greek drama. We know that each of the great dramatists told a select set stories from Homer's *Iliad*, the houses of Atreus, Oedipus, Hercules, and Theseus. We can see it at work in the retelling of the story of Electra that Aeschylus, Sophocles, and Euripides each had a hand at writing.

A similar dynamic is at work in the Christian tradition that understands all Old Testament stories as prophetic prefigurations of the story of their savior Jesus Christ. In this respect, the sacrifice of Isaac is a precursor to the sacrifice of Christ. It is as if the story of Abraham's sacrifice of Isaac was God's first draft or dress rehearsal for Christ's crucifixion. An early Christian audience would have been encouraged to look for similarities and differences between both testament tales. And so, for this audience, they are experiencing two stories in one. In this dual telling there are two fathers; one human, the other holy. Both are intent on sacrificing their sons. This may help us understand why several of the Isaacs we will encounter seem so otherworldly since they function more as prototypes for Christ rather than just children. Let us begin with the Isaac from N-Town who, upon hearing the news of his soon-to-be demise, tells Abraham, without a moment's hesitation, that:

> Almyghty God of his grett mercye,
> Ful hertyly I thanked be, sertayne
> At Goddys bidding here for to dye
> I obeyed me here for to be slayne.[6]

Not exactly the sort of response one might expect from a child. But then again, the N-Town Cycle is the most schematic of extent Medieval Mystery Plays, often sacrificing human behavior for doctrinal demands. The York Isaac is less otherworldly, more like a terrifically precious child doing as he has been told; even when what he has been told is the unthinkable. Here is his considered response to Abraham's revelation:

> And I sall noght grouche peragayne
> To wirke his wile I am wele payed;
> Sen it is his desire,
> I shall be bayne to be
> Brittynd and Brent in fyre,
> And perforce morne noght for me.[7]

Both responses, ultimately, feel less concerned with capturing the truth of how a young child might respond and more in keeping with how such responses might prefigure Jesus and his question-less faith, even when faced with the most horrific of fates. The Townley Isaac is perhaps the closest to behaving like a child in frightful circumstances. This Isaac has no intention to be as compliant as the other Isaacs have been. The Townley Isaac, recoils with shock:

> I am hevy and nothing fayn,
> Thus hastely that shall be shent.[8]

And then, the Townley Isaac does what any child, faced with this situation, should do. He begins to run from Abraham. His father calls after him, suddenly sounding like some big, bad wolf let loose from a Grimm Brothers' tale:

> Come heder, bid I;
> Thou shal be Dede, whasoeuer betide.[9]

These fatalistic words do the trick and the Townley Isaac relents, giving himself over to his father like the Isaacs of York and N-Town; but the Townley Isaac, is not completely compliant, he tries to work on Abraham potential sense of guilt:

> When I am Dede and closed in clay,
> Who shall be your son?[10]

But his Abraham refuses to entertain any thought but what his God has demanded he do. It is the Isaac of the Chester Cycle who is ultimately the most challenging, the most capable of penetrating his father's resolve. The Chester Isaac wastes no time:

> Alas, father, ys, that your wyll,
> your owne chylde for to spyll
> upon thys hilles bryncke?
> If I have trespassed in any degree,
> with a yarde you may beate mee.

> Put up your swords yf your wyll bee,
> for I am but a chylde.[11]

It is this Isaac who strays the furthest of being a precursor of Christ and remains rooted in a child trying to comprehend the cruel and inhuman fate that awaits him. He asks pointedly,

> Is yt Godes will I shalbe slayne?[12]

And his Abraham answers:

> Yea, sonne, yt is not for to leane;
> to his bydding I will be beane,
> ever to him pleasinge.
> But that I doe this deolfull deede,
> my lorde will not quite mee my meede.[13]

Isaac, hearing this response, counters with the following answer, it is eight simple lines, but within them he goes from child to adult:

> Marye, father, God forbydde,
> but you doe your offeringe.
> Father, at home your sonnes you shall fynde
> that you muste love by course of kynde.
> Put I once out of your mynde,
> your sorrowe may soone cease.
> But yet you must doe Godes byddinge.
> Father, tell my mother for nothinge.[14]

What an extraordinary request: "Father, tell my mother for nothinge." The child is thinking beyond himself and worrying about protecting his mother from the knowledge of his father's terrifying deed. One can feel the profound difference between the rather one-dimensional Isaac of the N-Town to this Isaac of the Chester Cycle who has reached a level of deep maturity in the span of eight lines. What we witness here is the moment where the child becomes the parent, for now it his father who is in need of care. The author of the York Cycle will take this idea of maturity one step further with his Isaac (ever the precocious child) ultimately helping his overwhelmed father complete the remaining duties of the sacrifice. Most importantly, he bids Abraham to bound his hands and feet as tight as his father can since he is unsure of his courage and worried that he might otherwise try to escape. Ever the good son, he does not want to be the cause of his father's failing in his divinely ordained task.

This is the concept of difference, with a capital D, at work. It is similar to the different approaches we found in Agamemnon's walk across the carpet. Although in this instance, it is a series of authors, rather than actors, that are exploring the range of revelation that this particular event can show. With Agamemnon the difference was open and interpretative; with the story of Abraham and Isaac, the difference is being scripted from play to play. Both require an event (the walking on the red carpet, or the sacrifice of Isaac) for us to arrive at a core moment of understanding of these characters. It is intriguing to note that in the story of Abraham and Isaac, the fundamental difference (variation) always concerns how Isaac responds, rather than with anything that has to do with Abraham. This suggest that the emphasis is not on whether Abraham will do the deed (we know he will) but rather on Isaac's capitulation. This is where, for these authors, the real meaning of the story resides. Again, their interest is in how Isaac prefigured Jesus. What we are experiencing in these variations in the story is how these authors slowly arrive at fully dimensional rendering of young person acquiring true, Christ-like faith in the face of the direst of circumstances. Each author gets closer, capturing how this nearly impossible leap of faith actually might happen; each iteration brings us closer and closer to the messy, human and honest way we arrive at such a miraculous vantage point.

And so, it is through these differences that we are able to tease out the unified thematic meaning that exists at the heart of these medieval renderings. There is also another, somewhat subtler difference at work in the unfolding of each of these variations. Again, the fact we know the outcome of the story helps us in discerning this slightly more elusive difference which has more to do with our experiencing rather than our understanding of the scene. When we know a story's outcome, we not only become more sensitive to the how of its telling, but also to the when of its climaxes. The great climax in the story of Abraham and Isaac is, of course, the intervention of God's Holy Messenger. Most medieval audiences would watch this horrific scene unfold and remain comforted in the knowledge that God's Heavenly Messenger will arrive at any moment to save the day. But that moment of arrival has a significant degree of variance from one rendition to the other. In the N-Town version it takes a swift 55 lines from the drawing of Abraham's knife to the arrival of the Messenger. The Townley version takes a slightly less brisk approach, clocking in at 85 lines, while York requires a solid 100. The Chester Cycle trumps all three rival versions with 145 lines ensuing before the Messenger actually intervenes. Do these slight variances actually make a difference? In the theater the answer is yes. Theater, like music, is a time-based art form where we are hyper-sensitive to time's passage; or, to be more precise, hyper-sensitive to when time does not pass as we expect it. The author of the Chester version plays with this sensitivity of ours. By delaying the intervention of the Heavenly Messenger, he heightens the tension of the scene. The author of the Chester Cycle seems to intuitively understand that with the telling of an old tale, we may lose the element of surprise, but gain the element of suspense.

Now there is also an intriguing byproduct that comes with the use of this suspense, it inadvertently makes us aware of a rather ephemeral and often forgotten aspect of our existence: time's immanence. Time is, in many ways, the shyest of phenomenon. It seems happiest when it is invisible, like the air we breathe; but when there is a delay in the anticipated outcome a story, time begins to congeal and shows itself as duration. The experiential result is as though theater were able to liquefy time. When this happens, time feels as though it has indeed taken on the physical properties and tendencies of water, flowing at varying rates. It can be a steady stream, a rushing river, or an absolutely still pond. This is what we mean by theater's liquefaction of time. In short, we can feel how time secretively moves. Theater has the power to not only make time manifest but also to remind us that time does not always behave with the comforting mechanical regularity of the clock. In the theater, clock time gives way to the more relative and unpredictable realm of felt time.

And so, certain moments, like Abraham revealing the knife he will use on Isaac, lures time from the shadows and out into the open. Once revealed, it moves swiftly as Isaac attempts to dissuade his father from this cruel act and then slows to almost a standstill when Abraham lifts his knife high over his head, about to plunge it downward into his child's breast. In such moments, time itself becomes ek-static, it stands outside of itself, crystallizing into what Shakespeare calls, "the interim." A concept introduced in his *Julius Caesar*:

> Between the acting of a dreadful thing
> And the first motion, all the interim is
> Like a phantasma, or a hideous dream.[15]

We have been here before, with Agamemnon, when he was faced with sacrificing his own child and, ten years later, when challenged to walk on fine fabrics that are reserved for the gods. These are the moments when the pressure of the events lead to core moments of revelation. And these core moments have a palpable time signature, where time itself seems to stop. This is where the actor becomes interpreter again, since there is no marking denoting how long the moment from the knife being suspended above Abraham's head should last before it is plunged downward toward the cowering Isaac. The length of this dramatic caesura is left to the discretion of each actor who takes on the role of Abraham. He must use his own inner sense of how long such a moment can sustain itself before it becomes overindulgent. These are the variances that can change a performances night to night, based on what the actor actually feels in the moment and whether he senses the audience is with or ahead of him. And so, the slight variance of time is a reality of every performance.

This is the mercurial nature of theater, its very life-blood. Those who are familiar with the inner vicissitudes of putting on a play, learn quickly that live performance is very much like Heraclitus' river: the same and yet ever-changing. An added two minutes to a performance can turn an otherwise engaging evening into deadly theater; whereas, the loss of two minutes can reduce what was a profound experience into something hollow and inconsequential. Such is theater's susceptibility to time, no wonder it is so sensitive to its every alteration. It is ultimately the alertness to these variances that keeps the theater unique and very much alive. When we return to a book, or a movie, or a painting, whatever variance we experience is in us, not in the work itself. The work of the book, movie, or painting remain the same sequence of words, images, or pigments that they were from our last encounter; they may seem to have altered, but we know that the real alteration is always in us; that is what effects our re-viewing of the work. Not so, when we return to a theater piece; it is, like us, a living organism, shifting just as we shift. We find the same words and actions, but when in the mouths and bodies of actors, these words and actions cannot help but vary, given the actor, his scene partner, the particular historical moment, and the idiosyncrasies of each audience. Theater must be awake to all these variances. When it is not, it can be a deadly affair. In the theater, difference makes meaning; variance gives life.

But we must move on, we will return to how time is made manifest in theater when we come to Chekhov's *Three Sisters*, a play besotted with the issues of a temporal nature. Meanwhile, our next tableau beckons.

Notes

1 Anonymous, *The N-Town Play: Cotton MS Vespasian D.8*, edited by Stephen Spector (published for the Early English Text Society by Oxford University Press, 1991), 54.
2 Anonymous, *The Chester Mystery Cycle*, edited by R.M. Lumiansky and David Mills (published for the Early English Text Society by Oxford University Press, 1974), 68.
3 Anonymous, *The York Plays: A Critical Edition of the York Corpus Christi Play as Recorded in British Library Additional MS 35290*, edited by Richard Beadle (published for the Early English Text Society by Oxford University Press, 2009), 60.
4 Anonymous, *The N-Town Play*, 55.
5 Anonymous, *The Chester Mystery Cycle*, 69.
6 Anonymous, *N-Town Play*, 54.
7 Anonymous, *The York Plays*, 60.
8 Anonymous, *The Towneley Plays*, edited by Martin Stevens and A.C. Cawley (published for the Early English Text Society by Oxford University Press, 1994), 53.
9 Ibid.
10 Ibid., 54.
11 Anonymous, *The Chester Mystery Cycle*, 70.
12 Ibid.
13 Ibid., 71.
14 Ibid.
15 William Shakespeare, *Julius Caesar*, edited by David Daniell (Arden Shakespeare, Third Edition, 1998), 201 (II.1).

15

EXHIBIT THREE: *ROMEO AND JULIET*

Love and other spatial relations

It is night, she is above in her balcony; he is below in her garden. She is looking at the moon; he at her. Is there a more iconic theatrical tableau than this? Share this description with anyone walking down the street and they will tell you, without hesitation, that the characters depicted in the above sentence are none other than Romeo and Juliet. But this young ingénue and her inamorato are not the first stage lovers to be rendered in such a fashion, they hail from a long and illustrious pedigree that began with the dawning of the commedia dell'arte. Long before Romeo became Romeo he was Flávio, Ottavio, Orazio, Silvio, Leandro, Lelio, Mario, and Fulvio. And she, long before she became Juliet, went by the names of Isabella, Flaminia, Celia, Lidia, Lavinia, Auerelia, Valeria, Silvia, Graziosa, and even Ortennsia.[1] In other words, our Romeo and Juliet are the culmination of a veritable army of star-crossed lovers that graced the theaters and public squares of Italy. Now they find themselves transplanted on the stage of the Rose Theatre, trading in their innate Petrarchan octaves for Elizabethan iambics.

Leave it to the Italian masters of theater to bequeath us a tableau as captivating as this, with the same oddly arresting power of a tarot card image. In fact, it feels as though this tableau might have escaped from one of those infamous decks of divination. It is probably not by accident that the commedia and the tarot deck are both invented during the same period. Both share a fascination with a series of stock figures, situations and resulting tableaux that could be combined and recombined to tell an infinity of stories. With each shuffle or performance, these same figures and situations would rearrange themselves into new meanings, the best of which would somehow overturn Fate. This is fate with a capital F, that ancient power, left over from pagan times, still holding everyone firmly in their place according to their preordained status; a hierarchy determined in some dark, distant and unalterable past. Its days are actually numbered, for Fate is about to be overturned by a new metaphysical force that goes by the name of Fortuna and takes on the comely shape of a woman. She is half Muse and half Madonna and she seems to take an actual concern for human kind. If you are cunning and industrious, she will smile on you and, low and behold, anything can become possible. Fortuna becomes a new metaphysics for a new age. After all with the advent of the big cities, capital, and the rising mercantile class, everything was opening up: minds, pocketbooks, status. The structures that held everyone and everything in its place were dissolving thanks to the new marketplace.

This change is best represented in a profound paradigm shift in storytelling. The primary story of the Middle Ages dealt with a young and worthy knight who falls in love with a fine and noble lady. She is the wife, or about to become the wife, of his honorable king, or lord, or just plain superior. The knight must abjure his love, placing himself and his desire in a state of perpetual suspension; he may yearn for his lady, but it must be at a distance. If he should dare to traverse the moral dividing line that separates him from his love, then what awaits is disgrace, destruction, and death. Those who cross this invisible line are such lovers as Lancelot and Tristan. They end condemned to death with their respective loves, Genevieve and Isolde. The only mobility possible in this world is in death; other than that, everyone must remain fixed in their preordained social relations. This is the story of the Middle Ages, a time of immobile hierarchies and concepts like the great chain of being, all fashioned to keep everyone in their proper orbit, like the stars in the night sky. It warns: shift from those positions and all will be chaos. It is a story in praise of social stasis.

The commedia scenario, which begins at the dawn of the Renaissance, reverses this tragic trajectory.[2] It begins with a reshuffling of its central characters. The king becomes an old man; the lady, a young girl half his age; the knight, a young man of boundless love and usually little means. Or, rather, at least means enough to employ a wily servant to aide in his winning of the lady. This new character, the servant, hails from an equally illustrious line that began with the ever-resourceful slave characters drawn from Plautus and Terence (recently rediscovered in the Renaissance) and goes all the way to Beaumarchais' Figaro. These figures bravely enter the abyss that exists between their master's desire and the unobtainable loved one that engenders it; bringing them, by the end, together. They do so, with the Renaissance perquisite of wit and ingenuity; thereby winning Fortuna's favor, overturning Fate, and allowing the young lovers to live happily ever after. A new story for a new age. An age of merchants, who have invented the middle man. Between a person and their desire, there is now someone who, for a price, can procure it for you. Juliet's nurse harkens from this tradition of inestimable go-betweens.

So powerful is this new story that Shakespeare immediately appropriates it and, being Shakespeare, can't help but subvert it. Shakespeare seems particularly sensitive to transition from medieval to modern storytelling as personified by the secret battle between Fate and Fortuna. In *Romeo and Juliet* and *Othello* he begins both plays with the promise of a fun-loving Renaissance commedia piece, but ends each with an irrevocable return to the tragic. It is as if he were saying that Fortuna is nothing more than a Renaissance fairy tale and therefore no match for so ancient and intransigent an opponent as Fate. In *Romeo and Juliet* Shakespeare borrows both the commedia storyline and the popular tableau of the woman imaged above and the man below. Shakespeare adapts this to the architecture of the Rose Theatre, dispensing with the usual window that frames the woman and utilizing the Rose's handy inner balcony. The rest, as they say is history.

It is a richly evocative image that has its basis in a fundamental socio-historical fact. Young women were not given easy access to the streets and marketplaces of sixteenth-century Italy and were primarily sequestered to the confines of their homes and inner courtyards. The result of these precautions led to the simple reality that the best chance for a young man to catch a glimpse of a beautiful young lady would be to cast his gaze upward to the windows of Italy's finest homes. This was as close as these ardent suitors were going to get, as far as the parents of these young girls were concerned; without the entree of a distinguished family name, or a newly forged fortune, a glimpse of their beloved in the window was all these poor souls could expect. In Flaminio Scala's *Il theatro delle favole rappresentative* (*Scenarios of the Commedia dell'Arte*) we find that more than half of its scenarios have the young inamorata discovering his loved one framed in a window above.[3]

But this tableau transcends its socio-historical moorings; it works on us, compels us. But why? Perhaps part of the tableau's appeal has a certain phenomenological foundation, where love becomes associated with verticality. Isn't this, after all, our first experience of love? Think back to our time as infants in a cradle, lying on our backs, waiting for what we will eventually identify as our mother to reappear above us. Don't we reach upward to touch her smile, to feel that she is still real, still ours? And doesn't that touch fill us with all the properties that we will come to associate with the idea and sensation of pure love? Perhaps it is on this very primary level that we begin to conceive of love as something above and just beyond us.

This idea of love and verticality is given further credence with Socrates who builds his image of love as a ladder. Its first rung begins with the concrete love of the parent and works its way upward to the highest and most abstract rung, where we discover a love for the "good." Somewhere at the midpoint of Socrates' ladder is the love we are most desirous of, the kind of love that Romeo feels when he sees his Juliet. But, in the realm of love and verticality, it was most likely the poets of Islam, rather than Socrates, who were behind cementing this iconic image of the unobtainable woman on her balcony as a metaphor for our yearning toward the divine. Here, through these extraordinary poets, we find our longing for a heavenly union cloaked in the imagery of an amorous desire for a loved one forever out of reach. Such poems found their way West after the Crusades, and came to rest in far-flung regions like Provence, giving birth to the Troubadour tradition, flowering in the garden of their Courtly Love, then spreading throughout all of Europe, creating a bridge between the Middle Ages and what will become the Renaissance. Where Amor will battle Roma (the home of the Holy Catholic Church). Amor, after all is an anagrammatic inversion of Roma, created to show the world how easy it is to upturn the rules of the church and free lovers from any authority that stands in the way of their love. Romeo and Juliet are the inheritors of this rich tradition.

And so, our lover's tableau contains not only a certain socio-historical reality, but also intimations of a phenomenological, philosophical, and quasi-theological/mystical meaning as well. What all these readings have in common is this notion of a vertical distance which is very much on the mind of the Renaissance as it looks upward to the heavens in the hopes of deciphering God's secrets. It has a new plaything for this endeavor, the telescope, which is just too inquisitive to be pointed in only one vantage point and quickly turns its attention to every possible direction, bringing the world into ever-sharper view. As the world seems to contract, its painted canvases begin to deepen with the discovery of perspective. Piero Della Francesca, one of perspective's greatest practitioners, will claim that the world has finally been distilled down to its simplest terms: there is you, the object you desire, and the distance that separates the two. All this is made possible by perspective's use of the imaginary vanishing point, a methodology that becomes the perfect metaphor for desire, since the vanishing point lures the eye deeper and deeper into its ever-receding center. The world itself, like its paintings, is now no longer flat, but deep and traversable; one may sail off into God's vanishing point and return with whatever one might desire. It is as if distance itself was the inventor of desire; the more out of reach something might be, the more desirous it becomes. Distance and desire now commingle to create: spice, silk, wealth, women. But now, more than ever before, these distances are traversable and the objects of desire all the more obtainable. The world now radiates with the anticipation of infinite acquisition.

Italian scene design flirts with this newfound perspective and its ever-alluring vanishing point, but quickly realizes that such artifice is not necessary in the theater, which has its own God-given depth and dimensionality. Its inhabitants play an intricate game of distance and proximity with a variety of objects of desire, these can be a loved one, riches, or a letter that might promise both. Space becomes a part of the play of desire; its traversal becoming the very drama of the Renaissance, Baroque, and Rococo periods. Everything is just out of one's natural grasp, just a step or two away from becoming yours, all you have to do is break out of the decorum of the times, make a leap, and seize it. Now it's yours until someone else comes along and takes it. So, whatever you do, keep your distance. A new language of space is beginning to be fashioned with its own particular syntax. A grammar of distances and spatial punctuations are being re-scripted on the stages of the Renaissance theater for all to learn and emulate. Space is suddenly broken into discreet units of meaning. It gains a grammar, a secret syntax.

Anthropologist Edward T. Hall rechristens these discrete spatial units, calling them Intimate Distance, Personal Distance, Social Distance, and Public Distance.[4] The first and most proximal, in terms of our sense of space, is Intimate Distance. Hall characterizes this spatial relation as the presence of another person's body, sound, smell, and feel of breath to the point where it can become overwhelming. Hall calculates this distance to be anywhere from zero to 18 inches. Personal Distance is our default comfort zone in terms of normal spatial relations. Hall likens it to a small protective sphere or bubble that an organism intuitively maintains between others. Personal Distance, according to Hall, is anywhere from one and a half to two and half feet. Social Distance is space in terms of varying degrees of domination: there are those of whom one must maintain a certain respectful distance and then there are those whose personal space does not warrant such respect and can be encroached upon at the whim of a dominate interlocutor. Hall calculates that those who maintain a strong social distance require seven to twelve feet of distance from others. Finally, there is Public Space which occurs outside of what Hall calls "the circle of involvement" (which is basically the three previous distances). This gives one a maximal view of one's surroundings. Hall calculates that this is a space of about 25 feet or more, a distance commensurate with the reaction time necessary to readjust to any sudden changes in the surroundings. Each of these zones and their dimensions are so culturally ingrained upon us at an early age, that most humans observe them without even thinking. One is reminded of these unspoken boundaries, when they're accidentally or purposefully transgressed. When this happens, the seemingly invisible space around us wakes and makes itself known. In such a moment, one feels as though a swarm of subatomic particles were suddenly mobilizing to maintain their little pocket of reality.

Nothing woke up the spaces of the Italian Renaissance theater more than the introduction of actual women onto the stage. This was culturally unheard of at the time. Suddenly audiences were presented with young women and allowed to view them not only at a "Public" distance, but see these same young women as they would behave with men in the most "Intimate" of distances. Talk about the dance of subatomic particles—this was a truly epochal event for Renaissance audiences and explains why so many of the extant love scenes that come down to us seem longer than dramatically necessary; clearly it was the eyes of the audience, rather than their ears, that were being so captivated. When we turn to the letters of the time, we find that those who attended such performances speak very little of the plot, or clowning, but have a great deal to say about the various ingénues that graced the stage, whether this was Isabella, Flaminia, Celia, Lidia, Lavinia, Auerelia, Valeria, Silvia, Graziosa, or even Ortensia. These appearances alone had the capacity to electrify a performance. So popular was Isabella Andreini, a leading ingénue and theater impresario, that attendance for her funeral was one of the highest in all of Renaissance Europe, rivaling that of popes and kings. Now Shakespeare, did not have the advantage of putting an actual woman, like Isabella, in the role of Juliet; thanks to the continued conservatism of his English homeland, he would have to make do, paradoxically, with the most gifted boy actor he could find. This forced him to make Juliet's poetry the event of these scenes and, as is the case with Shakespeare, he does not disappoint. The language is indeed some of the most glorious every uttered by two young lovers.

But let us stay focused on their spatial rather than verbal language. This other language speaks in terms of distance and proximity and yet acquires its own poetic power. She, as we have said, is above; he below and the distance between them is nothing short of formidable. This space that separates them has its own expressiveness, we feel both the tension and the ache that it creates. Distance can be as evocative as words and proximity as expressive as music. Both carry a meaning that happens more in the body than in the mind. When it speaks to us, it is direct and almost visceral. It is as if these spatial relationships were more like moods than geometric coordinates. All of this becomes heightened in the three dimensions of theatrical space. The power of distance and proximity is also joined with questions of balance. Is something centered or off of center? A certain tension can be created in the audience when a person or object is not properly placed within the frame of the proscenium arch; engendering a kind of spatial dissonance. And so balance and imbalance become another powerful anti-thetical coupling; playing with our eye's natural inclination toward symmetry to create new relationships to the experiencing of space. But also, in such moments of imbalance, we can discover how quickly our eye will adjust; reminding us that space, like time, has its own relativity. Or, as Merce Cunningham once slyly noted, "center stage is wherever I am." This brings up another trick of theatrical space: it feigns a pictorial flatness, until there is movement. Movement wakens theatrical space, shows us its actual density, its third dimension. This contributes the final and equally powerful antithesis of movement and stasis in theater. Such a coupling, can become a story in itself. Take Don Juan who begins Molière's play with great mobility, only to find himself slowing down, more and more, act by act, until he becomes as still as the statue of the dead commander. Don Juan's journey is from movement (life) to stasis (death).

But nothing is quite as electric as how two lovers negotiate the space that separates them. The journey, from one to the other, registers both before our eyes and deep within our own bodies. First there is that insurmountable distance. Look at her, so far above and him, down below with us. Experience his slow and arduous ascent upward, toward her. Feel the sense of relief when he reaches her and the con-comitant ecstasy that fills us as they embrace. In that moment, our feeling rhymes with the feelings Romeo and Juliet. Each inch of theatrical space becoming the keys of an invisible piano, what we are sensing is the music of space. Theater, in such moments, can makes another ineffable manifest.

Notes

1 For a more in-depth look at the parade of young lovers that emerged during the age of commedia see Pierre Louis Duchartre, *The Italian Comedy* (Dover Publication, 1996).
2 For a wonderful evocation of the world which birthed commedia see K.M. Lea *Italian Popular Comedy Vol. 1* (Russell and Russell, 1962).
3 The best English edition of these scenarios is: Flaminio Scala, *Scenarios of the Commedia dell'Arte*, translated and edited by Henry F. Salerno (New York University Press, 1967). For a wonderful analysis of these scenarios, see Natalie Crohn Schmitt, *Befriending the Commedia dell'Arte of Flaminio Scala* (University of Toronto Press, 2014).
4 Edward T. Hall, *The Hidden Dimension* (Anchor Books, 1990), 7–14.

16

EXHIBIT FOUR: *THE WINTER'S TALE*

Seeing being

She stands there before him, immobile and yet so lifelike. He believes that what he is seeing is a statue of his late wife, Hermione, who he lost some 16 years ago. A loss that he caused by his irrational jealous rage. It was a relentless force that ultimately hounded her into an early grave. But none of this is evident in the almost other worldly face that now confronts him. How to describe it? Serene? Indifferent? Perhaps, to a statue, these states are ultimately the same. A statue is a paradoxical creature. It is there and not there. There like a chair, but not there like a person. It occupies space, but nothing occupies it. There is no consciousness, memories, hopes, dreams, loves, fears, beliefs, questions. If anything, it is a frozen moment completely dependent upon the ability of its sculptor to try to capture one simple expressive trait. The usual default expression ends up existing somewhere between the indomitable and the implacable. And yet, what is it about this trick of stone and light that can make one think mute matter might actually, if properly prompted, speak? And if, in this case, it could—would it forgive this husband, the once great Leontes, for what he has done? For all the ruin he has left behind him? The statue remains silent to this, its eyes never quite meeting his ever-intent gaze; it is focused elsewhere, toward a horizon just beyond him. If he could only make eye contact, as if an exchange of glances could do the magic trick and bring this statue to life. After all, it seems just on the verge of such a miraculous transformation.

On this matter, Leontes is not far from the truth. For, as the viewer might have guessed, his beloved never died. Her death was feigned by an ever resourceful lady-in-waiting to protect her from her jealous husband's unjust punishment. This is, after all, a late Renaissance romance where such plot turns are to be expected. The statue before him is his actual wife. She has been convinced to pose as a work of art to see for herself if her husband has, after all these years, repented for his wrongful acts. And so, it is not just he who is examining her; but, more importantly, she who is studying him. If he should prove true, she will reveal herself; if not, she will return to her safe seclusion and let him live out the remainder of his days believing that he is the central character in the most tragic of tragedies. Little does he know that, thanks to the late Elizabethan taste in storytelling, his tragedy is about to become a tragic-comedy. All of this, by the way, is merely alluded to, rather than shown. It can be deduced from a few veiled clues by Shakespeare and our own hermeneutic acumen. Shakespeare does not necessarily need us to reach this conclusion before we encounter the tableau. He seems perfectly content to have us discover this in time with Leontes.

It took Shakespeare most of his career to arrive at this tableau. We can see him begin working on its first iteration as far back as his *Much Ado About Nothing*. There, if you remember, the young lover Claudio is tricked into believing he sees his beloved, Hero, at night on a balcony embracing another man. This sends Claudio into a Leontes-like fit of jealousy where he cruelly rejects Hero in the very midst of their wedding vows. Hero, like Leontes' wronged wife Hermione, faints as Claudio storms off, renouncing his love of her forever. Thankfully, there is a wily friar, cut from the same cloth as his compatriot in *Romeo and Juliet*. This friar has an idea of how to protect Hero and bring about a change in the now recalcitrant heart of Claudio. It is what we could call, for lack of a better dramaturgical term, "the Juliet gambit," similar to the plan proposed by Friar Lawrence, and requiring everyone to maintain that Hero has died of grief. At least in this version there is no need for potions, pretending will do, clearly these friars have learned their lesson. Such a pretense will, according to this sage-like friar, bring about a remorse in Claudio's breast and will make him all the more thankful when he sees his Hero restored to life.

Shakespeare moves us through a brisk Act IV and V where Hero's innocence is easily proven and the once-jealous Claudio is now overcome with a life-altering sense of guilt. In recompense for his rejection of Hero, he agrees to marry Hero's alleged sister, which, for those still not savvy to Renaissance plotting, will be none other than his Hero in disguise. This is what the Italians, like Boccaccio, called a "Befa" or "trick." These simple "pranks" became something of a narrative tic, finding their way into all manner of Renaissance stories. For the Italians, a "Befa" usually manifested itself in a cruel form of comeuppance; but in Shakespeare's hands, it could become the prelude to a restorative transformation. Such a magical turn is at the heart of the final scene of *Much Ado*. Claudio is brought before a masked woman, told that this is his intended, and that he may not see her face until he swears to marry her. A resolute Claudio says to his unknown bride to be, "Give me your hand; before this holy friar I am your husband if you like of me." Hero responds as she unmasks herself, "And when I lived I was your other wife; And when you loved you were my other husband." A startled Claudio gasps, "Another Hero!" The friar quickly intervenes with the proper Shakespearean wrap up:

> All this amazement can I qualify,
> When, after that the holy rites are ended,
> I'll tell you largely of fair Hero's death.
> Meantime let wonder seem familiar,
> And to the chapel let us presently.[1]

There are two key words in the friar's brief speech that will return years later in the *Winter's Tale* tableau. They are "amazement" and "wonder." Just prior to this speech, the word "strange" was also evoked. These three terms form a kind of trinity that runs throughout the endings of many of Shakespeare's comedies and romances. This movement of strangeness through amazement to wonder breaks us out of our habitual relation to the world before us and allows us to reconnect with the initial magic of when it first presented itself to us as children. It is a pathway to re-enchantment. But this is just the first, almost hasty pass at such a reversal in perception. We get a glimpse or taste of what this might be; but we will have to wait until the romances, where Shakespeare continues to play with these terms and their sequencing, to sound out the true depths of such moments of altered awareness. Shakespeare will also need to go through the crucible of the major tragedies to further refine and deepen the impact of this heightened state of awareness.

The next important iteration of *The Winter's Tale* tableau can be found in *King Lear*. It may, at first, seem difficult to tease out the shared concerns between a comedy like *Much Ado About Nothing* and a tragedy of the scale of *King Lear*. At first glance, they seem antithetical to one another in every way. But upon closer examination we begin to see a series of discrete linkages, starting with the notion of nothing that is found in the very title of *Much Ado* and very much at the center of the thematic concerns of *King Lear*. The nothing of *Much Ado* can refer to the fact that nothing untoward actually happened; or the nothing can refer to its slang usage, becoming another way of discussing a woman's private parts; or, the nothing can be construed as noting, a common occurrence in the Elizabethan pronunciation of nothing. This, intriguingly, turns the title of Shakespeare's comedy into *Much Ado About Noting*, an equally apt subtitle for *King Lear*. Remember Kent's injunction to Lear: "See better." There is a deep ocular concern that runs through *Much Ado*, *Lear*, and *Winter's Tale*. Claudio, Lear, and Leontes must learn to see more, further, deeper, through, and beyond. Hero, Cordelia, and Hermione are each mis-noted by their lover, father, husband. It will take the entirety of each play to right these initial misapprehensions. To see these women for who they really are—"the thing itself."

A turning point for Lear and an important development toward the final tableau in *The Winter's Tale* happens in Act III, Scene 4 where Lear looks on "Poor Tom." Here we see Lear, his fool and Kent watching this seeming beggar man, we know him to be the noble Edgar in disguise, but Lear mis-sees and utters the following famous pronouncement:

> Thou wert better in a grave than to answer with thy uncovered body this extremity of the skies. Is man no more than this? Consider him well. Thou owest the worm no silk, the beast no hide, the sheep no wool, the cat no perfume. Ha! Here's three on's are sophisticated. Thou art the thing itself. Unaccommodated man is no more but such a poor, bare, forked animal as thou art.[2]

At this point, the stage directions tell us that Lear tears off his clothes as he cries, "Off, off, you landings, come, unbutton here." We will come back to seemingly inconsequential last line about unbuttoning later, for the moment let us focus on how the above passage relates to the body of Poor Tom, who is actually a disguised Edgar. Lear uses the evocative phrase "the thing itself," as though what he is encountering is the primordial essence, a state worthy of a return. The irony is that Poor Tom is not Poor Tom but Edgar disguised. What does Sherlock Holmes say to Watson? Naked is the best disguise. Edgar seems to have taken a page from Conan Doyle's book. Lear thinks he is following Kent's injunction to "see better." But he still misunderstands what is before him. One could go a step further and say that what he sees is not "the thing itself," or Poor Tom, or Edgar, but a Renaissance actor playing these various incarnations. Such meta-theatrical insights will have to wait till the very end of this play when Lear, in the Folio edition, is cradling the dead Cordelia in his arms. It is at this juncture he tells us:

> Why should a dog, a horse, a rat have life.
> And thou no breath at all? Thou'lt come no more.
> Never, never, never, never, never.
> Pray you, undo this button. Thank you, sir.
> Do you see this? Look on her, look, her lips,
> Look there, look there.[3]

And then the stage direction tells us simply, bluntly that "He dies." Many scholars put the onset of death at Lear's "Never, never, never, never, never," which is a series of trochees. A trochee, you will remember, is the inversion of an iamb. Iambs mirror the rhythm of our heart beat: de-dum, de-dum, de-dum, de-dum, de-dum. A trochee is a kind of heart attack. dum-de, dum-de, dum-de, dum-de, dum-de. And so, it is on this line that Lear's heart is literally and figuratively breaking. He asks, again, for the button of his tunic to be loosed, which reminds us of his mad scene when he wanted a similar freedom from the constriction of his clothing, and before he shuffles off this mortal coil, he sees something. His very last lines bare repeating:

> Do you see this? Look on her, look, her lips,
> Look there, look there.[4]

At the very end he is still trying to follow Kent's injunction, trying to "see better." And what is it that he sees emanating from his daughter's lips? Breath. Not the breath of Cordelia but the breath of the actress playing Cordelia who has, all along, been surreptitiously breathing. It is at this juncture that we could say that Lear has finally seen deeper and further; right through the theatrical circumstances and into reality. A reality that none of the other play-bound characters can see. Is this not the "thing itself." We are at the threshold of the meta-theatrical. Shakespeare will explore the full possibilities of this kind of seeing when he arrives, at the end of his career, with the final scene in *The Winter's Tale*.

Let us return to Leontes, viewing the statue of Hermione, his long-lost wife. Regardless of whether we are aware of the ruse that is being perpetrated on Leontes, we know that the actress who played Hermione is now playing her statue. We laugh, knowingly, when Leontes says of the statue:

> Chide me, dear stone, that I may say indeed
> Thou art Hermione …[5]

And here, on the heels of this, is our first clue that this is indeed a ruse:

> But Hermione was not so much wrinkled, nothing
> so aged as this seems …[6]

The more discerning audience members laugh here because they know that 16 years have passed since Hermione's alleged death and these are the wrinkles of time rather than the inaccuracies of art. But soon, Leontes questions, asked in outright simplicity, begin to bare deeper implications and we find ourselves no longer laughing, but beginning to marvel at what Shakespeare is up to. Leontes notes:

> What was he that did make it? See my lord,
> Would you not deem it breathed? And those veins
> Did verily bear blood.[7]

Polixenes notes that there is a warmth upon her lip and Leontes ascertains a kind of motion in her eye. "It is," he says, "as though we were mocked by art." Slowly but surely, we are moved from our superior vantage point. We are now seeing and feeling in rhythm with Leontes himself. We also find ourselves no longer so critical of the actress' failed attempts at absolute stone-like mimesis. Something has happened to her and to us. She is no longer an actress trying to be a statue; but a human being that we are beginning to see as the ultimate work of art. And it is just when we make this leap of signification that Leontes asks his simplest and most profound question:

> Still methinks
> There is an air comes from her, what fine chisel
> could ever yet cut breath.[8]

And the unspoken answer on our lips is "God's." And in this moment the statue before us makes one final transformation. The first transformation was as a poorly played statue; the second as a work of art; and now, in this third and final metamorphosis, as something of divine origin. Is this not what Lear called, "the thing itself." The very quintessence of being which is indeed worthy of both amazement and wonder. Those two key terms from the ending of *Much Ado* return in this scene. Paulina, the ringmaster behind all this, agrees to bring Hermione to life, imploring her to:

Be stone no more; approach;
Strike all that look upon with marvel; come;[9]

In the late romances of *Winter's Tale* and *The Tempest*, Shakespeare begins these scenes with an immediate invocation of wonder. That is the state of perception that we first encounter with his characters. It will lead to a period of amazement, a sense of dizziness and lostness and will result in either a desire to marvel (*Winter's Tale*) or feel strange (*Tempest*). Wonder, in Shakespeare's hands, always returns us to the essential mystery or magic of the world. A relationship that we once had as children; but, thanks to the relentless force of habit, has been dulled in our adulthood. It is the trick of re-enchantment and it can reconnect us to something almost forgotten and yet truly wondrous, like the simple fact that we breathe, that taking in and letting out air sustains us. And so, in *The Winter's Tale* we can indeed marvel, once again, at this simple, ever-occurring miracle of the inhalation and exhalation of breath which separates us from stone. In the rush of our day-to-day world, breathing and forgiving lose their extraordinary magic; Shakespeare, in his late works, has found a way to restore such things to us.

This becomes an ek-static moment, another example of theater's ability to make manifest phenomena which have a tendency to recede from our awareness due to their habitual occurrence. Theater has the ability to tempt such phenomena out from the background and restore them to the foreground of our awareness— such dynamics as time, space, or, in this instance, being itself. When Agamemnon took his step across the red carpet an aspect of his psychology was revealed, but when Hermione steps down from her pedestal we have moved from psychology to ontology. What is made manifest in this moment is the most elusive of phenomenon: being. What Lear called "the thing itself." How easy it is to forget this basic miracle of existence, especially since it is a part of every moment of our day to day lives. This makes it all the more difficult to see thanks to habit's ability to dull our senses to all that is essential in life. It is similar to joke about fish being incapable of comprehending the concept of water. Or, as Ludwig Wittgenstein has said, "The aspect of things that are most important to us are hidden because of their simplicity and familiarity." One is often unable to notice something because Wittgenstein warns, "it is always before one's eyes."[10] Engendering wonder becomes Shakespeare's way of bringing these things back into view.

Notes

1 William Shakespeare, *Much Ado About Nothing*, edited by Claire McEachern (Arden Shakespeare, Third Edition, 2016), 352 (V.4).
2 William Shakespeare, *King Lear*, edited by Kenneth Muir (Arden Shakespeare, Second Edition, 1959), 121–122 (III.4).
3 Ibid., 218 (V.3).
4 Ibid.
5 William Shakespeare, *The Winter's Tale*, edited by J.H.P. Pafford (Arden Shakespeare, Second Edition, 1966), 155 (V.3).

6 Ibid.
7 Ibid., 157 (V.3).
8 Ibid., 158 (V.3).
9 Ibid., 159 (V.3).
10 Ludwig Wittgenstein, *Philosophical Investigations*, revised 4th edition, translated by G.E.M. Anscombe, edited by P.M.S. Hacker and Joachim Schulte (Wiley Blackwell, 2009), 56e, section 129.

17

EXHIBIT FIVE: *TARTUFFE*

The not-so-secret life of inanimate objects

The plan is simple. He will hide under the table, while she "entertains" the man she claims is trying to seduce her. This way, her husband will hear, with his very own ears, that the man he once believed in is a charlatan of the first order. The husband is Orgon, his wife is Elmire, and the soon-to-be-exposed-charlatan is none other than the titular Tartuffe whose very name has made its way into numerous modern dictionaries as a worthy synonym for a religious hypocrite, dissembler, dissimulator, Pharisee, and just plain phony. But we are less interested in this swindler and his victims and more concerned with the instrument of this villain's undoing: a simple, relatively nondescript table—an object usually employed for dining, or writing, or gaming. But during the next 16 or so minutes it will go through a series of less than ordinary usages. It will become a hide-away, an obstruction, a bed in service of seduction and, ultimately, the unnameable itself. Molière's usage of the table conforms to one of Jasper Johns' basic definitions of art-making: take something, change it, change it again. Our table will go through one transformation after another, like an actor assuming multiple roles; in this respect, our simple little table proves to be as versatile an actor as its master Molière. Let us look at the table's first and perhaps most well-known characterization.

The table as table

There it is, just on the periphery. It waits, like a worthy servant: patiently, unobtrusively just as a piece of furniture should. It is complacent in its nondescriptness, an exemplar of the unostentatious. Although it stands, it does not stand out. Unless, that is, it should be needed and then it shines forth with the assured dependability that we look for in our furnishings. Upon closer inspection, its commonality remains remarkably like the Platonic idea of a table that we all carry in our mind's eye: four sturdy legs supporting a flat wooden expanse that has seen an infinity of meals. It is adorned with a modest white table cloth that covers its otherwise well-varnished surface and makes its way downward, until it almost touches the floor. But then Elmire, in a fit of inspiration, suggests that it is just this very average table that should serve as Orgon's place to hide. After a quick back and forth between her and her dubious husband, Orgon acquiesces to his wife's wishes and the table assumes its new role.

From table to hideout

It is a bit of a stretch, but our table has played this role before, usually for Orgon's children when they were young and had a penchant for hide and seek. For a while our table was quite respected in this role but was ultimately passed over due to the increasing popularity of the nearby closet and the large and imposing grandfather clock whose interior could fit a child of six or seven and still keep proper time. The table looks almost as uncertain about its new deployment as Orgon does in his new role as spy. Suddenly both the table and Orgon's deficiencies seem to stand out: the damn tablecloth just won't completely touch the ground and Orgon is just not as flexible as he used to be. The combination is, to say the least, worrisome. But no matter, Tartuffe has entered the room and now the table is called upon to play yet another role.

Table as obstruction

This is not the table's favorite role. It has been, on occasion, an obstacle; or, if you must, an obstruction. But never of its own volition and it could always be easily moved when there was cleaning that had to be done or a party to be celebrated. But now, thanks to its central placement in the room, it will become a useful impediment, keeping Elmire from the ever-desirous hands of Tartuffe. The table rises to the occasion, it seems to have grown in dimensions and thickened in construction so that it gives Elmire her much-needed protection. All she has to do is keep the table between herself and her interlocutor. A game of he-moves/she-moves ensues with her always on one side of the table and he on the other. Our stalwart table has become wall-like in its defense, warding off Tartuffe's attempts at trespass. But after one rotation around the table, Tartuffe, with sudden swiftness, has his arms around her and is now moving her backward onto the table, where ...

The table becomes a bed

This is completely new territory for our table and it is as taken aback by this as Elmire. When it arrived at Orgon's house it expected to be of use, but never in such a fashion as this. It is familiar with bearing food, or cards, or even an occasional aperitif where a woman's hand might, accidentally, touch the hand of a man—but *this*—well, this is simply beyond the pale, as well as beyond its basic weight-bearing capabilities.

Elmire now finds herself on her back with an emboldened Tartuffe mounting her. This is perhaps the most iconic image from this play, yet there is no stage direction from Molière describing such a configuration. Tradition has collaborated with this scene to create such a tableau and have it passed down from production to production. The result is as pleasing as certain mathematical equations: Elmire, trapped between a Tartuffe that towers above her and Orgon who cowers beneath her. As though Tartuffe and Orgon were fractions with the table as the bar that divides them.

Let us pause here for a moment.

It was the wonderful French critic, Alfred Simon, who first noted Molière's penchant for objects and his ability to bestow upon them a kind of anthropomorphic life. As we can see with our hard-working table, it becomes as integral a character as its living scene partners. Simon says that the poetic theater of Molière:

> Confers upon certain things an intense presence and quite often a sign value. Certain objects are thus privileged. The objects of Molière's comedies have the magical presence of props on the table of a vaudeville magician, or of the acrobatic fittings that mysteriously shine at the top of a circus tent. Among those which most often appear in Molière's comedies, the following are significant: Objects that stand for possession: the chest, the purse, the key ring. Those which stand for enjoyment: the snuff box, the bottle, the dish of food. The signs of frivolity (mirrors, ribbons, jewels), denunciation (letters or portraits) and repression (stick or sword). In Molière's theatre, these props are always thrown into relief with a particular sharpness.[1]

But how, exactly does Molière work this magic spell over seemingly inanimate objects? This artistic alchemy is, like most theatrical practices, a combination of both high-flown aesthetics and down-to-earth practicalities. The traditions begun before Renaissance and the continuing vicissitudes of touring favored settings created out of language rather than raw materials; the latter being difficult and costly to transport from city to city. This meant that whenever an actual object was employed, it was due to its absolute necessity. The object, freed from competing with a field of rival objects, already begins to easily stand out. Theater, by its very nature, begins as a limit field: the actor, language, and an occasional object. The objects can be of the knife and crown variety (knives are, after all, usually employed to get the crowns in the first place). This is more than enough to hold an audience's attention. Practitioners from the Greeks to Molière learn quickly that such a limited field is part of the actual imaginative power of theater. Being intentional creatures, we have a tendency to confer an infinitude of meaning to the field of objects before us. The less objects to view, the more intentionality we bring to bear on what remains. Theater, due to this inherent selectivity, elicits a kind of hyper-intentionality toward whatever finds its way up on stage. In short: things have the tendency to mean more when placed within the otherwise empty space of the stage, their meaning multiplying under the collective pressure of an audience's gaze.

Molière takes this a step further by fixating on an object to the point of fet-ishizing it. Take the incriminating letter in his *Misanthrope*. Alceste, who has spent most of the play in a jealous fit over his beloved Célimène, finally has proof of her infidelities. Or so he thinks he does. He produces an incriminating letter from his person with the theatrical flourish of a prosecuting attorney, displaying it for all to see. She takes a casual look at the letter, as though it were as significant as some long-lost laundry list, and hands it back to him saying she wrote it to a lady friend. He looks again at the letter, which now seems to have lost all its former confidence. Rereading the letter in this new light, he stops midway and again in full prosecu-torial mode insists she kindly explain how the sentence he is pointing to could be construed for a woman. She refuses. He follows her, letter in his extended hand, imploring her to decipher this one little sentence. She informs him that she is tired of his games and of him. She realizes now that she can never love a man who doesn't trust her. He tries to calm her, placate her, anything to stop her from leaving. What can he do? He loves her, he's mad about her, he can't live without her and so, to prove this love, he tears up the incriminating letter right then and there, into a thousand little pieces that he sends flying above his head. He embraces her as pieces of the letter fall, like confetti, to the floor.

First and foremost, this is what, those in the trade would call a lazzi, a piece of business worked out, often with objects, to gain laughs and show off the virtuosity of the performer. Here, the lazzi is in how many ways Molière can treat this letter: with reverence, contempt, doubt, concern, condemnation, etc. But there is an intri-guing byproduct to such comedic play. The obsessive use and reuse of the letter has the ability to bring the object to life, endowing it with an agency that is otherwise absent from inanimate objects. There is something invocational in how Molière employs this object, conferring on it this newfound life and status.

Molière's table is more than a table. Theater has the power of transformation of the material world. In such moments, we are reminded that objects, whether we like it or not, precede and exceed their names. Names, no matter how much faith we put in them, are no more than temporary restraining orders for objects. Even the inanimate is on the lookout for ways to escape its linguistic confinement. In theater, unlike literature, objects are returned to their natural habitat, free from the tyranny of words on a page which limit their possibilities. Thanks to these the-atrical circumstances, their meanings can shift with one's perception of a given situation. Children, when learning language, are most awake to the feeble nature words have on the magical things that make up their pre-linguistic world. A world where objects are much more mysterious and polyvalent in their use and meaning. Molière's table begins to shimmer, when we sense it slipping out from under its lexical moorings, it is at such moments that they feel alive and full of surprises. Wittgenstein notes, "Why should dreaming be more mysterious than the table? Why should they not be equally mysterious?"[2]

Let us return to Elmire lying atop the table as though it were a bed, desper-ately trying to escape the amorous entanglements of a Tartuffe who has gone from religious zealot to sex-starved lover. Orgon is just underneath this entire affair and is profoundly unforthcoming in any display of even the slightest out-rage; so much so, that one wonders if he is even still there. Orgon's seeming lack of intervention becomes not only an interpretational question but also some-thing of a staging conundrum, all of which is left to the imagination of each production to answer for themselves. There is no stage direction from Molière suggesting that, at such and such moment, Orgon sticks his bewildered head out from underneath the table. And yet who could resist the temptation? Especially when we know that Molière himself was the first to play the role of Orgon. Is it conceivable that the great Molière would forgo a gallery of shocked "reveals," comically choreographed to match the action just above him? Most productions cannot resist such a delicious invitation for laughter and pepper the scene with such moments of Orgon's head popping out, here and then there, to the mounting delight of audiences.

Let us, for a moment, ask ourselves, what happens if Molière was able to resist this comic invitation? What happens if he remains unheard and unseen throughout the entirety of the scene? Such a prolonged absence begins to beg a series of questions in regards to Orgon's intentions: Is he too shocked to interrupt? Too cowardly? Enjoying hearing his wife suffer a little? Each refusal to intervene seems to deepen and complicate our understanding of Orgon. It also increases our awareness of the table, which begins to loom larger and larger in our imagin-ation. It seems to grow with import, its resolute silence endowing it with mystery. It seems less and less like a table and more and more like some solemn creature whose silence is otherworldly.

We may go home haunted by this tableau. Asking ourselves over and over again these same basic questions: Why didn't he reveal himself? Why would he let something so terrible continue? Why wouldn't he intervene? And perhaps these questions lead us to an epiphany of sorts, allowing us to see the image of the mute and monolithic white table as a symbol for the divinely unnamable itself. After all, are these not the same questions we often ask our seemingly invisible God? In a play that questions all things religious, is this perhaps Molière's sly answer? God, in Molière's symbolic universe, is there like the man just underneath the table. He may seem absent, but he is just hiding, why he will not come out remains for us to answer. If this is indeed Molière's intention, then our humble little table has gone from playing itself to the role of a lifetime: "He who has no name." Also known as "I am I." Not bad for our four-legged friend.

Notes

1 Alfred Simon, *The Elementary Rites of Molière's Comedy*, in *Molière: A Collection of Critical Essays*, edited by Jacques Guicharnaud (Prentice-Hall, 1964), 36.
2 Ludwig Wittgenstein, *Remarks on Philosophy of Psychology*, Vol. 1, translated by G.E.M. Anscombe, edited by G.H. von Wright (University of Chicago Press, 1980), 74e, section 378.

18

EXHIBIT SIX: *FAUST*

The persistence of allegory

It is almost dawn. The cell is dark. At first he can hear but not see her. It is a hollow breathing that punctuates the dark. His eyes adjust and for the first time he can make her out, crouched in a corner of the cell. He is there to save her, but she does not want to be saved. No amount of reasoning will help, for she is mad, and therefore beyond reason's reach. All that is left is the silent vocabulary of a lover: an outstretched arm, a beseeching hand, his imploring eyes. He tries to hold her, console her, kiss her. She is tempted, for a moment, a vague memory of a former, happier time comes to her; but it is replaced with a fear that the man who is holding her is someone or something wholly other. He takes her again, this time by force, dragging her to the door of the cell. She resists. The two are locked in an impossible embrace. How did we get to this heart-wrenching tableau? Let us begin at the beginning.

He is Goethe's Faust, not to be confused with Marlowe's Faust, or the Faust of Johan Spies' *Faust Book*, or the actual Faust who inspired all these flights of fancy. The real Johan Faust was a traveling necromancer who brought Greek heroes from antiquity back to life. He would conjure them before the dumbfounded masses and quickly move on to the next town or village before any one was the wiser. In short, he was a kind of medieval Barnum or Bailey of the spirit world. It seems somehow fitting that he would find an afterlife in the theater since so much of his own work borrowed from the same repository of stage tricks. Somewhere along the way, legend got hold of Faust and elevated him to the rank of a university professor in Wittenberg. This, intriguingly, would have been around the time that young Hamlet was deep in his studies. Not that Hamlet has anything to do with our hero; unless, perhaps some future playwright brings these two together in a Stoppard-like work of meta-theatrics. But this Faust has chosen a far greater sidekick to share his days and nights. For this Faust, it is alleged, has made a pact with the Devil. The *Faust Book* collects all these legends that swirl about our mysterious magus and puts them under one cover, becoming one of Europe's first bestsellers. The work makes its way across the channel and into the capable hands of the playwright Christopher Marlowe. It is he who is the first to seize upon the theatrical possibilities of such a story. He quickly transposes the piece from the page to stage, adding his mighty iambic line to the whole affair, and forever transfigures our medieval prankster into the mightiest of Renaissance transgressors.

By the time young Johann Wolfgang Goethe encounters Faust, our magus has fallen on hard times. He has, it seems, been relegated to the stages of puppet theater. It was Gotthold Ephraim Lessing, the great Enlightenment philosopher and some-time playwright, that we have to thank for rescuing Faust from a life consigned to a tangle of strings and the easily distractible eyes of children. He did this in a simple open letter to fellow German intellectuals. It is here that Lessing points out the somewhat embarrassing fact that Germany had not yet produced its great national masterwork. The Italians had *The Divine Comedy*; the Spanish, *Don Quixote*; the English, *Paradise Lost*. But where was the great Germanic figure or theme that would rival such works? Lessing found both in the Faust myth and penned a draft of Faust's pact with the Devil to prove his point. Goethe, who always had a healthy sense of his own poetic prowess and promise, picked up the gauntlet and, at the tender age of 23, dashed off a first draft of the play. He would, throughout the remainder of his long life, return to this work, fashioning and refashioning it into the national lit-erary monument that Lessing had prophesied.[1] Goethe, being Goethe, cannot help but tinker with the myth and develops his own unique pact scene that is radically different from all the authors who came before him. In most versions, prior to Goethe, Faust was satisfied with a somewhat metaphysically straightforward *quid pro quo*. In other words, the Devil serves Faust on earth and Faust will return the favor when he goes down below. Goethe's Faust adds an intriguing existential loophole to this standard agreement that if he ever grows lazy or wants to freeze the fleeting moment, by saying "This moment is too beautiful I must stay." *Then and only then does Mephisto get Faust's soul.*[2] This is an intriguing and radical departure from previous Fausts. It thrusts him out of his medieval moorings and makes him a true child of modernity. A new species, *Homo Consumerus*, whose aspirations can be summed up in a simple little word: "Next." It is a new life where fashion trumps tradition, where the "new and the next", become more important than "the old and the status quo." It is the same engine at work in the invention of both capitalism and modernism. All this energy and appetite is rolled into one voracious man whose rallying cry to the ages might as well be "Consume!" And this consumption will become all-pervasive. You name it, Faust will partake of it: food, pleasure, fashion, treasure, knowledge, why the list is as endless as Faust's appetite. It is, in part, this little escape clause that makes and keeps Goethe's Faust so unrelentingly modern, a significant improvement over Marlowe's Faust who remains, at the end of the day, a burned-out Renaissance Roaring Boy. It is this clause that has made Goethe's version of the myth our pre-ferred Faust. That and his other great invention: Margarete.

She is the girl from our tableau, the one locked in Faust's infernal grip. She is the second and equally profound variation to the myth. Our previous Fausts went from one demonic prank to the next, seemingly oblivious to the lure of love. At most, one would get a brief conjuring of Helen of Troy, but this was more for the titillation of Faust's audience than Faust himself.

Granted, this makes way for Marlowe having Faust ask, "Is this the face that launched a thousand ships?"—perhaps the most glorious line in the entire history of iambic pentameter; but these ten beats of poetic perfection are more about the love of language than the love of another. We must wait for Goethe to turn Faust's attention from acquisition to love.

Some scholars attribute the invention of the Faust and Margarete's affair to an early chapter in Goethe's own love life. It seems young Goethe carried on relations with a girl considered beneath his station. The affair, like most of this kind, ended badly, with the girl's reputation ruined and Goethe guilt-ridden. As to the tragic turn and subsequent trial of Margarete, most scholars agree that these incidents are taken straight from an actual scandal that found its way into the newspapers of the time. Goethe has a penchant for mixing classical material with contemporary events. Here the Faust myth meets contemporary scandal. Goethe revels in trafficking in topicality. His Margarete has one foot in high art by aping Shakespeare's Ophelia and the other foot in the tabloids of the times, where peasant girls commit the then-uncommon crime of infanticide. But we are getting ahead of ourselves. Let us begin at their beginning, with Faust passing Margarete on the street. It will lead to a series of firsts for Faust. Love at first sight and Faust's first command: "Get me that girl." This will be no small feat since, according to Mephisto, she is the quintessence of innocence. And it is true, Margarete is indeed innocent, chaste, poor—everything these men are not. We get a glimpse of her interior life when Faust and Mephisto, under a magical cloak of invisibility, enter her room and overhear her sing a song while she undresses. The song is entitled "The King of Thule,"[3] and it is instructive to study, especially in light of Faust's earlier credo to Mephisto. The ballad tells of a king given a cup by his dying lover, one he cannot bear to part with, until he himself dies years later. Through this song, we see that Margarete's worldview is the very antithesis of Faust's. If Faust's great rallying cry can be thought of as, "Next!" Than Margarete's gentle rejoinder would be, "Stay." Such a sentiment is at the very center of Margarete's song, it is one of constancy, fidelity, tradition. Life, in the world of Margarete, is about staying true to that which was, is, and will always be. In this respect, she is very much a product of the Middle Ages, a time where the links in the great chain of being are unbreakable, where the celestial order is one of perfect clockwork, and life, like the seasons, is one of dependable, ever-returning cycles. The same as it ever was, until the end of time. Such a worldview is forever severed by Faust. He is no longer in thrall of the old; the new is his God. He is not content with one cup, he wants to partake of every cup, filled to the brim with new experience. Everything must be grasped, tasted, digested. Faust is the great progenitor of us. We are his children, for his pact ushers in our modernity. It breaks the great medieval circle and flattens it out into a straight line that extends to infinity, just like our insatiable wants and desires.

And so, with Faust and Margarete, we have the collision of two worlds: the old and the new. Each is attracted to the other but neither can ultimately remain in a mutual embrace. It is at this very moment where we have suddenly moved from the realm of the real and found ourselves in the land of allegory. It is a realm of particular interest to Goethe, who trafficked in alchemy and the arts of the Masons. He tells us: "True symbolism is where the particular represents the more general, not as a dream or a shadow but as a living momentary revelation of the inscrutable."[4]

We could define Goethe's "particular" as the story of Faust and Margarete, which points to something "general," the co-mingling of the old and the new. But even these allegorical coordinates do not answer the fundamental question of why opposing forces are attracted to and ultimately destroy one another. This question moves us beyond both the particular and the general to the "more general," or what Goethe ultimately defines as the "inscrutable." In other words, to the very heart of a mystery that taunts our answers.

The dream of the alchemist is to transmute lead into gold; the dream of the poet is to transmute people and things into symbols. This is what Goethe achieves in the final scene of *Faust Part I*. Margarete is in prison for having drowned her and Faust's illegitimate child. This, coupled with the inadvertent poisoning of her mother, has driven her mad. Faust has stolen into her cell, in the dead of night, and is trying to convince her to come with him. She refuses his entreaties. There is something beyond her madness that is making her stay. Faust, thanks to his pact with the Devil, can do anything but stay. If she is condemned to her past, Faust is condemned to the future. And so Faust takes Margarete by force, into his arms to carry her across the threshold to her freedom. And in this moment of embrace, suddenly before our very eyes, it is no longer a struggle between Faust and Margarete that we see, but a struggle between the old and the new. It is as if the very engine of the plot has broken down in the land of allegory where people are no longer people but symbols. Faust and Margarete have been transmuted; no longer flesh and blood, they have become, momentarily, pure ideation and the intimation of an another order of understanding. Past and future are now locked in an immortal battle over the present. An indelible image. Goethe, late in life, noted:

> We ought to talk less and draw more. For my part, I should like to lose the habit of conversation and, like nature, express myself in images. That fig tree, this little snake, the chrysalis lying there in the window quietly awaiting the future—all these are pregnant with meaning. Indeed, anyone who knows how to decipher them properly would soon be able to do without writing and speech.[5]

Faust and Margarete locked in their final, futile embrace, is such a moment where the image itself speaks without words. It is the moment where the history of an entire epoch, the transformation from the medieval to the modern, is captured through two human beings holding onto one another. It is the moment when theater reminds us that everything is a potential symbol, even our very selves.

Notes

1 For a look at Lessing's letter in English see Johan Wolfgang von Goethe, *Faust: A Tragedy*, edited by Cyrus Hamlin (Norton Critical Editions, First Edition, 1976).

2 Johann Wolfgang von Goethe, *Faust Parts One and Two*, translated by Howard Brenton (Nick Hern Books, 1996), 41–42.

3 Ibid., 77.

4 Quoted in Warren Breckman, *Adventures in the Symbolic: Post Marxism and Radical Democracy* (Columbia University Press, 2013), 31.

5 Johann Wolfgang von Goethe, *Goethe On Art*, translated and edited by John Gage (University of California Press, 1980), 73.

19

EXHIBIT SEVEN: *WOYZECK*

Reading other minds, or the discovery of subtext

It is 1837 and one man is shaving another; or, more precisely, a soldier is shaving a captain; or, for those who are more politically inclined, a servant is shaving his master. This master is only referred to as Captain, but the servant goes by the name Woyzeck. The name and the basic story are drawn directly from the tabloids of the day but the implications remain sadly pertinent to a new millennium. The great dramatist, Heiner Müller, upon receiving the Büchner Award in literature, astutely noted, "The tragedy of Woyzeck is that there are still Woyzecks, all across this globe, shaving Captains." Müller pulls this iconic image from the political unconscious and forces it out into the open: The oppressed are still shaving their oppressors. And with this observation comes the deeper, perennial question, what keeps the Woyzecks of the world from taking their collective razors and drawing them across the fat throats of the men who are the very cause of their despair?. Ultimately, as we know, Georg Büchner's Woyzeck will take another steel blade and plunge it into the chest of the one person he cares for more than anything else in the entire world, his lover Marie. It is she, not the Captain, that becomes the victim of Woyzeck's anger. Especially since the Captain is in collusion with the Doctor. The two are performing a series of experiments on Woyzeck to see how little an infantry man needs to be fed and still be effective in his duties. Currently Woyzeck's diet is restricted solely to peas. The results have been dubious, weakening poor Woyzeck's stamina and exasperating his propensity to hear certain voices. But this is part of Büchner's dramatic conceit, it is informative to compare Büchner's rendering of the story with the known facts of the actual case. It will help us understand why Büchner believes we will be closer to truly understanding Woyzeck on the stage than in the contents of even the most astute medical file.

The facts of the case are as follows: The incident occurred on June 21, 1821, at half past nine in the evening; the barber Johann Christian Woyzeck, 41 years of age, dealt a decisive series of stab wounds to the 46-year-old widow Johanna Woost. Dr. Johann August Clarus' report explains that these seven wounds were executed with:

the broken blade of a rapier … penetrating breast wound that cut through the first intercostal artery and both sacs of the pleura and punctured the descending part of the aorta in a location completely inaccessible to medical help.[1]

It takes less than a paragraph to understand the causes of Johanna's Woost's death. But it will take Clarus and his community the next three years to comprehend the underlying motivations that lead to Johann Christian Woyzeck's decision to murder the woman he loved. The issue being: was Woyzeck in his right mind when he murdered Woost or under the influence of strange voices that compelled him to do this horrific deed? Such delineations were new to the judicial processes of 1820s Leipzig. Clarus will ultimately conclude that there are no grounds whatsoever for the assumption that Woyzeck was of unsound mind at the time of the murder. Büchner will beg to differ with Clarus. What took Clarus three years to misunderstand, Büchner will prove can be properly understood within 90 minutes of an audience's time. Although it will take Büchner roughly four drafts to arrive at such a hermeneutic distillation.

The iconic scene of Woyzeck shaving his captain seems to be one of the earliest, if not the first experiment in dramatizing Woyzeck's story, although it differs significantly from its other iterations. In this fragment we have a character designated not as Woyzeck but simply as the Barber who is speaking as he shaves an unidentified client. In subsequent drafts this Barber will be replaced by Woyzeck, who earns a little extra pay for tending to his Captain's toiletries. It is intriguing to compare this early draft with Büchner's last iteration of the scene. In this first version it is the Barber, rather than the Captain who does all the talking.[2] This Barber's diction sounds more like that of the Doctor, and yet he, like Woyzeck, earns extra money by giving himself over to scientific experiments. Perhaps he is simply another example of a poor soul who is being meddled with by the Doctor and the Captain. Whoever he may be, he disappears in subsequent drafts, replaced by a more simple-minded Woyzeck. Beyond that, all similarities between the scenes ends. This subsequent scene, with Woyzeck as barber, is a complete inversion of the original barber scene. In this variation, it is the Captain who does all the talking while Woyzeck is reduced to an occasional, "Yes, Captain," or semi-evocative utterances on the poor in heaven, who will no doubt "have to help with the thunder." Beyond these scant interjections, Woyzeck places his full attention into shaving his superior. The result on stage is breathtaking.

The Captain speaks incessantly about anything and everything: time, eternity, the rotation of the earth, weather, conscience, morality, the church, the good, the poor, love, sex, and the efficacy of naps. His loquacious-ness borders on glossolalia. He talks and talks and yet we begin to hear less and less. What comes out of his mouth is nothing more than meaningless human noise whose only purpose is to keep any encroaching silence at bay. Because with silence comes thought, real thought, about life and how one lives and loses it. And who can bare to think of that? Not our Captain. And so, he talks and we hear nothing he is saying. Woyzeck, on the other hand, is mostly silent and yet we "hear" everything: the furrow of his brow, the incessant shaking of his hand, the bead of sweat on his temple, the itch where the collar of his uniform meets his Adam's apple. All these things speak to us in the language of the body and all its regional dialects: facial expression, gesture, pallor, posture, ease of being. This is the power of theater that Büchner finds at his disposal. Its tendency to create in the audience a kind of hyper-intentionality that helps him as he shows things that would otherwise elude his audience in the lecture halls of science. But now, all these things that no microscope can reveal, are shining forth in the unfolding of this scene, telling us about the secret Woyzeck, the Woyzeck that even Woyzeck might not know. The real Woyzeck, who eluded Johann Clarus for all those years. In this moment, as Woyzeck shaves his Captain, we feel privy to his private thoughts; as if we could read his mind, follow the stream of his consciousness to the very source of all his pain and longing. Büchner certainly makes the situation much easier than most dramatists, within the first several scenes we are introduced to the entire repertory of Woyzeck's limited thoughts: Freemasons, nature, Marie, the child, the Bible, and roll call. That pretty much constitutes the entire "cast" of Woyzeck's mental theater. It is not that hard, with so few principle players, to predict the contents of Woyzeck's mind at any time. We know he must be thinking about: Marie, the nape of the captain's neck, the baby, just beneath the Captain's chin, that passage from the Good Book, the asymmetry of the Captain's mustache, something to do with "suffer the little children," more lather, the Freemasons, be careful, don't think about the Freemasons, the Captain's right cheek, concentrate, the Captain's left cheek, steady, what did the Captain say? Just nod.

Such are the potential thoughts of Woyzeck, coming to us as we watch him shave his Captain. It is as if Büchner has transformed us into some exotic mind-reader, making us right at home in the world of the carnival that Woyzeck and Marie visit early on in the play. We could rival the carnival barker's mathematical horse; it may instill wonder by counting with its hoof, but we can now read the inner workings of people's minds. Büchner has made all of Woyzeck's thoughts manifest to us. As well as what goes unthought, including that one thought that we cannot help but think for him: What if Woyzeck just changed the direction of his razor and added just a little more pressure? Or, put more succinctly: what if he just slit his Captain's throat? But we intuit no such thought. Büchner, by taking away Woyzeck's speech in this scene, forces us to look at those other languages that his body speaks. The language of his face, his hands, his very muscles and sinews, all of which whisper to us: he is innocent of any foul thoughts. We will take this new-found knowledge and apply it to future scenes, to where Woyzeck kills Marie and know, on a certain level, contra Clarus and his report, that Woyzeck is not in complete control of his faculties. Faculties that, thanks to Büchner, we have been schooled in watching carefully. And so we see that it is not Woyzeck that condemns Marie, but the "voices" in his head. Voices that have gotten louder and louder thanks to the handy work of the Captain and the Doctor.

Büchner accomplishes all this thanks to the unique blend of his skills, for he possesses both the exactitude of a scientist and the intuition of a poet. He is, after all, a product of a new age. A time when the rigors of a new, materialist science had begun to assert itself without yet completely casting out the romantic idealism that had so dominated the culture. The two, in this briefest of historical moments, co-exist in a somewhat uncomfortable embrace. This is why Büchner can be both an anatomist at the University of Zurich by day and a secret playwright at night. He does believe, with the help of science and art, that he can pluck out the heart of Woyzeck's mystery and show it to an audience. Man's actions, for Büchner, must be set within the framework of society that can curb or encourage certain pre-given tendencies.

In the process of doing so, Büchner treats Woyzeck as an "open book" and patiently shows the audience how to "read" this tragic figure. It is a kind of dramaturgical anatomy lesson that lays bare the inner workings of Woyzeck's mind.

Büchner begins with a very modern mistrust of language, treating it like skin and muscle, which must be stripped away so that we can get to the real human being. This is part of the secret power of the shaving scene. Büchner intuits that language tends to cover up more than it reveals. He shows how language is a kind of clothing, it protects us from the elements, and helps us identify one another. The Captain and the Doctor have gone to great lengths to dress themselves in the distinguished language of power and science. Woyzeck and Marie have had to make do with what they can find, their language is rag-tag, found bits and pieces: Bible quotations, folk wisdom, superstitions, snippets of songs. These are scraps that don't necessarily go together, but it was the best they could assemble to keep themselves warm in an existential sense.

But through this dissection of language, Büchner inadvertently discovers the underneath of characters. What will become the unconscious of the modern subject. Before Büchner, characters spoke their minds: what they said was what they meant (think of almost any character in Shakespeare). If a character was going to dissemble, he would tell you in aside, usually just before he or she did so (think Richard III). Once in a while, a character would play at being something of an enigma, but that was just play (think Iago). With the advent of *Woyzeck*, all this changes. For the first time, the characters themselves are often detached from their own language, saying things they might not mean or actually feel. Here the wires of speech and intention are often crossed. Or sometimes the thought is just incomplete, trailing off, back into the silence that it came from. Such verbal tics come under the grammatical rubric of ellipsis, the omission of one or more words that at first were left out for a variety of reasons (they are implied, unknown, or lost). The word is Latin but borrowed from the Greek *elleipien*, which meant to leave out or fall short. This sort of expression (or lack thereof) is virtually absent from all dramatists before Büchner. In their hands, language flowed all the way until it reached its conclusion, rarely getting lost in the process. It would stop when it made its point, made all the more literal by the period at the end of each sentence. There were, of course, caesuras, but those were to catch one's breath, rather than lose one's thought. It is not till Büchner that language was allowed to break down, or fall short of ambitious conclusions. This opened up a series of gaps which would revolutionize the history of dramatic language.

An entirely new epistemological landscape opens with the advent of these gaps. Those three little dots, one after another, that designated the beginning of an ellipsis, was like an X found in pirate maps, it marked the spot where treasure was buried. But here, the treasure is not gold but subtext. An indeterminate space somewhere just underneath the speech of a person, where another unspoken set of intentions hides, often from the very one who is doing the speaking in the first place. And often, this buried meaning, was richer than anything that was ever spoken. This is what made it as valuable as gold. The trick became knowing where to look, how to intuit these hidden intentions. It required all our hermeneutic acumen, which meant looking to the other languages of human behavior to understand what is really going on.

We are also reminded that just because one speaks well does not mean that they are close to speaking the truth. This, in many ways, is Büchner's final revelation. In Woyzeck's world we learn that the one who struggles with speech the most, is often closest to stumbling on what really matters. Those with a smooth and well-refined language always at the tip of their tongues, like the Doctor and Captain, feel somehow suspect. As though their language was ready-made, or pre-scripted, rather than honest and immediate. The language of the Captain and the Doctor seem constructed to actually keep the surprises of the world out of their well-ordered lives. Büchner is a precursor to practicing what Paul Ricoeur called the hermeneutics of suspicion.[3] In this respect, our young scientist turned playwright is a forerunner of other such practitioners in the art of the suspect as Nietzsche, Freud, and Marx, although there is a delay in his dramaturgical revolution since his drafts of *Woyzeck* would not be discovered until the beginnings of the twentieth century. By that time such authors as Chekhov would anticipate the advances of Büchner on his own. But it is still important to note that in 1836, Georg Büchner got one of the first glimpses into modernity and left us an extraordinary message in a bottle called *Woyzeck*.

Notes

1 Georg Büchner, *The Major Works*, edited by Matthew Wilson Smith, translated by Henry J. Schmidt (W.W. Norton and Company, 2012), 160.
2 Ibid., 201.
3 Ricoeur, Paul, *Freud and Philosophy: An Essay in Interpretation*, translated by Dennis Savage (Yale University Press, 1970), 32.

20

EXHIBIT EIGHT: *THE THREE SISTERS*

The invention of the pause and intimations of the void

There they stand, stiff, uncomfortable; suddenly and irrevocably aware of themselves, their bodies, and the bodies next to them. Everything feels suspended and oddly concrete. This includes the most ineffable of qualities, time itself, which seems to have wandered off somewhere, leaving them in this stultifying, unending, unendurable present. What was to be a brief interim has turned into a veritable eternity; standing there, waiting, before this strange black box with its unblinking mechanical eye. A technological epiphany was supposed to occur in just a moment or two, which turned into three, until they lost count. There was the promise of some grand illumination. An explosion of light was to fill the room and somehow—now this was the tricky part—the part they didn't quite catch, but it had something to do with the light and the impression it would make on … oh, it's impossible to understand. Suffice to say, through the magic of modern ingenuity, this light would somehow forge their image into a picture for subsequent generations to ponder. So there they are: Olga, Masha, and Irina. The three sisters. They are surrounded by family, friends, and prospective lovers, all trying to look their best for a posterity that they can't quite begin to comprehend; making themselves presentable for a future us, who, they hope, will look kindly upon them. So, they continue to stand: frozen, while time's "winged chariot" has raced off, leaving them behind like relics from a forgotten past.

The Three Sisters is besotted with issues of time. We are not even four lines into the play before a nearby grandfather clock begins to inform the room that it is now twelve noon; as if to announce to all that the subject of this great work will be time itself. In fact, you could say the three sisters themselves are variations on the theme of time. One could identify each sister not only by what they do but how they are tensed. Olga is forever falling backward into the comfort of the past, Irina projects herself ever-forward into a more hopeful future, and poor Masha cannot escape the relentless pressures of the present. We can see each sister venture out from their particular temporal comfort zone, only to watch them quickly retreat to what seems to be their default setting. Time, as a theme, runs throughout Anton Chekhov's plays. One could argue that *The Seagull* deals with the past in the form of nostalgia, *Uncle Vanya* with the present as purgatory, and *The Cherry Orchard* with the future as something to be avoided at all costs. But it is *Three Sisters* that brings all three of these tenses under one roof for our investigation. In Chekhov's other works, we get intimations of the phenomenon of time, but it is with *Three Sisters* that time, in all its manifestations, is thoroughly interrogated. To fully understand and appreciate the power of this particular tableau, it behooves us to look at the development of these moments throughout the span of Chekhov's dramatic works.

The prototype for this moment can be found in Chekhov's third full-length play, *The Seagull*. It is here that Chekhov finally, fully, discovers himself as playwright. It begins inauspiciously, like any other boulevard comedy of the day, with a quick succession of scenes that play out the farcical equation of A loves B but B loves C. This translates into Medvedenko loves Masha, but Masha loves Treplev, but Treplev loves Nina, but Nina loves Trigorin; and so on and so on, until we reach Doctor Dorn, who seems to love everyone. One can imagine the first St. Petersburg audience enjoying this la-ronde-like opening and the promise of further amorous complication that comes with such frolics in the country. But then Chekhov does something strange and unexpected. He has these thwarted lovers all assemble to watch young Treplev's symbolist play. It is, as symbolist plays are wont to be, the very opposite of the boulevard farce: All theme, little character, and no sex. Before the audience can get their bearings, Arkadina, Treplev's mother, makes fun of the entire affair and her son calls the performance to a halt and storms off. There is a kind of Hegelian rigor to this sequencing. Think of the first boulevard comedy scenes as a kind of thesis, the ensuing symbolist play as its antithesis, and what follows—what we will call the Chekhovian moment—as the very synthesis of all that proceeded it. It is in this moment that Chekhov becomes Chekhov. He blends the surface realism of the boulevard comedy with the thematic intimations of Treplev's symbolist play and thereby founds a style that has earned the name Chekhovian. The moment is as follows:

Treplev has run off and the assembled onstage audience is left somewhat undone by all that has transpired. The play-within-a-play's meaning eludes them, the only thing that is clear is the animosity between mother and son. Arkadina says, "Let's talk about something else, shall we? What an marvelous evening," referring to the night, the stars, and the full moon above. And then, as if by magic, she enquires:

ARKADINA
You hear that singing?
(Listens)
Absolutely marvelous.

PAULINA
It's coming from the other side of the lake.[1]

And then something relatively new to drama. A little word appears: pause. If Shakespeare is the master of the caesura; Büchner, the ellipsis; than Chekhov's artistry is found in the dramatic pause. It is not of metrical import like the caesura, nor of grammatical clarification like an ellipsis. No, this is a longer, deeper, and somewhat more suspended interval; slower than any caesura and harder than your average ellipsis to excavate. Something is happening in this new form of time-taking, a vague feeling is growing into a concrete mood. In this case, it is nostalgia, time's most lyric manifestation. Arkadina continues:

> Ten or fifteen years ago there was music and singing here by the lake almost every night. There were six big country houses on the lake then. I remember the laugher, and the parties—people were always shooting off guns, all night long—and the love affairs, oh, the endless love affairs.[2]

And in this moment, everyone is swept up into the evocative magic of this collective sensation. It is, in many ways, an actual manifestation of Treplev's idea of a universal soul. Much later in the play, Dorn will describe his time visiting Genoa as the best approximation of such moments:

> Evenings, when you left your hotel, the entire street was full of people. You drift along with the crowd, no destination in mind, just back and forth; it becomes a living thing, and you become a part of it, spiritually, as well as psychically; you begin to believe that a universal soul is possible.[3]

Such moments in Chekhov maintain an intriguing blend of realism *and* symbolism. There is the realism of a group of people relaxing by lake, or strolling down a foreign street at night; yet, at the same time, there is also the tincture of the symbolic, pointing to another realm of meaning, just beyond our articulation. As though we were given a glimpse at Plato's secret universals.

This is the first of three pauses that happen in quick succession in this scene. The second pause occurs when the future lovers Nina and Trigorin meet and the final pause happens after Shamrayev tells a bad joke. You could say there is something of physic's second law of thermodynamics at work here, a kind of entropic trajectory which takes us from the sublime, to the erotically charged, to the just plan awkward. After the third pause, Doctor Dorn jokes that an angel has passed. Actually all three pauses could be construed as variations on this theme since the phrase itself escapes a clear-cut definition. For the French, "Un ange pass" (an angel passed) is the result of an awkward pause that an angel tries to mend. For the Germans, "Ein Engel flogs durch zimmer" (an angel crossed the room) conjures the sublime passage of angel whose magnificence momentarily subdues the noise of the world. This German iteration seems a worthy characterization of the Chekhov's first pause. The French translation captures the final pause, where we have gone from the sublime to the ridiculous. Between these two extremes lies the pregnant pause that envelops Nina and Trigorin. This is perhaps the oldest intimation of angelic

intervention: the angel as messenger. In this instance, bringing Eros to our unsuspecting couple.

The culmination of such moments can be found in Chekhov's final masterpiece:
The Cherry Orchard, his last portrait of a disenfranchised aristocracy that will soon
vanish from history. Here a group of them are somewhere just outside of their
estate, enjoying the setting sun when, as Chekhov tells us in his stage direction:

> They all sit in silence. The only sound we hear is old Firs mumbling. Suddenly
> a distant sound seems to fall from the sky, a sad sound, like a harp string
> breaking. It dies away.[4]

It is hard not to hear this and think that some sort of celestial warning is being
sounded for all to hear. Perhaps the metaphysical thread that held this precarious
world and heaven together has been irrevocably severed. The characters, like the
audience, try to domesticate the sound's source; bringing its origin back down
to earth. There are several theories: a cable breaking, an echo from a mine shaft, a
bird, a heron, perhaps an owl. The old servant Firs remembers a sound just like it
long ago when the "troubles" first started. "What troubles?" Someone asks. "The
day we got our freedom," Firs replies. Who is passing over these poor souls now?
The Angel of Death? Or perhaps Walter Benjamin's Angel of History? Again we
are confronted with a moment that is both absolutely real and symbolic at the
same time. Here we have a group of people, out in the countryside, watching
the sun set *and* the symbolic evocation of the end of an era. The sound itself
is both quotidian, most likely a cable breaking in mine shaft; as well as mythic,
signifying the end of the world as these people know it. Out of the chrysalis of
a real moment cracks open something otherworldly, which takes flight in our
imagination. We are at the very heart of Chekhov's magic art. Chekhov would
later write in a letter about *The Cherry Orchard* that he was so pleased to make it
through an entire play without a pistol going off. There is no offstage gunshots
like in *The Seagull*, just the metaphysical gunshot of this mysterious sound that
cuts through all assembled. Where our collection of lost souls in *The Seagull* could
wrap themselves in the universal feeling of nostalgia for a time long gone, our
new-found aristocratic friends can only feel a collective shiver for an end-time
that is just around the corner. The sound itself seems to be the harbinger for an
approaching figure in the twilight. Not the Angel of Death or of History. Just a
man, down on his luck and in need of a little something to help him make ends
meet. Another of Chekhov's dualities: a homeless man who foreshadows a revolution to come.

The Prozorov family and friends of *The Three Sisters* are caught between *The
Seagull's* intimations of a lyric past and *The Cherry Orchard's* fear of a foreboding
future. The Time we encountered in the unfolding of *Abraham and Isaac* has
returned, but now rather than a knife over the head of Isaac, it is like the sword
of Damocles over the heads of all who pose for this innocent photo. Here we feel
the full weight of theatrical time in this pause. This is Time with a capital "T." It

has metastasized into a kind of endless purgatorial present. In such moments we become aware of the relentless industry of Time as it goes about its quiet work. All is still and yet Time is busy preparing that first random grey hair that one will see tomorrow morning in the mirror, or the beginnings of a wrinkle in an otherwise porcelain-like face. One senses these infinitesimal alterations happening as we wait. As if we were an illustration that time was gently erasing, one tiny feature at a time until (if that damn photograph isn't taken soon) we might very well disappear. It is as if Time whispers to us, "you are here now, but how many more 'nows' do you have until you are no more?" And with the shuttering of the camera comes a shudder of mortality.

This is the beauty and the terror of the pause. Something is occurring, happening, coming into being. It is an intimation finding its way from sensation to articulation. Perhaps this is why such moments are called, "pregnant." An understanding is about to come into the world. Sometimes this is a discovery, sometimes this is a remembrance that has been long forgotten or repressed. But within this interim, something is at work on us, coming into being. This is what happens to the Prozorovs and company as they pose for their photo. Each is having their own private intimation of time's passage on a micro and macro level. Each senses how they are, ever so slowly, becoming memory.

Chekhov, juxtaposes this tableau of the family and friends posing for a photograph with the same group later engaged in watching a toy top spin. What is our playwright attempting with this second image? What is he trying to tell us that he could not do with the earlier tableau? What happens when we compare waiting for a photo to be taken with watching the spinning of the top? Are they the same experience of time? The photo seems as though it takes forever. The spinning top is another experience of the same amount of time that somehow does not feel so interminable. This delay is somehow captivating; or rather the top's gyration upstages our sense of duration. And yet, the phenomenon is somewhat misleading, giving us the sense of motion that does not transport. The top, for all its effort, simply spins in place; letting physic's second law of thermodynamics go about its entropic work. Are we like that top? Is it our minds that are spinning in place, giving us the illusion of movement while, in reality, we are going nowhere?

Perhaps the real meaning is in the juxtaposition of our sense of terminus. In the case of the photograph, we can't wait for the photo to be over and done with, for this interminable interval of time to end. But with the top, we want it to spin and spin for all eternity, defying entropy, to be immortal. We know such a thing is not possible and yet, perhaps this time; each subsequent gyration giving us the intimation of immortality. The same swath of time experienced in two radically different ways. Each gives a divergent understanding of our being and its limit. Both the moment of the photo and the moment of top bring our end in sight. An end we'd rather go about forgetting, like time itself.

Beckett will take this idea one step further with his ominous notation: Silence. Let us look at this stage direction in action. The play is *Waiting for Godot* and two tramps, Didi and Gogo, are doing just what the title tells them to do. As they wait, they pass the time with talk; all manner of talk, from the sublime to the ridiculous. Well, to be honest, their talk is mostly in the key of the ridiculous with moments of an accidental kind of sublime. They talk of ill-fitting shoes, what they might eat, their difficulty sleeping, and their eventual meeting with the mysterious Mr. Godot. All of these subjects are punctuated by what Beckett designates as moments of silence. We have noted earlier that pauses are characterized as being pregnant with potential meaning, an intimation just on the cusp of realization. Silences, on the other hand, tend to intimate a kind of stillbirth of such potential. Nothing grows within them, or if it does, it dies before being articulated. The silence is a kind of wasteland, nothing flourishes there. Subjects, thoughts, understanding can only die and be buried in such a space. An overextended Chekhovian pause brings us to the very border of Beckett's silence. This is particularly true of the fourth and final acts of Chekhov plays where the pause becomes so interminable it presages Beckett's silence. It is beyond a sense of time passing and brings us face to face with the void, with nothingness. What does the great poet Valéry say? "God created everything out of nothingness, but the nothingness shows through." A silence in Beckett is one of the ways nothingness shows itself. It is the final and perhaps most unnerving manifestation of the theatrical apparatus. Silences in life, tend to be unnerving. In the theater, a space of hyper-intentionality, they can become unbearable. In the hands of Beckett, it makes us aware of the nothingness that seems to always be lurking just beneath time itself. It reduces all our words and action into a series of failed diversions to keep this silence and its concomitant nothingness at bay.

This is, of course, our "fallen" Western/secular relationship with silence and nothingness. The East and early Western traditions found ways to make peace with the nothingness that Chekhov and Beckett bring onto stage. But if Western theater traffics in the realm where words become actions, than silence and nothingness are its ultimate adversaries. At least for most modern, secular spectators. To them, such silence equals a figurative death—something very difficult for the West to process. It remains the most palpable of ineffables.

In some ways we could chart the progress of theater through the movement that begins with Shakespeare's caesura, opens up to Büchner's ellipsis, grows into Chekhov's pause, and ends in Beckett's silence. Each is a widening of the gap where speech, a primary function in theater, is withheld for an ever-widening length of time. Each of these intervals carries with it a different experience of meaning. The caesura remains somewhat technical, the ellipses and the pause within the bounds of the quotidian, with silence pointing to something uncomfortably other. It is Chekhov who becomes the first to begin to explore these varying intervals and make a new kind of dramatic music out of their interplay. This is part of Chekhov's great gifts. In the process he did more than just change the rhythms of theater. He was also able to lure such ineffables as Time, Mortality and the Void out into the open for all us to experience.

Notes

1 Anton Chekhov, *The Plays of Anton Chekhov*, translated by Paul Schmidt (Harper Perennial, 1998), 121.
2 Ibid.
3 Ibid., 150.
4 Ibid., 358.

21

EXHIBIT NINE: *GALILEO*

"Making strange": the fine art of seeing otherwise

There he sits. Ancient. Naked. Alone on stage. Our sense of decorum tells us not to look; but our curiosity gets the better of us. We sneak a peek. Time has not been kind to this old man. It has made a mockery of his body. So much so, we feel compelled, once more, to look away. It is as though his very flesh was weeping for the long lost muscle and sinew of his youth. His skin is milk white, suggesting that it is phlegm rather than blood that now courses through his veins. From a certain angle, this old fellow resembles some evolutionary misstep: half man, half overgrown amphibian creature. Two young apprentices enter and, as our scene ensues, slowly dress this half-toad, half-man. They begin with a variety of white undergarments, followed by an ornate robe, matching floor-length cape, vestments, and, the crowning touch, a miter. Slowly before our eyes, this feeble evolutionary misstep has become God's representative on earth, leader of the Holy Roman Empire, Pope Urban VIII.

This, as many may quickly recognize, is the famous scene from Bertolt Brecht's *The Life of Galileo*, a play Brecht wrote while on the run from Hitler. It was begun in Sweden, revised in Santa Monica, and finalized upon Brecht's return to East Berlin. It marks the beginning of Brecht's final mature phase. These are the great works of Brecht, they include *Mother Courage*, *Good Person of Setzuan*, *The Resistible Rise of Arturo Ui*, and *The Caucasian Chalk Circle*. They follow on the heels of Brecht's *Lehrstücke* (learning plays) where his work was at its most radical, both in terms of content and form. These experiments in theater were to prepare a new audience (the proletariat) for a new world (the communist future). It was a world that was not to be. The Weimar Republic gave way to fascism rather than communism, and this fatal choice sent Brecht into a self-imposed exile.

Bereft of his homeland and his native language, Brecht was forced to rethink his future writing. He had to face the fact that it may not be performed in his lifetime and therefore must be for "all time." But what makes such a dramaturgy? This sent him back to Shakespeare and other writers who have withstood the test of time. It forced him to return to more "classical models" to found his new work upon. To give his work a presentable cover, because he did not want to forgo his radical relationship to the world at large, Brecht became a dramatic black-marketeer, under the guise of a more traditional narrative he smuggled in his radical critique.

Brecht tells us, in a manner that never makes complete analogical sense, that *Galileo* is really about Oppenheimer and the Bomb; but, upon closer inspection it seems the play bears a closer tie to the Moscow show trials where the great revolutionary Nikolai Bukharin was forced to confess to false charges of treason. The real question of the play seems to be, how does one go on believing in the cause (whether it is science or communism) when those who inspired us fall short of our hopes and dreams. How do we keep the faith that others have lost?

Along with playing "hide and seek" with the content of his work, Brecht must also modify much of his formal intervention. This had been a big part of his artistic signature during the Weimar Republic. Much of these "bells and whistles" went under the rubric of the *Verfremdungseffekt*, a collection of theatrical methods "borrowed" from Meyerhold and Piscator that would help support the larger argument of the given play.[1] Brecht's great achievement was not in inventing these devices, but in putting them together into a semi-coherent alternative methodology to normative (Aristotelian) theater. Even Brecht's *Verfremdungseffekt* has its origin in the Russian formalism of the time; specifically, Viktor Shklovsky's concept of *ostranenie*. Brecht's term is often, awkwardly, translated as the "alienation effect." Such a translation misses the directness that Shklovsky's *ostranenie* offers. *Ostranenie* literally means: "to make things strange."[2] Shklovsky used this word to talk about how literature, as a form, is capable of breaking us out of our habitual relationship to the world and thereby making us look at things anew. Shklovsky found that prose tended to reinforce the habitual; whereas poetry, in its pursuit of heightened language, had a propensity toward restoring a sense of wonder to what was often dismissed as the commonplace. Brecht takes this notion of "making strange" and politicizes it. He wants us to see that certain situations, attitudes, and relations are not *a priori* like nature but are, in actuality, social constructions. By showing us the naked man underneath the religious robes of the Pope, he dispels much of the aura that we attribute to such a figure. The Pope is, in the end, just like us. This is the quintessence of the Brecht's mature use of the *Verfremdungseffekt*.

Other examples of *Verfremdungseffekt* can be found in Brecht's early use of music, projections, placards, and the unadorned theater itself. To undo the power of a patriotic song, he projects images of war's inhuman devastation; to undercut the emotional power of certain dramatic moments, he has them underscored with a comedic melody; to focus on an audience's attention on a particularly dense scene, he displays a placard announcing the scene's fundamental intent; and, finally, to counteract the theater's overall illusory capabilities, he reveals the lights, ropes, and pulley systems that are responsible for creating such moments of enchantment. All of this, again, is at the service of "making strange" the trappings of bourgeois reality as it manifests itself in the theatrical apparatus. By doing so, Brecht shows that this reality is nothing more than a social construct. Since it is a construct, Brecht reminds us, it can be reassembled into a better world. Brecht's goal is twofold, to get the audience to see the badly constructed seams and cracks in the facade of bourgeois reality as it is depicted on stage, and then take this new found visual acuity and apply it to the world just outside the theater.

As Brecht continues working on the potential of such *Verfremdungseffekt*, he begins to see the contradictions inherent in a character as another powerful form of making strange. The fact that Mother Courage could be a mother and a businesswoman in the same scene begins to fascinate him. Showing such contradictions becomes another way to alert the audience to the faulty construction of bourgeois character. The contradiction momentarily throws us out of the scene, making us ask, "How can a mother, who loves her children, engage in the business of war which will ultimately destroy the very family she strives to protect?" Such a contradiction gets right to the heart of the bourgeois dilemma. These contradictions become, for Brecht, another example of the badly concealed seams and cracks that belie the authority of bourgeois reality. In short, just as reality is a construction, so too is the subject. In Brecht, both are shown as flawed and therefore ultimately changeable.

The dressing of the Pope in *Galileo* shows us this dialectic at work. First and foremost, it does so without the theatrical "fireworks" of Brecht's earlier *Verfremdungseffekt*. There are no projections, music, or revelations of the theatrical apparatus. There is just the simple, straightforward unfolding of a contradiction: a man who displays absolutely no singular marks of distinction whatsoever is, through the arrangement of certain fabrics, made out to be a figure of otherworldly significance. All *Verfremdungseffekt*, whether they are technical (use of projections) or behavioral (how the actors comport themselves), are based on the revelation of a fundamental contradiction. It is the contradiction that interrupts our interiorizing of the event (just experiencing it as it unfolds) and, momentarily, throws us outside (making us re-aware of the event as construction and suddenly critical of what is unfolding). Thanks to having been brought "behind the scenes" and witnessing the dressing of this ordinary figure, we can no longer view the resplendent final results without thinking back to how the image came about.

It is as if Brecht were staging Hegel's offhand comment that "For the valet there is no hero"; meaning, it is hard to take most people seriously after you've seen them in their underwear. In this case, this revelation short-circuits our innate desire to respect the signage of a religious potentate. We cannot easily fold back into the image; but remain outside of it, in a critical frame of mind.

The irony of this is further compounded by the fact that this Pope seems less and less powerful the more and more he is dressed. He opens with a commanding, "No! No! No!" as the scene begins, rejecting his inquisitor's desire to force Galileo to recant. After all, this Pope is a friend of Galileo's and a man of science himself. The Pope tells his inquisitor, "I will not set myself up against the multiplication table. No!"[3] But as more and more vestments are placed on him and the inquisitor's argument becomes more and more strident, we find the Pope pleading rather than ordering, "This man is the greatest physicist of our time. He is the light of Italy, and not just some muddle-head." Finally, by the end of the scene, dwarfed by the grandiosity of his robes and the responsibilities that the inquisitor reminds him of, he consents to Galileo's trial with the following caveat, "It is clearly understood: he is not to be tortured. At the very most, he may be shown the instruments." The inquisitor bows, and in perfect Brechtian understatement says, "That will be adequate, Your Holiness. Mr. Galileo understands machinery." Before we leave the scene, Brecht's stage direction tells us that the eyes of our newly dressed Pope "look helplessly at the Cardinal Inquisitor from under the completely assembled panoply of Pope Urban VIII." Brecht, the master of contradiction, shows us how the robes that adorn this new Pope enslave rather than empower him. The more regal he becomes, the more burdened by tradition. The supposed master is no more than a well-dressed slave.

This is Brecht in a nutshell, reminding us, through the art of making strange, not to take anything at face value. Once we see things in this light, Brecht hopes, it will be all the more difficult to un-see them. It is a kind of double sight; or, perhaps more technically, a kind of dialectical seeing where we hold these two contrary images in our mind: The Pope endowed with otherworldly might and the Pope as construction. It is a kind of seeing through that Brecht wants to cultivate in the theater so that, upon learning this new way of seeing, we might leave the darkened auditorium and go out and re-see the world for what it really is. A tall order, that we, as theater practitioners and audiences, are still learning to live up to.

Notes

1 See Bertolt Brecht, *Brecht on Theatre*, edited by John Willet (Hill and Wang, 1992), 91–100.
2 See Viktor Shklovsky, *Theory of Prose*, translated by Benjamin Sher (Darkley Archive, 1990), 1–15.
3 See Bertolt Brecht, *Galileo*, translated by Charles Laughton, edited by Eric Bentley (Grove Press, 1994), 108–110.

22

EXHIBIT UNDER CONSTRUCTION:
ANGELS IN AMERICA

Seeing double

We have almost come to the end of our tour. There is one last room that will house our latest installation. You are more than welcome to take a quick look. As we said, it is not quite finished. The tableau has not had the benefit of time going about its quiet, painstaking work of conferring full universality. Such things can only happen when a significant distance emerges between the work and its future reception, such a passage has a cleansing aspect. It erases certain contemporary elements that may have made the work meaningful for its original audience. Once such contemporary trappings recede, we learn what the work really has to say or not say to subsequent generations. Keep in mind this tableau is, after all, not yet three decades old, a veritable infant when compared to the other works we have viewed.

And yet this image has already shown great promise. From its first staging it has immediately captured the imaginations of audiences all around our beleaguered globe. This particular tableau has become ubiquitous, emblazoned in every audience member's memory, its photographic double finding itself multiplied *ad infinitum* in review after review, as well as on the covers of a growing body of books about theater itself. This now iconic image occurs at the very end of the first part of this ambitious two-part epic where a young man, Prior Walter, who is stricken with AIDS, awakens in his bed, to the sounds of a strange "creaking and groaning from the bedroom ceiling." What happens next we will leave to the poetic stage directions of the author himself:

> A sound, like a plummeting meteor, tears down from very, very far above the earth, hurtling at an incredible velocity towards the bedroom; the light seems to be sucked out of the room as the projectile approaches; as the room reaches darkness, we hear a terrifying CRASH as something immense strikes the earth; the whole building shudders and a part of the bedroom ceiling, lots of plaster and lathe and wiring, crashes to the floor. And then in a shower of

unearthly white light, spreading great opalescent gray-silver wings, the Angel descends into the room and floats above the bed.[1]

Not bad as far as grand finales go and it came at just the right time. Not only to save poor Prior Walter, but also to save late twentieth-century theater from the relentlessly tight grip of realism that was threatening to squeeze all the imaginative life-force out of theater. The image, which heralds a future theater, draws much of its power from theater's neglected past. The play, unlike its contemporaries, revels in such theatricality with the appearance and disappearance of ghosts and books of spouting fire. Tony Kushner, in his notes on the play, suggests that all these moments:

> Be fully realized, as bits of wonderful *theatrical* illusion which means it's OK if the wires show, and maybe it's a good thing that they do, but the magic should be at the same time thoroughly amazing.[2]

The idea that "it's OK if the wires show, and maybe it's a good thing that they do," harkens back to one of Kushner's most significant influences: Brecht and the idea of seeing double. Brecht's impulse, as we saw in *Galileo*, was first and foremost to dismantle the illusion and show the theatrical machine that produces the effect. In Marxist terms, if we see the means of production that go into the creation of illusion we will be less likely to be in the thrall of what we see. We move from a passive spectator to a critical one. This becomes something of a metaphor for looking at our own reality which we often forget is a social construction. "Seeing the wires" in the theater allows us to go back into the world and begin to see the "wires" and "seams" that hold our reality together. If we can see our reality as a construction as opposed to some immutable *a priori*, then we can conceive of changing it.

But an intriguing and perhaps unforeseen aesthetic byproduct of such an approach is that revealing the inner workings of the theatrical machine has its own kind of beauty; like looking at a clock's inner mechanism, there is something sublime in seeing the intricate interplay of one gear interacting with another. The attempt to dispel illusion also leads to a strange kind of re-enchantment of the theatrical experience. We get to experience a piece of magic and see how it is done at the same time. It bestows on theater a kind of inadvertent metaphysical tincture. This is no doubt what Kafka was after in the last chapter of *Amerika* where the main character stumbles in to a shabby theater that is in the midst of rehearsing a heavenly pageant replete with the gaudy trappings of all things otherworldly. At such a moment the reader wonders whether our main character has actually entered a rundown theater or has arrived at heaven itself. In Brecht's technique and in Kafka's novel theater easily lends itself to this whimsical metaphor for heaven. Such a conflation is as old as theater itself. Kushner's very first play was entitled *The Heavenly Theatre* and dealt with a medieval acting troupe during the time of carnival. This was followed, several years later, just before *Angels*, with his free adaptation of Pierre Corneille's *The Illusion*, another play that also conflates magic and theater into an intoxicating evening of entertainment. This semi-magical current runs throughout much of Kushner's early theater work which has been called the Theater of the Fabulous.

Finally, this image, tells us something fundamental about how we see. Upon first glimpse of this image we see an actress, with wings, suspended in the air, by wires. We understand, perhaps from previous experience in the theater, that this represents an angel in free flight. At which point, we mentally edit out the wires to better enjoy the image. We make an active choice to re-script what we see. This does not mean that we longer see the wires, just that we have momentarily bracketed them out. The image is now split for us, we can move back and forth from seeing an actress suspended in the air by wire and, with a slight mental blink, we can see an angel in mid-flight. This is what we mean by a kind of double sight. It is, in essence, what we have been doing throughout this essay; moving back and forth from an image to an intimation of something else, something other, something more. This is part of our innate, human capacity to take what we see and transform it from the realm of reality into the realm of poetry. It is a gift acquired in childhood and mostly forgotten by the time we reach adulthood. It is in the theater where this innate capacity of ours can be rediscovered and brought back into the world at large.

The angel of Kushner's *Angels in America*, upon descending from on high tells Prior Walter: "Greetings, Prophet/The Great Work begins." And so it has thanks to such contemporary theater artists like Tony Kushner who has returned theater to its metaphoric foundations, allowing it to re-enchant ourselves and the world.

Notes

1 Tony Kushner, *Angels in America* (Theater Communications Group, 1995), 124.
2 Ibid., Playwright's Note.

23

RECAPITULATION #2: OR TOWARD THE HOW OF THEATER

In this chapter we have been primarily dealing with "the how of theater" through its use of ek-stasis. Our argument has been that theater goes about its fundamental work by making things stand out. This is, in part, thanks to the basic hyper-intentionality of the medium where theatrical space is ultimately a limited field, capable of showing only so much. The inherent selective nature of theatrical space leads to a kind of condensation of representation that is further animated by the pressure of an audience's collective gaze. The collision of these two forces results in making manifest aspects of existence that usually remain in the background or just under the radar of our consciousness. They exist on the periphery of our comprehension, where they take on an ineffable half-life, waiting to be brought back into focus.

We have designated nine and a half aspects that theater helps to make legible:

1. Actions (*Agamemnon*).
2. Time (*Abraham and Isaac*).
3. Space (*Romeo and Juliet*).
4. Being (*The Winter's Tale*).
5. Thing-ness of objects (*Tartuffe*).
6. Symbolization/surplus meaning (*Faust*).
7. Other minds/subtext (*Woyzeck*).
8. Ellipses/the pause (*The Three Sisters*).
9. De-familarization/"making strange" (*Galileo*).
9½. Duality/seeing double (*Angels in America*).

All exist, but are often difficult to see, read, or verbalize. Some are forgotten out of the force of habit, like time, space, or being; some can only be felt or intuited invisibly by our second nature, as is the case with actions, subtexts, and ellipses; some are domesticated by our activity of naming, in such instances the naming of a thing can often deprive it of its initial strangeness or surplus meaning. We call this spectrum of occluded phenomena "ineffables." As you can see, such ineffables come in all shapes, sizes, manners, and degrees. What draws these disparate phenomena together is that they tend to escape immediate comprehension in words, often first coming to us as feelings or intuition that then find their way to verbal expression. We could re-categorize these ineffables into three basic categories that are grouped in terms of their actual scale of ineffability, i.e., how hard they actually are to bring into words. The re-categorization would look like this:

1. Big Ineffables:
       (scaled to the conditions of being-in-the-world)
          Time
          Space
          Being
          Nothingness

2. Medium Ineffables:
       (scaled to the conditions of human interaction)
          Actions
          Subtexts
          Ellipses

3. Discreet Ineffables:
       (scaled to the conditions of objects and naming)
          Thing-ness
          Strange-ness
          More-ness

We could say that "Big Ineffables" are often occluded by the sheer force of habit. They are like the water in the old joke about two little fish who are completely unaware of their actual surroundings. The joke finds these fish swimming past an older fish who says to them, "Hiya boys, how's the water?" The two little fish say, "Fine." But as soon as they swim out of earshot of the older fish, the one little fish asks the other, "What the hell is water?" In other words, such huge existential givens, like the water for fish or consciousness for us, are so large and all-encompassing they become actually hard to see. We would say that this is also true of such dynamics as time, space, being, and nothingness. The common denominator of these differing existential givens rests in their enormity and persistence that dulls us to their active presence. As a result, these givens have the tendency to move to the background of our consciousness, waiting for the right moment to be re-experienced in all their profundity. And so, even though time is a constant, we are often not aware of it until we have to wait for a subway train; or, like when the three sisters pose for a photograph to be taken. Suddenly, at such moments, time returns to us in all its concreteness. Think, for instance, of how we become aware of the nature of being as we contemplate a living Hermione posing as a statue in *The Winter's Tale*; or, how the distance and proximity of Romeo and Juliet invokes in us "the music of space," which we are so often deaf to; or, finally, the sense of nothingness that can emerge within the silence between one Beckett character and another. These are the "Big Ineffables" that theater can restore to our apprehension.

"Medium Ineffables" primarily have to do with the reading/understanding of various human attributes and energies that we are often unconscious of processing. These aspects of being are part of the many pre-verbal languages that we first learn in infancy. These languages actually precede the acquisition of words and remain in the background throughout our lives, helping us to continue to decipher the world at large. Over time, these pre-verbal languages become a kind of second nature, almost as invisible as the very ineffables they were developed to decipher. But it is these essential pre-lingual understandings that allow us to read the language of actions, bodies, faces, the grain of voices, and certain ellipses. All of these behaviors have their own secret syntax and grammar that we learned to read like words. In many instances they speak louder to us than words since they are tied to something more primordial and immediate. Think of how we read the action of Agamemnon walking across the red carpet, how his body language, in that moment, speaks to us, and reveals something profound about his interior motives; or how we can intuit the stream of consciousness that flows through Woyzeck's head as he shaves his Captain; or finally, understand the missing words in an ellipsis by one of the three sisters. In all these cases, we are able to do so thanks to our almost unconscious, pre-verbal understanding of the many languages of human nature.

Finally, there are the "Discreet Ineffables" that often result from the tyranny of naming and can lead to intimations of estrangement (strange-ness) and surplus meaning (more-ness). Naming, as we know, is our major way of ordering the world; but, in such naming, it also has a side-effect of denuding aspects of the world's inherent mystery. This is particularly true when names are attached to objects, these objects often lose their surplus meaning or strangeness, having been constrained or domesticated by the word that suddenly references them. The strange thingliness of the object disappears in the process and yet, at certain points, when we return our attention to the object at hand, it can assert its non-verbal autonomy as sheer thing. This returns us to James Joyce's use of epiphany where, "the mind recognizes that the object is, in the strict sense of the word, a thing, a definitely constituted thing … its soul, its what-ness, leaps to us from the vestment of its appearance."[1] It is in such moments that an object, person, or situation can achieve its epiphanic status. This is true not only of our example of Molière's table, but also Brecht's Pope, and Goethe's Faust and Margarete in prison. Here an object, a person, and a situation break from the shackles of their signifier (i.e., name). In the case of Molière's table, the object is released from its name (signifier) and meaning (signification) to return to a brief moment of pure, shimmering thingliness (sign). During this pre-lexical reprieve, it is free to become anything it wants: a barrier, a bed, or even a belated God. In the case of Brecht's Pope, the meaning (signification) of otherworldly authority breaks down since the name Pope (signifier) proves to be nothing more than a literal and figurative garment to clothe an otherwise very ordinary man (sign). In other words, under Brecht's rubric of de-familiarization, he "makes strange" the correspondence between Pope (signifier) and ordinary man (the actual sign), thereby short-circuiting its otherworldly meaning (signification). This negation of the sign is reversed in the hands of Goethe where he allows Faust attempting to free Margarete from prison (signs) to mean more (signification) than the situation (signifier) intended; thereby endowing both Faust and Margarete with a surplus of meaning, in this case of an allegorical nature. Here Faust and Margarete mean more, they shimmer before us as both characters *and* as symbols of a larger authorial message about the clash between modernity (Faust) and tradition (Margarete). It is a kind of seeing double, which Tony Kushner makes more evident with his angel/actress-on-a-wire dichotomy in *Angels in America*. In these latter examples, theater allows us to see both possible readings simultaneously and to remind us that such an enhanced acuity can be brought back with us into the world at large.

At the center of the decipherment of all these ineffables is the ek-static moment itself. In this miraculous instant, the ineffable is re-cognized. Often this arrives as a profound feeling or intuition before it is translated into words; in fact, words, for such experiences, often arrive long after the ek-static moment has passed. This is true for the overall meaning of certain theater works where their actual intent usually accrues over time. Often the point of a play eludes us until its last moments; we are given intimations like breadcrumbs that eventually lead us to a destination of understanding. The artist William Kentridge talks about the moment in the actual sketching of a horse when the observer can actually discern the figure at hand; when what had previously been an indecipherable set of lines suddenly coalesces into horse-ness.[2] Duchamp goes further and calls all of his art works "delays" since, even when the artwork is presented in all its completeness, it still can require time for the viewer to grasp the work's deeper significance.[3] There is a certain wisdom to this observation of how art's meaning is ultimately made manifest. The exact "when" is open to each viewer; but, at some point over the course of the event's unfolding, the work's own ineffable core of meaning becomes ek-static and "stands out." In the case of Shakespeare's *King Lear*, Kent's injunction for Lear to "See better" is one potential meaning that gets louder and louder as the play continues. In the case of *Hamlet*, the meaning of the play can demand multiple viewings and still escape our complete comprehension.

Regardless of the time signature of a work's given meaning, when these moments finally do coalesce into an insight, we often marvel that such revelations had indeed always been in-sight. We realize that we were just too close, or too habituated to see what was in front of us. The very nature of the *theatron* (made possible by a conjunction of distance, condensation, and the collective pressure of an audience's gaze) engenders a hyper-intentional state that enables of us to re-engage with such phenomena. This makes the *theatron* the perfect machine to retrieve these ineffables and bring them back to our attention and contemplation. The result is that the audience is allowed to see afresh, see more, and even see double. Each of the authors we have examined use theater to arrive at such fundamental revisionings of our reality. Theirs is a battle against our often-impoverished relationship with the world at large. A world that can be dulled to the point of obscurity by the day-to-day force of habit. By bringing many of these ineffables back to the fore, we have an opportunity to re-enchant our world that has slaved under the tyrant of habit. In these moments theater returns us to the realm of intimation and reintroduces us to the secret tools of decipherment that were first bestowed upon us in childhood. It reminds us how they work, and how they can be used when we return to the world at large; enabling us to extract even more potential meaning from this rich, varied, and ultimately mysterious thing we call existence.

Notes

1 James Joyce, *Stephen Hero*, 211–213.
2 William Kentridge and Rosalind C. Morris, *That Which Is Drawn* (Seagull Books, 2014), 41.
3 See Elena Filipovic, *The Apparently Marginal Activities of Marcel Duchamp* (MIT Press, 2016), 121–122.

PART III

From Sophocles' urn to Wittgenstein's box

Theater and the engendering of fellow-feeling throughout the ages

24

BRIEF INTRODUCTION: THEATER'S TELOS

The engendering of fellow-feeling

In these past chapters, we have been interested in the "what" and "how" of theater. Now it is time to address its "why." It is all very well and good to surmise that theater is a machine of hyper-intentionality and to suggest that how it goes about its secret work is through the art of ek-stasis (making things stand out) but the larger question still remains: why? To what end?

The answer we will pose is quite simple; although its realization is often rather elusive. We will argue that theater's goal, when you get right down to it, is a modest one; its basic impulse, humble. It simply wants to *move us.* Not just me, or you, but *us.* Theater is a plural affair. When it works, it does indeed transport. At the beginning of a play we sit down in our seat as an isolated I amongst a sea of other isolated I's, and by the time it ends, we discover we aren't as isolated as we thought. We have moved from that isolated I to a collective us. How does this magic trick happen? Through the prism of our emotions. What a curious word: emotion. Tap it with an imaginary hammer, break it in two, what do you have? E motion. There's that word: motion. Feelings take us places. Huge distances. They can take you all the way from I to we.

The argument of this section is that theater brings things "to light" in order to engender a collective response of fellow-feeling. This is theater's endpoint. It gathers a group of individuals together, sits them down, makes them all face the same direction, and asks them to watch a living representation come into being; having collectively experienced this, it wants to know whether this representation speaks to ourselves and those around us. This "speaking to" is addressed, like all art, to both the mind and the heart of an audience. Although, in theater an interesting form of synesthesia is at work. Thanks to the embodied playing of the actors, the audience has the opportunity to both *feel* a thought and *think* a feeling. These two forms of understanding (the mental and the emotional) are so intricately threaded together in theater, that it is often difficult to not only untangle them, but to understand whether one form of comprehension is superior to another.

This battle between thought and the feeling has been waged throughout the history of theatrical aesthetics, with each struggling for supremacy. It reminds us that our understanding of something like fellow-feeling is not a universal given; but rather, a series of very specific historical and cultural constructions that have competed with one another over an immense swath of time. We want to examine this ever-shifting relationship from its inception to our current practices to better understand how these dynamics have worked in the past and why they might be misfiring today.

Perhaps the tangled history of fellow-feeling could best be charted by comparing the distance we've come from Sophocles' urn to Wittgenstein's box. Wittgenstein's box is part of a modern philosophical thought experiment; while Sophocles' urn is a prop from his play *Electra*. Now, this thought experiment and this prop are separated by 2,500 years; but, when placed side-by-side, they have something intriguing to tell us about the evolution of our feelings for one another. They form a kind of alpha and omega of this history.

Wittgenstein's box

This paradox can be found in the very center of Wittgenstein's posthumous *Philosophical Investigations*. This marvelously elliptical work takes on the very loose form of a Socratic dialogue. The conversation takes place between an unnamed interlocutor and a patient, all-knowing, respondent who sounds very suspiciously like Wittgenstein himself. The book chronicles their discussion of such subjects as Augustine's theory of language, the nature of what Wittgenstein calls "language games," "rule following," and a host of other topics. When taken all together, these theories upend Wittgenstein's first published and most famous work: *The Tractatus Logico-Philosophicus*. Amid these topics is a brief conversation on the issue of knowing another's sensations, most notably pain. It is out of this discussion that Wittgenstein crafts his famous paradox of "the beetle in a box." Somewhat prior to its deployment, the unnamed interlocutor has exclaimed, "How am I filled with pity for this man? How does it come out? What is the object of my pity?" Our unnamed respondent, who, for clarity's sake we will call Wittgenstein, surmises, "Pity, one may say, is a form of conviction that someone else is in pain." The unnamed interlocutor goes on to question whether his conception of pain is similar (or identical) to someone else's, "If I say to myself that it is only from my own case that I know what the word 'pain' means—must I not say the same of other people too?"[1] And it is at this point that Wittgenstein unleashes his grand paradox:

> Now someone tells me that he knows what pain is only from his own case. Suppose everyone had a box with something in it. We call it a "beetle." No one can look into anyone else's box, and everyone says he knows what a beetle is only by … looking at his beetle. Here it would be quite possible for

everyone to have something different in his box. One might even imagine such a thing constantly changing. But suppose the word "beetle" had a use in these people's language? If so it would not be used as a name of a thing. The thing in the box has no place in the language game at all; not even as something: for the box is empty. No, one can "divide through" by the thing in the box; it cancels out, whatever it is. That is to say: if we construe the grammar of the expression of a sensation on the model of object and designation, the object drops out of consideration as irrelevant.[2]

Even though Wittgenstein's paradox was intended to dispatch our interlocutor's doubt, its image of doubt (an unknowable beetle in a box) is so vivid that it threatens to overshadow Wittgenstein's whole grammatical moral. Sitting at the center of Wittgenstein's paradox is an image that could be found in a Kafka parable: a world where everyone carries boxes of shape-shifting beetles that are for their eyes only, no one truly knowing the content of another's box. And, horror of horror, these boxes might, upon further inquiry, prove to be empty; built on the foundation of nothing!

In this respect, we have a parable in the center of a paradox. A parable that feels like a nightmare version of our modern times, capturing one of those moments of epistemological vertigo that seem to be a byproduct of modernity. It taps into those momentary lapses of certainty when relativism bends toward nihilism. When we doubt how we can know another; let alone collectively feel for them. Wittgenstein believes such moments are due to a "grammatical misunderstanding," our language playing tricks on us (or rather our endowing language with too much ontological authority). It is, with such moments of doubt, hard not to wonder if our suspicion is tied to something deeper, more insidious than a trap in language. But before we can answer such a question, we must first pose another: has it always been so? To begin to answer that, let's move backward in time, some several thousand years ago, in amphitheater where Sophocles' *Electra* is being performed.

Sophocles' urn

Sophocles' *Electra* centers on the aftermath of the great King Agamemnon's murder. Clytemnestra, his wife and "co-author" of her husband's death, now reigns with her lover and co-conspirator. Everyone in Mycenae has made their peace with this turn of events and has resumed their lives. Everyone that is, save for Agamemnon's daughter, Electra, who still, 20 years after the day of his death, mourns for him outside the palace walls where she now lives like some feral creature. She cannot forget nor will she let anyone who passes by forget this heinous crime. That is the amount of agency she has in this world: a wail and endless reserves of venom. Her only hope for revenge is the return of her younger brother, Orestes, who she had whisked away to safety when he was just an infant. No one has since seen or heard of the boy who has, by now, turned into a young man. But return he does, to do the deed his sister hoped for. He arrives disguised, pretending to be a messenger bearing the news of Orestes' death and the urn of his ashes to prove it. He hands what we know to be an empty urn into his sister's hands. She holds the urn, contemplating it, thinking that its meager contents hold what is left of her brother and her hopes. It is, in many ways, an ancient analog to Wittgenstein's beetle in a box. Electra does not doubt the contents, cradles it in her arms like a babe and delivers one of the great laments in all of Greek drama:

> OIMOI TALANIA.
> All my love gone for nothing.
> Days of my love, years of my love.
> Into your child's fingers I put the earth and the sky.
> No mother did that for you.
> No nurse.
> No slave.
> I, your sister without letting go, day after day, year after year and you my own sweet child.
> But death was a wind too strong for that.
> One day three people vanished.
> Father. You. Me. Gone.
> Pity, PHEU PHEU PHEU oh beloved, OIMOI MOI.[3]

If Wittgenstein's box is a paradox about grammar, than Sophocles' urn is a metaphor for theater. We, like Electra, cry over nothing, over a fiction that is less substantial than a shadow. The crucial difference is that Electra does not know this, but we do and *still* we cry with her. It is truly extraordinary when one thinks about it. Our unnamed interlocutor was surprised that we can feel what another person feels, but how much more wondrous that we can feel for a fiction! For theater is indeed nothing but an empty urn. The last time someone reminded us of this extraordinary fact was Shakespeare's Hamlet, after experiencing the Player King's portrayal of "the marbled queen." Our melancholy prince tells us, in a fit of amazement, "What's Hecuba to him, or he to her/That he should weep for her?" But weep we do, as the Greeks did, for their fictitious Electra and her empty urn. We and the actor fill that empty urn with meaning, or a memory, or in the case of Polos (the great Greek actor and most famous interpreter of the role of *Electra*) with the actual ashes of his dead son. Legend has it that Polos was once asked how he accomplished this penultimate scene. He explained that he secretly put the ashes of his own son who died in the wars into the empty urn. This allowed him to find "the real living grief and lamentation" necessary. But ashes or no ashes, we the audience, make a certain emotive leap; without thinking, we instantly feel.

Or we thought we did. Now, ever since the advent of modernity and the rise of new variations in the realm of relativism, the question of fellow-feeling has returned. We find an ever-growing constituency of individuals who, like Wittgenstein's unnamed interlocutor, wonder about our ability to really know and feel for another; or, for that matter, know how to feel anything about ourselves. In addition to this concern, we find a growing number of individuals from around the world for whom this is not a rhetorical question but an actual psychological condition. Clinicians call this growing phenomenon "alexithymia" and use the term to characterize those who have become incapable of describing their own feelings. The operative word here is "become" as opposed to being born with this inability (as in the cases of patients suffering from autism or Asperger's syndrome). Franco Berardi, in his book *Heroes*, calls alexithymia an, "extreme form of un-empathy, which annuls not only the ability to perceive other people's suffering, but also blurs and un-tunes emotional self perception. The human being is transformed into a sort of automaton."[4] How did we get from a culture that could feel for the empty contents of Sophocles' urn to the culture where the parable aspect of Wittgenstein's box is becoming a reality? To begin to answer this question, it behooves us to take a brief look at the history of fellow-feeling. We will begin with the foundational thinking of the Greek and Sanskrit cultures, followed by a very quick tour of fellow-feeling from its rediscovery during the Renaissance, to its apotheosis in modern times. Finally we will look at the current state of emotional affairs in the twenty-first century. What we will find is not a linear tale, that directly connects Sophocles urn to Wittgenstein's box, but rather a dialectical argument over fellow-feeling that has been waged throughout the centuries.

Notes

1 Ludwig Wittgenstein, *Philosophic Investigations*, translated by G.E.M Ansombe, P.M.S. Hacker and Joachim Schute (Wiley-Blackwell, Revised Fourth Edition, 2009), 105.
2 Ibid.,106.
3 Sophocles, *The Complete Sophocles,* translated by Anne Carson, edited by Peter Burian and Alan Shapiro (Oxford, 2010), 207.
4 Franco "Bifo" Berardi, *Heroes: Mass Murder and Suicide* (Verso, 2015), 116.

25

THE ANCIENTS

It is the Greeks who have had perhaps the strongest influence on our culture of fellow-feeling, developing the basic terms and concepts that continue to haunt our understanding of emotion in the West. Along with instituting this emotional nomenclature, they also inaugurate the West's deep-seated suspicion of all feeling by introducing emotion's younger sibling, reason. The result is a rivalry, or dialectic, that has subsequently been played out through the centuries, continuing to today. But the Ancient Greeks do not have the final word on this subject. The Sanskrit culture is equally impressive in its conception of the role of emotion and is worthy of equal consideration as we try to tease out the complicated place of so ineffable an emotion as fellow-feeling.

The Greeks from *kardia*, through *thumos* to *psyche*

It was L.P. Hartley who wrote, in perhaps the finest first sentence of any modern novel, "The past is a foreign country, they do things differently there."[1] They do not just *do*, but they also *feel* things rather differently there as well. Case in point, this drinking song from the halcyon days of Greek antiquity:

> To see what sort of man
> each person happens to be,
> divide his breast in two
> and take a look at his *nous* (mind)
> then close him up again
> and think, with your undeceiving *phren* (discernment)
> whether he's still your friend.[2]

A sobering thought for a drinking song. And what are we to make of our singer's sense of anatomy? Open up his breast to read his mind? No, this is not a product of our companion's inebriated state. The Greeks believed that the seat of reasoning, as well as feeling, were both situated right there in our chests. Somewhere between our heart and lungs one would find a thicket of emotive faculties, such as: *thumos, kardia, kear, etor, splanchna, cholos, chole, menos, phrenes, nous,* and *psyche,* all jockeying to be the primary explanation for why we feel and do the things we do. Ruth Padel, in her astonishing *In and Out of the Mind,* tells us that multiplicity is a core condition of Greek thought. How this multiplicity might have actually functioned has not been passed down to us—we are, after all, only dealing with fragments. And so, in the case of the emotional life of the ancient Athenians, we are left with these shards of words to arrange and rearrange into some semblance of understanding; attempting to learn how they might have functioned in tandem with one another. This seeming lack of any sort of a systematized understanding on the part of the Ancient Greeks has led some scholars, like Bruno Snell, to wonder if the Greeks even had a unified sense of self.

What we can discern is that, in the beginning, we possessed a *kardia,* sometimes called *kear* or *ker* and at other times referred to as *etor.* All of these words coincide with our modern-day concept of heart. It, unlike many of the other Greek terms for our emotional life, was resolutely physical rather than psychic in its operation. The Greek heart beat like our heart. It would quicken with arousal and pound with fear, just as ours does today. And it could stop, ending life, then as it does now. But surrounding the *kardia* and forever encouraging it, this way and that, was the much more ineffable *thumos.* Sometimes the *thumos* was associated with blood, sometimes with breath, the only thing we know for certain is that the *kardia* was its plaything.

Thumos is sheer, unadulterated feeling. It is what wells up inside of us to the point where we are compelled to speak out, laugh, cry, pray, or sing. It is located in the same region as our lungs and, as we have said, is often associated with both breath and wind. This latter association is true of other words from other cultures. The Hebrew word *ruah* can mean both wind and breath, but also soul or spirit. A similar dynamic can be found with the Latin *spiritus,* which suggests both spirit and respiration. But the wind of *thumos* is rarely gentle or regular. Its root, *thuo,* pulls the word in the direction of seething, storming, and raging; associating it with angry men and even angrier seas. It is a breath that is quickened, a *thumos* that blows the prow of *kardia.* It is the seat of a vibrant energy. When activated, it can fill the entire body with tremendous force. That force can be joy, love, hope; or can just as easily turn to pain, grief, and anger. In short, it is susceptible to any strong emotion that the world engenders. Often it is imaged as a receptacle where emotions, like anger, drip into this container until it overflows and fills the body with, in this case, *menos* (rage). In such moments, it seems as though it is independent of ourselves, another force or person, who is trying to persuade us to take a certain action. Think of Homer's Achilles, whose *thumos* seems, from the first page until his death, filled with *menos* (rage). It is interesting to note that Homer's epic begins with the word *menos* and ends with a term for a horse being bridled, as though the whole poem were about properly harnessing one's *thumos.* This ambition to control *thumos* occupies much of post-Homeric culture.

Although *thumos* fills the a body with feeling, that does not mean it is easily read or understood. The ability to read another's *thumos* becomes a significant challenge for the Ancient Greeks thanks to Prometheus who, after making man from mud, placed *pulai* (gates) in the human breast so thought and feeling could not be seen. As a result, we can close these gates to outsiders, making it difficult to understand our inner inclinations. Ruth Padel tells us, "We are doubly masked. Our innards in themselves are hard to see, and they mask the feelings they contain."[3] This forces the Greeks to find ways to pry Prometheus' gates open. Two such attempts become *extispicy* (the reading of entrails) and the less messy invention of the *theatron* (theater). Thanks to these burgeoning disciplines, we have a growing number of seers and dramatists who begin their literal and figurative dissection of humankind. It is thanks to the dramatist that we have such a rich vocabulary to attempt to explain the complex question of why we feel what we feel and how we act on those feelings. But in the midst of this rich language, two words dominate our dramatist's understanding of our emotional processing: *nous* (which is often translated as mind/intellection) and *phren* (which we will attempt to define momentarily). More and more, these two words are utilized in the investigation of another's interior life. By the end of the fifth century the word *phren* has fully eclipsed its rival *thumos*. This marks an important step in our piecing together the interrelationship between feeling and thought.

Phrenes is a notoriously difficult word to not only translate but also locate in the body. Some say *phrenes* resides in the region of the diaphragm, others find it in the muscular membrane that separates the heart and liver from the lower viscera. It comes to mean the seat of deliberation and thought. If *thumos* compels, it is *phrenes* that deliberates. It weighs what the *thumos* desires and ultimately considers what might be the right choice. The Greek tragedians become particularly taken with the notion of *phrenes*. Where *thumos* dominates the emotional landscape of Homer's poetry (appearing more than 700 times), we find Aeschylus, Sophocles, and Euripides turning away from *thumos* and relying more and more on *phrenes*. *Phrenes* makes a 104 appearances compared to the 20 mentions of *thumos* throughout the extent work of Aeschylus; Sophocles uses *phrenes* 74 times throughout his surviving corpus, compared to 35 mentions of *thumos*. Euripides, surpasses both Aeschylus and Sophocles, deploying *phrenes* some 160 times, compared to the 30 mentions of *thumos*. What we see over the hundred years that span the beginning of Aeschylus' writing career to the death of Euripides is the advancement of *phrenes*/deliberation over the formally unmediated *thumos*/emotional compulsion.[4] This coincides with Jean-Pierre Vernant's theory that fifth-century Athens is moving from an archaic to modern culture. The pressure to do so grows out of the demands of democracy, which put more and more agency and responsibility on the citizen.[5] This means that deliberation/*phrenes* becomes more helpful than pure, unadulterated *thumos*. *Thumos* is still important, especially for a warrior culture where it contributes to a soldier's sense of patriotism and can summon his courage in times of crisis, but it is no longer as helpful when returning home to a democracy where compromise and consensus become more and more necessary. Here, in this new world of democracy, *thumos* is indeed bridled; becoming part of a process that aides in decision-making. One of the most famous examples of this can be found in Plato's *Phaedrus* where he introduces the notion of Logos as the charioteer that is driven by two horses: *eros and thumos*. As long as the charioteer can keep those two horses working together, they can indeed move forward.

Toward the end of the fifth century *phrenes* is slowly replaced by another ancient word *psyche*, which is given a new lexical life. Bruno Snell believes that this need for a new word or concept grows out of the arrival of a singular and unified self.[6] The emergence of this sense of self is no longer dominated by an emotional model but rather uses it, to achieve its ends. And so, we find *phrenes* suddenly subservient to *psyche*. *Psyche is* first found in Homer, where it means "life-spirit." It animates a person when they are living and departs them when they are dead. At that point it travels down to Hades where it spends the rest of eternity as a "shade," or "spirit," or "ghost," all of which signifies that it is now no more than an *edola* (image). Pindar and Bacchylides seize upon the idea of *psyche* being a spirit that animates the living *and* the point of origin for all our emotions. Aeschylus and Sophocles stay with a more traditional Homeric view of the word, but Euripides makes *psyche* the very seat of personality and uses it some 117 times in his surviving plays. Plato picks up from here and applies the finishing touches to this repurposing of *psyche*.

In Plato's hands, *psyche* begins to exhibit many of the features we now attribute to it. It moves from being our "soul" to (following Euripides) our very sense of self-hood. This new concept unifies all the other unruly emotional faculties that we have mentioned and gives them order. Plato, like the dramatists, wants to rethink the role of *thumos*, which, although vital on the battlefield, was proving not so helpful in the Acropolis. By the fourth book of Plato's *Republic* he has worked out a schema where one's *psyche* is made up of three key attributes that work together to help humans go about their daily decision-making ways. This schema imposes a new hierarchy where our old friend *nous* (intellection/control) is now established at the top, with *thumos* (passion/feelings) as the mediator for *epithumia* (appetite, desires). Plato envisions this hierarchical tripartite system leading to a well-integrated self who is able to navigate his or her life; with this system firmly in place, the modern deliberating person emerges, so they could function like the good citizens that fifth-century Athens needed.

Es meson protithenai: or, to set the course down the middle: the first stirrings of fellow-feeling

Theater historians often situate the birth of Greek theater within the nexus of ritual, bardic storytelling, and the emergence of the democratic ideals that will shape fifth-century Athens. But perhaps an equally important and often overlooked influence on theater grows out of the Greek tradition of *es meson protithenai*, which was practiced by Ancient Greek warriors. The expression can be translated as to "set the course down the middle," which was the Greeks' particular way of arriving at a path of agreed-upon behavior. To set something "down the middle" became a way of discussing the group's interests as a whole and can be found in such expressions as *phrerein gnome es meson* (take one's opinion to the middle) or *legion es meson* (to speak in the middle). The goal was to arrive at what the group held "in common." Or, as the herald at the beginning of each assembly would say, *"Tis there polei christen ti bouleum' es meson pherein echon?"* ("What man has good advice for the city and wishes to make it known at the center?"). Marcel Detienne, the great French classicist, describes this unique practice where the early Greek warriors, who considered themselves equals, would deliberate among themselves. Detienne explains:

> In warrior assemblies, speech was a common right, a *koinon* set down "in the middle." Each individual could exercise this right when his turn came, with the agreement of his peers. Standing at the center of the assembly, an orator found him-self equally distant from all his listeners, and each listener found himself, ideally at least, in a position of equality and reciprocity vis-a-vis the speaker.[7]

Detienne goes onto explain that the language of such assemblies was based in an interplay of speech and dialogue that was not only egalitarian but also secular. Here there was little mention of the non-human forces that might be at work in the moment. Detienne tells us that the Achaeans met to deliberate before every military engagement and were directly focused on the immediate concerns of every member of the group. Such speech is founded on a social agreement of either approval or disapproval. In such military assemblies, the value of speech depended for the first time on the judgment of the social group as a whole. Speech now submitted itself to the public space and drew its strength from the approbation of the social group. Here we have the seeds of both democracy and theater. Remember both Aeschylus and Sophocles were generals and Sophocles himself would go on to be one of Athens' elder statesmen. Detienne notes:

> Within these same circles concepts such as *proegoros*, *oaristus*, and *paraiphasis*, which defined the field of persuasion, emerged. A skillful purveyor of advice knew how to gain the audience's attention. He knew which words elicited assent, softened hearts, and won support. In Homeric vocabulary, *paraiphasis* (which, like peitho, could be either good or bad) means a persuasion born of reassuring familiarity; *oaristus* means mutual influence arising out of the social life of a brotherhood; and *paregoros* refers to exhortatory speech used to encourage a comrade-in-arms.[8]

All of these rhetorical devices are employed to move a social group toward a certain point of view, searching for a truth that can speak to everyone. This practice sits between a primitive notion of truth as intuition and the Greek moment of reason. Something becomes true for these warriors not because "I" feel it, but because "we" all feel it. The engendering of the "we" is not brought about by the invocation of divine force which insists on plural subservience; but rather on persuasion. This new form of communication is understood to be good and bad (one can be lead and mislead by it), which forces the rhetoric to find a balance between pure feeling and reasoning. This will lead to the necessity of such works as Aristotle's *On Rhetoric* where he puts forth three forms of persuasion:

1. Ethos, the upright character of the speaker as a person to be regarded with esteem.
2. Logos, the formation of logical arguments based on evidence and probability.
3. Pathos, playing to the emotions of an assembled audience, so that their collective feelings rhyme with that of the speaker.

You will note in Detienne's examples (of *proegoros*, *oaristus*, and *paraiphasis*) that these warriors knew how important it was to speak to the heart (pathos) of the audience as well as their head (logos). It is this balance that the Greek tragedians favor and that Aristotle both in his *Rhetoric* and *Poetics* will continue to advocate.

Aristotle and the "rethinking" of emotion: or, the physics of feeling

Aristotle, like any good student, questions his teacher Plato. One such question is the significance of emotion, particularly in the realm of art and the politics. As you may remember, Plato, in a moment of inspired provocation, banishes all artists, poets, and dramatists from his ideal state. The reason behind this rather severe treatment has to do with Plato's central concern that such work bypasses our reason (*nous*) and returns us to our irrational emotions (the realm of *thumos*). Aristotle's genius was in showing that reason and emotion were not opposite of one another as Plato would have us believe; but, rather inextricably bound together and next to impossible to separate. He would show that the *emotion* of anger comes from the *thought* of outrage, or how the *feeling* of fear is the result of the *idea* of vulnerability. In short, there is cognition at the root of every emotional response. In addition to this, W.W. Fortenbaugh astutely notes in his revelatory *Aristotle on Emotion* that Aristotle:

> brings the study of emotions within the framework of demonstrative science as explained in the *Posterior Analytics*. By building an efficient cause into the definition of individual emotions Aristotle was conforming to his own principle that questions of essence and questions of cause are one and the same.[9]

As a result of this coupling of cognition and emotion within the framework of essence and cause, Aristotle was able to recuperate the status of emotions within Greek culture. This quasi-scientific method becomes the focus of Book I of his *On*

Rhetoric. Book II shifts the argument toward the persuasive power of an emotional argument (*pathos*) and how it rivals the more accepted rhetorical modes of *ethos* (speech based on the ethical character of the speaker) or *logos* (persuasion gained by means of logical demonstration).

Pathos, according to Aristotle in his *De Anima,* unites mind and body. The word comes from the verb *paskhein,* which means to undergo, experience, or find oneself in a certain state of being. In such moments we discover that both mind and body are impacted simultaneously. And so, when a speaker uses *pathos,* he or she is using emotion to assist in the persuasion of a given audience. For, as Aristotle writes, "The emotions [*pathe*] are those things through which, by undergoing change, people come to differ in their judgements and which are accompanied by pain and pleasure, for example, anger, pity, fear, and other such things and their opposites."[10] This leads Aristotle to the categorizing of key emotions, by their positive to negative or negative to positive relationship (i.e., anger to calmness and friendliness to enmity, etc.). George A. Kennedy, in his commentary of *On Rhetoric,* explains:

> Emotions in Aristotle's sense are moods, temporary states of mind—not attributes of character or natural desires—and arise in large part from perception of what is publicly due to or from oneself at a given time. As such, they affect judgements.[11]

The body of Book II of *On Rhetoric* defines each of these emotion/moods. Although this text was not as well-known as many of Aristotle's other celebrated works, it has become increasingly important for twentieth-century thinkers, especially the young Martin Heidegger. Before Heidegger was to finish his seminal *Being and Time,* he devoted an entire 1924 lecture course to *The Basic Concepts of Aristotelian Philosophy* in which *On Rhetoric* takes on central importance and is examined in great detail. Heidegger would later write:

> Aristotle investigates the *pathe* (emotions) in the second book of his *Rhetoric.* Contrary to the traditional orientation, according to which rhetoric is conceived of as the kind of thing we "learn at school," this work of Aristotle's must be taken as the first systematic hermeneutic of the everydayness of Being with one another. Publicness, as the kind of Being which belongs to the "they" not only has in general its own way of having a mood, but needs moods and "makes" them for itself. It is into such a mood and out of such a mood that the orator speaks. He must understand the possibilities of moods in order to rouse and guide them aright.[12]

If we put aside Heidegger's penchant for his own idiosyncratic nomenclature, what we find is a keen understanding of the Aristotelian rethinking of emotion. Not only are we a "social animal," or the "animal that speaks" but, also, perhaps even more essentially, we are the creature of many moods; both positive and negative.

Thanks to the power of language (particularly emotive language), we have the ability to transport ourselves and our listeners from one mood to another; moving us from, say, the dangers of *orge* (anger) to the benign state of *praotes* (calm). What Heidegger understands is that a mood is not just a feeling but an orientation toward things at large; change a person's mood and you change their orientation of the world. In short, appealing to our emotions can yield powerful, life-altering relations with ourselves and others. In tandem with this view of the power of emotions, Heidegger insists that what is true in Aristotle's *Physics* is also true in his *Rhetoric*, "The *Being of nature* as it presents itself to us is not determined solely by material, but rather in *its being moved*." Here, Heidegger is thinking of movement (*kinesis*) in the fullest sense of the Aristotle's understanding of the word. This not only takes in account such things as moving from point A to point B; but also, and perhaps more poetically, the kind of transformation that occurs when the color of leaf moves from green to yellow. What we have with Heidegger's reading of Aristotle is a kind of *kinesis* of *pathos*. We can find such an impulse embedded in our own English word "e-motion." It reminds us, when we break the word apart, how easily feeling can indeed transport us from one experiential place to the next. For Heidegger, there is a physics of feeling. That is why Heidegger can move back and forth between Aristotle's *Physics* and *Rhetoric* to tease out the full dynamics of emotion. Heidegger can take a phrase like, "*Kinesis: entelecheia tou dynamei poietikou kai pathetikou he toiouton*" from Aristotle's *Physics* and apply it to how emotions and emotive language can impact human beings. Heidegger, in his own creative form of translation, understands this axiom to suggest, "every moving thing is the moving of something moved, and every moved thing is the moved of something moving."[13] Heidegger goes on to equate this with the role of pedagogy, telling us:

> This becomes visible in the discussion of teaching and learning. After all, according to its sense teaching means: speaking to another, approaching another in the mode of communicating. The genuine being of one who teaches is to stand before another, and speak to him in such a way that the other, in hearing, *goes along* with him.[14]

The danger still remains in how "the teacher" persuades "the student" to "go along." Heidegger himself was often accused of using a willfully obtuse and mystically inflected language to cast a powerful spell upon generation after generation of students. After the Second World War he was banned from teaching because of his questionable association with Nazism and for fear that this orientation, coupled with his powerful rhetorical skills, would potentially taint another generation of young minds. This brings us back to thinkers like Plato or even a professional rhetorician like Gorgias who condemn certain kinds of emotive speech acts since they can be like drugs (*pharmaken*), seizing the body for good or ill, causing distress, delight, fear, or boldness, leaving the hearer bereft of defenses. But, as Derrida reminds us, the *pharmaken* has the ability to poison *and* to heal.[15] Aristotle stays intent on the healing capabilities of the rhetor, where his or her language is used to make an emotional bond with the hearer, thereby bettering their communal status. This mode of communication, when performed responsibly, is oftentimes more persuasive than any logical or ethical argument. It can, on its own terms, participate in the further development of right judgment (*krisis*) and practical wisdom (*phronesis*).

And so Aristotle is ultimately able to allay the skepticism of fourth-century Athenians in regards to emotion by placing it within a larger system of rhetorical argumentation that appeals to the Greeks' newfound embrace of *logos*.

Pity and fear: the dramatic integers of Aristotle's tragic equation

Aristotle will attempt to create a similar reappraisal for theater; in doing so, he will borrow two key emotions that he has already defined in his *Rhetoric* to help with his new argument. They are now the famous and inseparable pair known as *elios* (pity) and *phobos* (fear). Just as Aristotle provides a kind of quasi-scientific method to rehabilitate the use of emotions in the realm of rhetoric, so too does he attempt to provide a similar reclamation of emotions in theater. He does so with the most innocent of sentences, telling us that tragedy "accomplishes through *elios* [pity] and *phobos* [fear] the *katharsis* [cleansing] of the experience." Or, perhaps less obliquely put: "through *elios* and *phobos*, we arrive at the *katharsis* of the [theatrical] experience." It is as simple and elegant as any logical theorem. But before tackling the larger implications of Aristotle's much-contested use of *katharsis* as the endpoint of tragedy, let us look at the two emotional integers, *elios* and *phobos*, that bring us to the shore of *katharsis*. Here is how Aristotle describes *elios* in his *On Rhetoric*: "Let pity be [defined as] a certain pain at an apparently destructive or painful evil happening to one who does not deserve it and which a person might expect himself or one of his own to suffer."[16]

Although Isocrates called his fellow Athenians the most *elemonestatous* (pitying) of people, it is important to remember that pity does not seem to rank very high when compared with other Athenian virtues such as *sophrosune* (self-control), or *dikaiosune* (justness), or even a general sense of *arte* (a kind of basic excellence in a particular field of endeavor). This is just the first of a series of difficulties that confront a modern sensibility as it tries to understand what *elios* might have fully meant to the Greeks. It is also important to remember that *elios* is not a synonym for compassion, sympathy, or our more modern notion of empathy. David Konstan tells us in his *The Emotions of the Ancient Greeks* that *elios* involves moral appraisals and required a certain,

> distance between the pitier and the pitied that allows for this ethical dimension: to experience pity one has to recognize a resemblance with the sufferer, but at the same time, not find oneself in precisely the same circumstances. Where complete identification occurs, one shares the emotion of the other

and that is not pity as the Greeks conceived it (the relative detachment characteristic of pity even today has led some to condemn it as a form of contempt).[17]

Let us look at one of the great passages in all of Greek literature and see what it might tell us about the dynamics of true *elios*. The moment that Priam, who is mourning the death of his beloved son Hector, confronts Achilles, the murderer of his son. Priam, with the magical aide of Hermes, has made his way from the his palace, past the battlefield to the Greeks' own camp, where he enters Achilles' tent, embraces Achilles' knees and kisses Achilles' hands, the very hands that murdered his son. There on his knees, tears streaming down his ancient face, he creates a speech to invoke Achilles' pity. Priam says to his son's murderer:

> Remember your own father, godlike Achilles,
> whose years equal mine, on old age's deathly threshold:
> him too, it may well be, those dwelling on his frontiers
> are harassing, with no one to ward off ruin from him.
> But at least, while he hears that you're still living,
> is happy at heart, and hopes from day to day that
> he'll see his dear son returning from the land of Troy–
> whereas I am wholly ill-fated: of the best sons I sired,
> in the broad land of Troy, not one, I tell you, is left
>
> [...]
> The one true son I had left me to guard the city and its people
> you slew untimely as he fought in defense of his country–
> Hector!
>
> [...]
> Revere the gods, Achilles, and to me show pity,
> remembering your own father: but I'm the more pitiable,
> for I've borne what no other mortal on earth has yet endured:
> I've brought my lips to the hand of the man who killed my son.[18]

It is, indeed, an extraordinary, harrowing speech; as well as being a perfect sample of language constructed for the purpose of creating pity in the listener. Pity, remember, does not mean that one should identify with the experience of another; that would be closer to our modern-day understanding of sympathy, where one looks for an equivalence of feeling. Priam does not do this. He does not say, "I lost Hector who I loved and you lost Patroclus who you loved; look how alike we are in our sorrow." Priam does not pursue this sort of rhetorical gambit. Rather, he creates a scenario of pity, where he shows how much more lamentable his situation is to Achilles' father. Such an approach is the very quintessence of the pitiable. Here one places oneself lower than the Other. Priam tells Achilles: "Your father is far more fortunate then I, he still has you to protect him; whereas I, I have lost all 50 of my sons, including my most beloved Hector." This is the language of *elios* and it works on Achilles in a way that no other speech-act has; not the apologies of Agamemnon, the reasonings of Odysseus, or the implorings of Patroclus. Let us look at how Achilles responds to the father of his enemy:

> So saying, he stirred in Achilles the urge to weep for his father:
> he took the old man by the hand, gently pushed him away.
> Both had their memories: Priam of Hector, killer of men,
> as bitterly weeping, he crouched at Achilles' feet,
> while Achilles wept, now for his own father, now again
> for Patroclus: their joint mourning resounded throughout the hut.
> But as soon as noble Achilles had had his fill of weeping,
> and the urge for it had departed from his heart and limbs,
> he rose from his chair, took the old man by the hand,
> and raised him up, pitying his grey hair, his grey beard ...[19]

Achilles' first tears are not necessarily of immediate *elios* for Priam. One could argue that it takes the entirety of the above passage for Achilles to actually arrive at any feeling of *elios* for Hector's bereaved father. First Achilles cries for his own father who Priam evoked, then for Patroclus who he cannot forget. The journey from tears for his father to tears for Patroclus brings him closer to tears for Priam, but the two remain on parallel tracks, their grief is symmetrical but not shared. Only after Achilles has lifted Priam to his feet does the feeling of *elios* enter Achilles' breast. For it is on seeing Priam's grey hair and grey beard that the gates of *elios* open in Achilles. Priam's words set the gum-stuck gears of *elios* in motion for Achilles, but it is his aged and enfeebled condition that ultimately moves Achilles. This spell does not last long, some 65 lines later we find Achilles warning Priam:

> Stop working on my emotions amid my sorrows, old sir,
> lest I might not spare even you, while you're here in my hut,
> supplicant though you are, and break Zeus's ordinances.[20]

So much for the staying power of *elios*. But what about the other part of Aristotle's theatrical equation: *phobos* (fear)? How does this relate to pity and ultimately help us arrive at the state of *katharsis*? Let's begin with a working definition of this second term of Aristotle as he describes it in *Rhetoric*, "Let fear [*phobos*] be [defined as] a sort of pain or agitation derived from the imagination of a future destructive or painful evil [that] do not appear far-off but near, so that they are about to happen."[21]

We often think of fear as something so immediate that it bypasses our cognitive faculties; the result of some vestigial wiring from our primitive past. But even fear, as Aristotle points out in his above examples, has a strong cognitive component. We have to know about knives to realize that the one in someone's approaching hand might be used to hurt us. Perhaps the cognitive assessment is far faster than usual, but it is there none the less. We find ourselves quickly assessing the person: do we recognize them? What about their face? Is it smiling? Is that the smile of someone who would like to be a friend? Or the smile of sadist? All of this heightened perceptual processing happens in the very first instance of encountering anything that might be the least bit fear-worthy. We actually find ourselves in a state of hyper-cognitive awareness. Heidegger shares Aristotle's fascination with fear,[22] no doubt for its similarities to anxiety, which becomes a key concept in *Being and Time*. Fear, like anxiety, can force our sense of self and our relationship to the world into a sharper focus; giving us an acuity to our actual state of being that is otherwise muted or forgotten. As a result, emotions like fear and anxiety have much to tell us about the inter-relationship of ourselves and the world.

Let us, briefly, look at an example of fear drawn from Aeschylus' *Agamemnon*. Agamemnon, against his better judgment has agreed to stride upon the precious silks that his wife, Clytemnestra, has laid before him. Such an act can be perceived as a sign of hubris to the gods and could result in some form of punishment; but Agamemnon, in an attempt to appease his much-wronged wife, does so. What follows is the chorus' response to this provocative act that bodes ill for Agamemnon and, by extension, themselves:

> Why does this fear float
> always in front of my heart—
> hungry for signs of the future—
> singing a prophetic song no one asked for or paid for?
> Why can't I thrust it off like a difficult dream
> My confidence drains away from the center of me.[23]

This sudden surge of fear in the chorus is triggered by Agamemnon's hubristic act which, for such a superstitious culture, suggests impending doom. As Aristotle has told us, fear tends to be something close at hand, on the verge of being (as opposed to a concept such as death from old age, which feels too far in the future to fully comprehend). But the "always" of the second line suggests that our chorus lives in a world beset by an almost unrelenting fear and laden with sign upon sign that something terrible is about to strike. This is a culture of fear. They try, like we all do, to put this out of their consciousness:

> Yet it was years ago the Greek ships tossed
> their ropes on the beach of Troy
> and I saw them come home with my own eyes.[24]

But even with the advent of this miraculous turn of events, this relentless sense of fear cannot be kept at bay:

> Still, at the edge of my heart, the song of the
> Furies keeps nagging—
> No one taught me this song and it has no music,

> All the same it shakes me. My thoughts go round and round.
> I know it all means something real but I
> hope not! I pray not![25]

Heidegger notes that there is a certain kind of fear where we do not know what it is exactly that we are afraid of, it is a feeling with no root or cause and therefore brings us to the threshold of what Heidegger designates as the uncanny. A sensation that forces one toward articulation and discourse. The uncanny engenders the need for understanding through communication with others. We see this is happening with Aeschylus' chorus, who in the next passage of the choral ode, attempt to understand the fear they feel and how to navigate it:

> Health and disease collaborate, don't they?
> They share a wall between.
> So a man's fortune runs a straight course
> then strikes a hidden reef.
> Yet if as a precaution
> we throw overboard a certain measure of wealth,
> our house doesn't sink,
> our ship sails on
> and Zeus keeps standing up field after field
> of grain to stave off famine.[26]

Here their discourse leads to way of comporting themselves in relation to their fear of impending misfortune. Their solution is an understandable cautiousness. Such a stance relates to Heidegger's observation where the fear of something can become a toning down of being. In the confusion fear causes, there can be a fleeing of one-self or a recoiling from myself, namely, from my being there. Often leading one to become, as this chorus confesses:

> I am a restrained person.
>   Otherwise …[27]

But there is always the "otherwise" in a state of fear. Instead of "fleeing" or "recoiling" in the moment of threat or fear, there is also the possibility for courage. In this case, the courage of the chorus to speak out. Such courage can only exist in relation to fear. Heidegger notes:

> It is evident that I can only be courageous in the right sense if I am afraid. *Fear is the condition of the possibility of courage.* Whoever is not afraid … does not yet get around to making a decision in the right sense, and being courageous. It is a question of *taking hold of courage.* It is a question of *being afraid in the right manner*, and thereby coming to resoluteness.[28]

And what about our chorus? Does it live up to Heidegger's possibility? Let's look at its final verse:

> Otherwise my heart would race past my
> tongue to pour out everything.
> Instead I mumble,
> I gnaw myself.
> I lose hope.[29]

It will not be until the final scene of *Agamemnon* that this chorus of elders finds its courage to stand up and speak out. But until then, they find:

> And my mind is burning.[30]

Let's pause here for a moment, mid-way through Aristotle's emotive equation, with our minds on fire. This is the final destination of fear: our consciousness in flames with a sense of danger. For Aristotle, theater leads us to the point of pity for the Other and a sense of fear for ourselves. How does this happen? A modern theater-goer would say that when he or she feels for another character on stage, this feeling is usually characterized by a very modern notion of "projection." We believe that we project ourselves into another person, hence phrases like, "what it is like to be in his shoes," or "seeing through her eyes." Upon returning to ourselves, we wonder whether such a situation could happen to us. Our experiment in emotive projection has lead us from pity (for the other) to fear (the other could be me). For the Greeks, the experiencing of another's pain was not a projection; but rather, an infection. It entered us, rather than we it. This is similar to how the Ancient Greeks understood the nature of optics. Aristotle thought that sight occurs when the watery part of the eye (what he believes to be the "seeing part") is moved by a given visual object and thereby assumes its qualities. A simpler way to explain this would be to think of how images are reflected in lakes. Aristotle believes that the sense organ becomes the sensible object. The image is *in* the lake as the piteous person's suffering is *in* us. Here vision becomes infection, the other's feelings are now inside of us. Pity begins its journey toward fear. It is at this point that we find our minds are on fire. But how does this lead us to Aristotle's notion of *katharsis*?

The mysteries of *katharsis*: where Aristotle's dramatic equation reaches its conclusion

As with *elios* and *phobos*, Aristotle gives us no working definition of *katharsis* in *Poetics*; we must look elsewhere for assistance. This time the help we need is not found in Aristotle's *Rhetoric* but rather *Politics*, where he describes *katharsis* within the following nexus of how music works on citizens:

> And since we accept the division of songs as some of those engaged in phil-
> osophy divide them, when they set down some of them as ethical, some prac-
> tical, and some enthusiastic, and they also arrange the nature of the scales in
> relation to their suitability to each of them, different for different songs, and
> since we assert that one must not use music for the sake of a single benefit

but for several (for it is for the sake education and cleansing—and what we mean by *katharsis*, we will now speak of in an unqualified way, but again in *On Poetics* more clearly—and thirdly as a pastime, for relaxation and rest from toils). For whatever experience occurs strongly in the case of some souls, it is there from the start in all souls, and it just differs by the less and more, for example pity and fear, and further enthusiasm; for by this latter kind of motion some are possessed and whenever they use the songs that excite the soul to frenzy, we see them get into this state from sacred songs and obtain as it were a *katharsis*. It is necessary that those liable to pity and those liable to fear, as well as those who are in general easily affected, experience the same thing, and everyone else does too to the extent that experiences of this sort befall each, and in the case of all a certain cleansing occurs and lightening with pleasure. In the same way too cleansing songs provide a harmless joy to human beings.[31]

Here, Aristotle, seems to be using *katharsis* in its current fifth-century medical meaning as being something curative. Aristotle had promised in *Politics* to explain his use of the word further in *The Poetics*. But, much to the future consternation of many a commentator, there is only the one sentence where pity and fear are yoked to *katharsis*. Either the alleged explanation from *Poetics* was lost between transcriptions of the text, or what we thought was an actual treatise by Aristotle is actually just the published lecture notes of an inattentive "graduate student." Regardless, the text of *Poetics* is of little help when it comes to any further elucidation of this word. *Katharsis* was originally associated with the ancient rituals of purification. It corresponds to the verb *kathairo*, which means to clean, purify, purge. The god Apollo is called *katharsios* (the "purifier" and also "the washer"). In Hippocratic medicine it takes on a slightly coarser character where it becomes the process of physical purgation, covering all manner of bodily discharges, including: defecation, menstruation, vomiting, and diarrhea.

This may make sense for emotions like "pity" and "fear" but what about the "other enthusiasms" that Aristotle speaks of in *Politics*? Remember that, for the Greeks, to be enthused was to experience the sudden indwelling of a god. Since the Greeks have a plethora of gods, there is an equal multitude of enthusiasms that could momentarily possess your average Greek subject. Not only are there gods of a traumatic variety like pity and fear; but also other gods of a more numinous kind. Let us, for a moment, replace pity and fear with wonder and awe. The shift in emotive integers makes us realize that certain readings of *katharsis* have been rigged to account primarily for only negative valences. This sends us back to a careful reading of the passage in Aristotle's *Politics*. Here it seems that pity, fear, and other enthusiasms all reside within us. These resting feelings wait to be awakened by a variety of matching exterior enthusiasms. Such exterior enthusiasms can be thought of as a song, play, or god, all of which are in search of the particular corresponding feeling that rests inside us. The reunion of the two reanimates the resting feeling. It is as though the resting feeling were invited to dance with its rhyming god, a dance that often ends in a "frenzy." *Katharsis* is the vertigo-like feeling that happens once the dance is over and the god has departed.

The addition of other "enthusiasms," beyond pity and fear are of particular interest to Heidegger. He sees Aristotle's forms of enthusiasms in light of his own notion of "attunements." For Heidegger "attunements" can be thought of as fundamental orientations toward ourselves and the world around us. Change our attunement and we see and feel the world in a new light. As we noted earlier, such momentous shifts can happen through a change in emotions, say from joy to sorrow. These shifts have a significant ontic impact on individuals. They are powerful, like a god; with the ability to change everything. The frenzy of such an experience can lead to a profound "confusion." Its disorientation can bring us into contact with what Heidegger calls "the uncanny." This is an experience that defies immediate understanding, setting our "minds on fire" like the chorus of elders in *Agamemnon*. When this sensation passes, it often leaves us feeling hollow, emptied out, with no immediate words to describe the intensity of what we just felt. This, emptying out, is what Heidegger believes Aristotle means, when he speaks of *katharsis*. We may feel purged, but this does not mean that the inner enthusiasm itself has been expelled. It simply returns to its resting place, deep inside us; waiting for the next opportunity to be reawakened.

For Heidegger, it is what happens on the other side of *katharsis* that is of particular import. It is at this point that one is filled with the overwhelming "need for discourse." This should not be confused with Freud's "talking cure." For Freud, *katharsis* is the purging of a suppressed trauma through the recounting of its origin in a story; for Heidegger, *katharsis* is the ensuing and mysterious opening up in oneself after the uncanny passing-through of an enthusiasm (god or attunement). We try to fill such openings by engaging in discourse with another. It is our way of *making sense* of such encounters with the uncanny; allowing us to develop a language to talk about it. Such a process does not, as in Freud, lead to the optimistic outcome of a "cure"; for Heidegger there is no "curing," or need for "curing," only a *sharing* that brings us within the proximity of understanding. This discourse is always provisional, there is no closure per say, only the potential for further approximations through language. Look at how much discourse is engendered in Plato's *Symposium* over the emotion of *Eros*. This is how strange, powerful, and perplexing certain fundamental emotions could be to the Ancient Greeks. Perhaps the missing explanation of *katharsis* that we do not find in *The Poetics* has something to do with Heidegger's "need for discourse." One of the intriguing dynamics of Greek tragedy is its propensity to ask difficult questions without directly answering them, leaving the audiences to decide among themselves once they leave the theater. Perhaps such subsequent discussions are part of the aftermath of *katharsis*. It would certainly fit into Aristotle's case for the necessity of emotions by showing how they engender further thought. But thanks to the fundamental lacunae in Aristotle's writings on *katharsis*, this issue will remain cloaked in mystery.

The deep-seated suspicion of emotion that runs throughout the foundation of our Western culture was not necessarily the case when it came to neighbors like India. We find that the Sanskrit culture also possessed a rather reserved and critical attitude toward emotions, ultimately favoring the attainment of *shanta* (a quiet repose) and *samaninveda* (a detached relationship with the world). Yet it still maintained an important place for the role of emotions in the private, civic and especially aesthetic life of its people. Their relation to these issues have much to tell us, not only about the nature of emotion, but also about the West's own blind-spots on this subject.

"Surely my ancestors are drinking for water the tears I shed": the Sanskrit theory for the "tasting" of emotions

The title of this section is taken from a lyric found in the sixth act of Kalidasa's renowned *The Recognition of Shakuntala*, perhaps the most celebrated of all Sanskrit plays. Kalidasa was a fourth-century CE dramatist who, like all dramatists of the time, based his work on the theories found in the *Natya Sastra*. This is a prodigious work of some 6,000 verses (*The Six Thousand* is its literary alias), it most likely began as a text entitled *The Actor's Sutra* written sometime before the third century BCE and was continually revised over the centuries right up until Kalidasa's own time. The work is attributed to the mythical sage Bharata and deals with everything from instructions on the building of a theater to the smallest nuances of intonation and gestures by actors. It defines the central task of theater as the representation of the emotional states and shows how, when these emotions (*bhava*) are experienced in their proper way, they can lead to a restoration of harmony in lives of its audience. This is accomplished through the complex work of *rasa*.

Rasa is a metaphor for tasting, it is often translated as flavor. The flavor we are savoring is *bhava* (the emotions). But these emotions are not our own, they are emotions once-removed, emotions that are found on the page or stage where this aesthetic distance allows us to enjoy the sensation of them in a calm and dispassionate manner. Another way of understanding the relation between these two terms would be in a the often sited analogy where *rasa* (taste) is to *bhava* (emotion) as wine is to grapes. In short: they are inseparable, there is no *rasa* without *bhava* and no *bhava* without *rasa*. One already senses a difference between Greek and Sanskrit aesthetics: where the Greeks can become easily "drunk" with emotions, the Sanskrit culture behaves like connoisseurs who know how to savor a vintage emotion.

Another way of thinking of *rasa* might be in terms of our own Western notions of "atmosphere" or "mood," it is a feeling or sensation and therefore is felt rather than seen. The "perception" of *rasa* happens through the doctrine of *paririanaveda* where the eight foundational emotions (*sthayibhava*) are transformed into aesthetic sentiments/feelings, becoming the property of poetry or of the stage. It is at that moment of transference from the real to the aesthetic realm that *rasa* makes itself felt. One could say that in this transmutation we become aware of the feeling-of-our-feelings; or, put another way, arriving at a state of meta-feeling. The following chart breaks down these eight fundamental emotions and their aesthetic equivalents:

Foundational emotions:	_Aesthetic sentiment_
Passion (_rati_)	Erotic (_srngara_)
Determination (_utsaha_)	Heroic (_virya_)
Revulsion (_jugupsa_)	Disgust (_bibhatsa_)
Anger (_krodha_)	Wrathful (_raudia_)
Fun (_hasa_)	Comic (_hasya_)
Fear (_bhaya_)	Fearful (_bhayanaka_)
Grief (_soka_)	Compassion (_karuna_)
Amazement (_vismaya_)	Wonder (_adbhuta_)

There is a ninth Rasa that is added around the eighth century, it is called _shanta_ and signifies quietude, tranquility, and enlightened repose. It is based on the foundation emotion of _samaninveda_, which suggests a detached relationship to the world. All Sanskrit dramatists had only these nine fundamental transformations to work with; allowing, as Sheldon Pollock tells us:

> The characters [to] move through different scenic contexts that stimulate their desire (moonlit nights, for example, or pleasure gardens), and can therefore be identified as "stimulant factors." No one experiences a basic emotion pure and unmixed, but rather conjoined with other feelings of a more ephemeral nature—"the transitory emotions," longing, disquiet, or despair, for example, in the case of sexual desire. These which number thirty-three, are more complex than the translation "emotion" might suggest … From an analytical perspective the play looks like a jumble of disconnected components, but the very performative—and almost alchemical-process … homogenizes them.[32]

Pollock concludes that the core of such an experience is a _rasa_ whose taste can be likened to the flavor of a drink made up of multiple ingredients that are complex and yet unified.

The ability to appreciate such a complex and yet unified aesthetic experience is not an innate trait, but something that is learned, over time, by availing oneself to a variety of such encounters with the arts, like poetry or theater. This builds our aesthetic sensitivity, allowing us to become an ideal reader or spectator. At such a point, we possesses _sahrdaya_, which literally means _to have the same heart_. The spectator now shares the same feeling as the author who created the work they are experiencing.

This allows for a very special response when one is watching a play like _The Recognition of Shakuntala_. Take, for example, the long-awaited reunion between King Dushyanta and his love Shakuntala. At such a moment the spectator undergoes a _bhogi-krttva_ (a "pleasuring") or what the Bhatta Nayaka calls an "experintialization" of pleasure.[33] This sensation, according to David Schulman, leads to an extraordinary form of self-absorption, "a 'coming to rest' in oneself (_visranti_) or turning inward (_antar-mukhatva_), a forgetfulness of the outer world, and above all, a 'tasting' (*asvada*) of the rasa in all its fullness."[34] Abhinavagupta breaks down this altered state of consciousness into three distinct mental planes of aesthetic experience:

1. *Druti*: deobjectification.
2. *Vistrara*: expansion.
3. *Vidasa*: illumination.[35]

It is the artists use of *sahharani-karana* that makes all of this possible. This is a difficult word to translate and sometimes is brought into English as "idealization" or now, in its more favored rendering, "universalization." It can be described as the generalizing of the particular, allowing the artist's creation to free itself from the distortions of our ego-based relationship. David Schulman explains that universalization:

> Transports the spectator beyond his or her normal, everyday awareness into a state of delicious self-forgetfulness and rapturous absorption, free from anxiety, doubt, and the usual background noise of consciousness. Abhinavagupta insists that such a state is, in fact, our true, radiant nature, the very ground of our being, though it is obscured by quotidian experience. It is the great merit of the aesthetic media of poetry, drama, and music that they can restore to 'ourselves,' at least momentarily, by inducing the radical self-forgetfulness that is defined as a flood of *rasa*, the fullness of liquid, pure, impersonal feeling.[36]

Let us take a brief look at Bhavabhuti's extraordinary *Rama's Last Act*, a work that is counted among the greatest of all Sanskrit drama and one of the most unusual variation of a love-in-separation story. Unlike many other Sanskrit dramas, it is not shy about the essential *rasa* that is at work in this masterful drama. We are told that the key rasa that runs throughout the play is *karuna*, which is Sanskrit for compassion; or, more literally, "the desire to remove harm and suffering from another." Midway through the play the author tells us:

> How complex a plot this is.
> There is only a single rasa—
> compassion—but it takes different forms
> since it changes in response
> to circumstances that are changing,
> just the way that water forms
> into a whirlpool, bubble, or wave
> though in the end it all remains
> the same: nothing but water.[37]

Karuna (compassion) is the *rasa* that is perhaps the closest in meaning to Aristotle's notion of *elios* (pity). But unlike Aristotle, Bhavabhuti does not team *karuna* (pity/compassion) with *bhaya* (fear); but rather by with *adbhuta* (wonder). This is an important coupling that we can find throughout Sanskrit drama. The results lead to a significantly distinct outcome from that of Aristotle's notions of tragedy.

"My heart reacts in ways I cannot understand": a brief look at *Rama's Last Act*

Bhavabhuti is the great eighth-century author of such immortal Sanskrit dramas as *Malati and Madhava* (*Malatimadhava*), *The Little Clay Cart* (*Mrcchakatika*) and his much celebrated *Rama's Last Act* (*Uttararamcarita*). This last play of his focuses on the final and highly controversial chapter of the *Ramayana*. It is here that King Rama, for no logical reason, suddenly doubts the chastity of his beloved Sita and banishes her to the woods while she is pregnant. Much later the two are reunited, Sita is proven innocent; but, instead of a heartfelt reconciliation, Sita refuses to forgive Rama for the wrong he did to her and his family. This conclusion to the story has become one of the most glossed sequences in the entire *Ramayana*, with scholar after scholar attempting to understand Rama's cruel and unmotivated banishment of his once-beloved Sita. So disturbing was this final chapter, that it was often left out of many future tellings of tale. Bhavabhuti's play begins on the fatal day that Rama, for no discernible reason, rejects his beloved and ends, years later, with their final reunion. The tale that unfolds, between these two singular events, defies linear storytelling; jumping in time, place, and between characters with a wild and virtuosic abandon. Bhavabhuti's work is particularly striking for the profound meta-aesthetics that bookend the play, with a first act taking place in a picture gallery and the final act at the theater. Between these two acts are a series of episodes where song, storytelling, and poetry are also enlisted to help tell the ongoing tale of Rama and Sita. The play revels in the many ways this couple has been captured and represented by the arts. Let us begin in the picture gallery.

Rama and his beloved wife Sita are strolling about an exhibition of paintings, each devoted to a significant moment from their past. The pictures follow the chronology of Valmiki's *Ramayana*. Here, as they walk past painting after painting, they re-experience their childhoods, their family, their meeting, their marriage, separation, search, war, victory, and reunion. The experience is more akin to encountering a memory than dispassionately viewing an artwork, these pictures still evoke strong feelings in both of our lovers, although it is Sita who seems the most openly affected by this artistic rendering of their past. She never hides what she feels, telling us immediately, "I almost feel as I were now there and this was then," or, "I shudder to look," and in the case of one particular painted incident, "Please, no more of that."[38] Rama, on the other hand, attempts to keep more distance from his feelings, he is uncomfortable re-experiencing his heroic acts, telling Sita and his retinue, "come now, there's so much more worth seeing. Show us something else," and gently chastising his wife, "Now, now, so afraid of separation—it's only a painting."[39] But he too is clearly taken with re-encountering the moments when they first met and fell in love. Finally, they come to the picture that anticipates the loss of Sita, the very turning point of their story from romance to separation. Rama's brother, Lakshmana, who has been guiding them through the gallery, sees beyond Rama's manly demeanor and says, "your distress, though you repress it/is perfectly clear to others/from your quivering lips and nostrils/and your chest heaving under the burden."[40] Rama, caught out, responds:

Dear Brother
At the time, the fire of sorrow ignited by losing the
one I love,
though sharp, was something the thirst for
vengeance made bearable.
But it continued to ripen in my mind and now
produces
the pain of a wound that reaches to the softest core
of my heart.[41]

Rama, like his wife, is being pulled back into the emotional vortex of their story; but, it is difficult for him to allow himself to be as open or vulnerable as Sita. Even in relating their tragic past, he tells us that he quickly shifted from sorrow to seeking vengeance. This is a man who favors doing over feeling. And yet Rama confesses that a sense of vulnerability persists, even after his vengeance has won the day. The event of Sita's abduction has left him with a wound that will not heal and with no cure in sight, save for the temporary salve of denial. The result is a strange and inexplicable malady, which is now feeding on the soft core of his heart. Meanwhile, their journey through the gallery has now brought them to the dark center of their story. Rama begs his brother to, "stop, please stop. I cannot take anymore."

Sita, reeling from the memories evoked, asks to rest and she does so in her husband's loving arms. While he embraces her, he muses out loud:

My beloved, what can this be?
Every single time you touch me
a kind of transformation
it can't be described as joy or sorrow,
ecstasy or sleep,
a state of intoxication
or all-suffusing poison—
confuses my senses and at once
excites and dulls my awareness.[42]

Sita responds, "You have always been constant in your affections for me. What could it be but that?"[43]

What indeed. This seems to be the central question that Bhavabhuti is attempting to address: How much does Rama actually understand of himself and his emotions? He can respond to the memories and feelings of affection that his wife has bestowed upon him, he can speak with warrior-like ease of the vengeance he exacted to rescue her, but he is at a loss for words when it comes to expressing the complex emotions he feels for Sita. Here he remains confused. He cannot find a name for the sensation he has while holding his wife. It contains too many extraordinary contraries as: joy/sorrow, ecstasy/sleep, intoxication/poison. He does not know what to do with the sheer cacophony of feelings that emerges when one is in love. He wants the joy/ecstasy/intoxication part of love (what he responded to in the paintings) but cannot make his peace with the sorrow/sleep/poison that also comes with giving one's heart to another. Nor has he expressed the central *rasa* of *karuna* (compassion) that Bhavabhuti tells us is the very theme of his play. When Sita was first stolen from him, it was vengeance for her kidnappers that he felt, rather than *karuna* for his beloved. And now, the thought of further separation brings *bhaya* (fear) of what will emotionally happen to *him*, rather than to her. Perhaps this is why Rama must lose Sita again, in order to truly learn and understand the nature of *karuna*.

Moments later, we find Rama overhearing a groundless rumor of Sita's unfaithfulness. Without the slightest hesitation, he believes it to be true. Immune to reason, he banishes his now-pregnant wife back to the very woods where he once lost her. This is not the first time Rama has done something that strikes us as inexplicably wrong. There was also, in the *Ramayana*, the moment where he killed Shambuka, the Shudra ascetic. This is another famous episode that has profoundly disturbed generation after generation of readers. Contemporary Sanskrit scholars tend to see these unexpected episodes as an attempt by ancient authors to create a degree of dramatic distancing. Such moments break the spell-like identification that can happen between the hero and his audience, reminding us that even a noble figure like Rama still has a long way to go before arriving at perfection.

The endpoint of Rama's new journey arrives four acts later. Years have passed. Rama, regretting his rash banishment of Sita, has searched the ends of the earth for his lost love. But to no avail. His sense of loss is so great that he has given up the world and taken on the strict vows of an ascetic. This is the state we find Rama in when news arrives that Valmiki, the actual author of his tale, the *Ramayana*, has now written a play detailing the lost years of Sita's exile. The court, with Rama, assemble at the bank of the Ganges to view Valmiki's play.

The director of our play-within-a-play begins by telling the audience: "Through deep insight made possible by a seer's vision we have produced a brief composition at once purifying and filled with *rasa*, the *rasa*s of *karuna* [compassion] and *adbhuta* [wonder]."[44] The play begins with Sita lost in the forest, suffering the first pangs of childbirth. Rama, exclaims, "My queen, my queen, look, Lakshmana, here!" His brother attempts to assuage Rama, just as Rama had done for Sita all those years ago in the picture gallery. He tells Rama, "But brother it is only a play." All Rama can see is the plight of his beloved, he cries out "my queen … this turn of events befell you because of Rama."[45] Here, unlike the encounter in the gallery, Rama displays immediate *karuna* (compassion) for his wife. He also seems attuned to the *karuna* of others who, like the two goddesses that attend Sita, bestow their care onto her, blending with Rama's own desire to aide his wife. He tells us:

> Waves of compassion have been sent surging
> and break in pools of astonishment and bliss,

reducing me now to some condition
that is impossible to describe.[46]

In the picture gallery when Rama contemplated the loss of Sita, the only pain he seemed capable of feeling was own; now, through the *karuna* that theater engenders, he moves beyond himself, to feeling his wife's own terrible situation.

Even though Sita learns of the survival of her two sons and their future fortune, she is inconsolable and asks the goddesses to take her to the netherworld, upon which Rama falls into a faint. Lakshmana cries out, "Valmiki, help! Is this the moral of your poem?" And at this point, the *rasa* of compassion turns to wonder. A voice offstage intones, "Behold the purifying miracle that Valmiki has vouchsafed."[47] And, at that very moment, Sita arises from the underworld to revive the unconscious Rama with her touch. Rama comes to but cannot believe his good fortune, especially in light of his earlier banishment of his wife. Upon awaking, Sita asks, "Does my husband know how to assuage Sita's sorrow?" Rama replies, "As the blessed one commands."[48] Valmiki, the author of the *Ramayana*, appears and asks his main character, "Is there some further good turn I can do for you?" But Rama is content, he turns to the audience and tells us:

This is a story that purifies from evil
and lavishes all benefits as well—
it is at once auspicious and enchanting
like the Mother of the world and Ganga.
May the learned come to relish it
embodied in dramatic performance,
the verbal art of a seasoned poet, a master
of the sacred mystery of language.[49]

So ends *Rama's Last Act*. The translation of the play's title smiles at us like Da Vinci's Mona Lisa, intimating a more-ness to the work than first might meet the eye. There is a multiplicity of meanings at work in this concept of a "last act." Is Rama's "last act" the banishment of Sita, as we first might have thought? Or rather, is it Rama's discovery of *karuna* (compassion), which also happens in the last (literal) act of Bhavabhuti's play? It would seem our story suggests the last and highest act a human being can achieve is *karuna* for another. Even a hero as great as Rama is somehow incomplete without such a fundamental facility. Indeed, the Sanskrit concept of *karuna* seems far more all-encompassing than the Greek *elios*. In *elios* we are restricted to feel for only those who are beneath our status, thereby allowing us to maintain a certain superiority in our relation to those less fortunate than us. In *karuna*, there is an immediate equivalency of feeling, our response is more open-ended, allowing ourselves to emotionally rhyme with anyone, no matter what their station in life.

There is also the difference of distance in terms of the audience's reaction to the emotions exhibited on stage. By having us watch a play where a character (in this case Rama) watches a play, we find ourselves twice-removed from the action. This is a perfect example of Sanskrit dramaturgy looking for ways to create an evaluative distance between ourselves and what the characters are feeling, enabling us to better "savor" their emotions. Instead of just feeling the feelings of a character, we can get a sense of ourselves suddenly conscious of our feeling their feelings. Rather than think a thought, we find ourselves suddenly thinking a feeling.

Finally it is interesting to note that Aristotle couples *elios* (pity) with *phobos* (fear); whereas, Bhavabhuti links *karuna* (compassion) with *adbhuta* (wonder). Bhavabhuti, by changing the second integer of the dramatic equation, drastically changes our reaction to the drama. This is not unique to Sanskrit culture, we can find such a dynamic happening in Euripides' *Alcestis* (as well as his *Helen* and *Iphigenia in Taurus*). It is at such a juncture that we have to remind ourselves how versatile a form Greek drama was and how it was able, with the advent of Euripides and other lost authors, to incorporate a much richer variety of dramatic unfoldings than what Aristotle initially outlines in his *Poetics*. We can also see a similar development in Elizabethan theater, moving from the tragedies of Marlowe, Shakespeare, and Middleton to the romances of Beaumont, Fletcher, and eventually Shakespeare himself. What we realize when we encounter such works is that fear is only one of several key modalities that are at the disposal of drama and that wonder can lead to another type of *katharsis*. Let us take a moment to understand how wonder works on us and our relationship to the world at large.

Wonder: an alternative dramatic integer

Wonder, as a concept, is often found in the company of other terms like "awe" or "amazement." It is easy, in our increasingly distractible age, to think of these terms as synonyms for one another and to use them interchangeably. This often hasty semantic carelessness blunts the extraordinary gradation of these words and their astute relation to the way the world works on us. "Awe" is something that we are supposed to feel toward gods, kings, and leviathans; it is our reaction toward anything larger and more powerful then ourselves. We bow or cower to such forces. "Amazement," on the other hand, is a kind of existential vertigo, a sense of being momentarily disoriented. The etymology is not so hard to see, since the word "maze" flickers like a neon sign at the center of the word. "Wonder" is similarly unique in its relation between the world and ourselves. It responds to anything that might ignite our imagination. Think of those sixteenth-century "wonder cabinets" that collected both natural and man-made artifacts from around the globe. There you might find everything from the rib-bone of a giant sperm whale to a gold-plated mechanical marsupial from Ancient China. Heidegger designates such things as "wondrous." The "wondrous" is, according to Heidegger, "what is striking, remarkable, an exception to the habitual."[50] Wonder becomes, for Heidegger, one of humankind's fundamental "attunements." These, as we noted earlier, are emotional dispositions that have the power to disclose unseen aspects of ourselves and the world. They include such notable experiences such as anxiety, love, and even boredom. In Heidegger's hands, "wonder" is not only reserved for what is out of the ordinary; but the ordinary itself. Or rather, those things that were once wondrous and have been domesticated by the gravitational pull of the quotidian, dulled by the unrelenting force of habit. Heidegger tells us: "The most usual—whose usualness goes so far that it is not even known or noticed in its usualness—this most usual itself becomes in wonder what is most unusual."[51] Heidegger continues:

> In wonder, what is most usual of all and in all, i.e., everything, becomes the most unusual. Everything has in everything at first the most usual to which attention is paid and which, it is glimpsed, but is not explicitly heeded. Everything bears in everything the most unusual, for this exists everywhere, altogether, and in every way. Everything in what is most usual (beings) becomes in wonder the most unusual in this one respect: *that it is.*[52]

Wonder becomes a kind of alchemy that transforms the usual back into its original state of unusualness. The key is how we can use our innate sense of wonder to create this in-between space and reanimate what has become commonplace (Heidegger's "everything" that has been dulled by its habitual presence) and, in so doing, restore the common place to its "wondrous" origins, bringing it back to life for us to fully appreciate.

We have already encountered a similar act of wonder in Shakespeare's *Winter's Tale* which, like *Rama's Last Act*, concerns another king, Leontes, who also wrongly punishes his innocent wife, Hermione, under the belief that she has been unfaithful to him. She, as you will remember, returned to him in the guise of a statue, putting Leontes into a state of wonder, marveling over how the shaping of stone could breathe, move, and become warm to the touch. In this glorious moment we are reminded that these simple acts are what we do from one moment to the next throughout all the days and nights granted to us. This is indeed something rather miraculous. Leontes' sense of wonder for what he thinks is a statue engenders our own wonder over what we know to be a human being. In short, we are reminded that we ourselves and those around us are all miraculous, all works of art. This is the wonder that Heidegger, Shakespeare, and Bhavabhuti are interested in bringing back to our attention. It is a simple reawakening or, better yet, a re-enchantment of the world. A world dulled by the force of habit, brought back to our full apprehension.

Heidegger notes that wonder is a "casting asunder," it "displaces the wonderer into the midst of what was cast a part. Wondering man is the one *moved* by wonder, i.e., displaced by this basic disposition into an essence determined by it."[53] Wonder engenders an in-between space between the usual and the unusual in which one can return to the primordial questions of existence. This feels very much akin to Brecht's theory of *Verfremdungseffekt* (de-familiarization) or Shklovsky's theory of *ostranenie* (making strange). Like Heidegger, these theorist are striving for a similar displacement which will allow the spectator/reader to pierce through the fog of habit and see the world anew, to see through "reality" to "the real." For Brecht and Shklovsky, such an approach is the precondition for any true revolution, either political or aesthetic. In Heidegger's thinking, such moments return us to a primordial orientation; as though we were suddenly Adam and Eve, looking at the garden of Eden for the first time and naming it.

Wonder, like fear, can both fill us and completely overwhelm us. Like fear, wonder also has, according to Heidegger, "discourse-inducing" possibilities that we have tied to the concept of *katharsis*. Both of these emotions compel us to bring these feelings into a provisional language for others to help us in our understanding of what we have experienced. Rama, when faced with fear or wonder, is at first without words, unable to articulate what he is feeling. Heidegger explains that in such states, there is:

> a certain inability to explain and an ignorance of the reason. This inability to explain, however, is not by any means equivalent to a determination and a declaration that the explanation and the reason are not available. On the contrary, the not being able to explain is first and essentially a kind of being caught up in the inexplicable, being struck by it; and upon closer inspection the amazement does precisely not want to have the marvelous explained but instead wants to be teased and fascinated by the inexplicable as what is other, surprising and uncommon.[54]

And so wonder, like fear, shares a propensity toward unsettling our already tenuous quotidian ease. There are no immediate words for the profundity we suddenly feel. But the feeling demands to be "teased out" through Heidegger's "need for discourse." By putting these complex feelings into words and then sharing those words with another, we begin to move toward a tentative understanding. The more powerful the experience, the more provisional our answers, and the more we must return to seek further elucidation. A great aesthetic experience should, by definition, persist long after the book has been closed or the curtain has fallen. The true power of *katharsis* should resonate long after the resolution of the story. When we can give language to such experiences, we have finally domesticated their unsettling nature.

What is "wondrous" in *Rama's Last Act* is no doubt Sita's return from the dead to comfort Rama. But what engenders "wonder" is the revelation that after what Rama has done, Sita is still able to *forgive him*. We leave the theater under the "spell" of "wondrousness," bathed in the magic of Sita's return from the dead to save Rama. But once the spell begins to subside, a question emerges: why would Sita do such a thing for the man who banished her? The question persists and out of this persistence the lost "wondrousness" of the story is returned to the center of our apprehension: human kind's limitless capacity for compassion and forgiveness. This is the true miracle of the play and of our lives; a miracle that often remains unseen. Wonder brings such forgotten aspects of being back to our awareness, reminding us of what we often take for granted.

Placing Greek and Sanskrit drama side-by-side

Both Greek and Sanskrit culture display a rich and somewhat suspect relation to human emotion. Both reveal a deep understanding of its centrality in human experience as well as its potential problematics when not kept in check or properly developed. Emotion is seen in both cultures as part of a dialectic where it is pitted against emergent concepts of either *logos* (reason) for the Greeks or *shanta* (enlightened detachment) for Sanskrit aestheticians. One could argue, that Sanskrit poets' handling of emotion is far more subtle and complex than Aristotle's theories; but, regardless, it is clear that both cultures argue for theater's unique ability to engender fellow-feeling. One can see this in Aristotle's some-what coercive theory of pity + fear = *katharsis* or in Sanskrit poetics more open preference for the use of compassion + wonder. Aristotle's approach may, when compared to the Sanskrit, seem more ham-fisted but then again, his argument happens during a cultural moment where the Greeks are infatuated with their further elevation of *logos*. We can trace a similar development with the rather late inclusion of *shanta* (detachment) as the final fundamental emotion in Sanskrit drama. The addition of this new concept coincides with development of a larger cultural impulse that will reach its apotheosis with the advent of Buddhism. And so, for the ancients of both the East and the West, feeling is subject to a kind of ongoing aesthetic surveillance.

This dialectical back and forth between emotion and logos/*shanta* will continue, unabated, well into the modern age with various epochs favoring one over the other. Intriguingly, our feelings about feeling may shift throughout the ages, but the acceptance of fellow-feeling remains relatively intact until the end of our twentieth century.

Notes

1　L.P. Hartley, *The Go-Between* (New York Review of Books Classics, 2002), 17.
2　Ruth Padel, *In and Out Of the Mind* (Princeton University Press, 1992), 14. My very brief gloss on the Ancient Greeks' emotional life is greatly indebted to Padel's extraordinary work.
3　Ibid.
4　See the work of Shirley Darcus Sullivan on the Greek Tragedians in *Aeschylus' Use of Psychological Terminology* (McGill-Queen's University Press, 1997), *Sophocles Use of Psychological Terminology* (McGill-Queen's University Press, 1999), and *Euripides Use of Psychological Terminology* (McGill-Queen's University Press, 2000). Her work in this area is perhaps the most in-depth analysis we have in English.
5　See Jean-Pierre Vernant and Pierre Vidal-Naquet's seminal *Myth and Tragedy in Ancient Greece* (Zone Books, 1988), particularly Chapter 1, which lays out Vernant's grand theory of the emergence of tragedy in relation to the advent of democracy.
6　Bruno Snell, *The Discovery of the Mind in Greek Philosophy and Literature* (Dover Press, 2011).
7　Marcel Detienne, *The Masters of Truth in Archaic Greece*, translated by Janet Lloyd (Zone Books, 1996), 99.
8　Ibid., 99–100.
9　W.W. Fortenbaugh, *Aristotle on Emotion* (Duckworth Press, Second Edition, 2008), 13.
10　Aristotle, *On Rhetoric: A Theory of Civic Discourse*, translated and edited by George A. Kennedy (Oxford University Press, 1991), 121.
11　Ibid.
12　Martin Heidegger, *Being and Time*, translated by John Macquarrie and Edward Robinson (HarperCollins, 1962), 178.
13　Martin Heidegger, *Basic Concepts of Aristotelian Philosophy*, translated by Robert D. Metcalf and Mark B. Tanzer, (Indiana University Press, 1992), 221.

14 Ibid., 221.

15 See Jacques Derrida, *Dissemination*, translated by Barbara Johnson (University of Chicago Press, 1981), 1–56.

16 Aristotle, *On Rhetoric*, 151.

17 David Konstan, *The Emotions of the Ancient Greeks: Studies in Aristotle and Classical Literature* (University of Toronto Press, 2006), 201.

18 Homer, *The Iliad*, translated by Peter Green (University of California Press, 2015), 452.

19 Ibid., 453.

20 Ibid., 455.

21 Aristotle, *On Rhetoric*, 139.

22 See Heidegger's *Basic Concepts of Aristotelian Philosophy*, 167–176, for what Heidegger has to say about fear in relationship to Aristotle.

23 Anne Carson, *An Oresteia* (Faber and Faber, 2009), 44.

24 Ibid., 44–45.

25 Ibid., 45.

26 Ibid.

27 Ibid.

28 Heidegger, *Basic Concepts of Aristotelian Philosophy*, 175, emphasis in original.

29 Anne Carson, *An Oresteia*, 46.

30 Ibid., 46.

31 Aristotle, *On Poetics*, translated by Seth Benardete and Michael Davis (St. Augustine's Press, 2002), 75–76.

32 Sheldon Pollock, *A Rasa Reader* (Columbia University Press, 2016), 7.

33 Ibid., 18.

34 David Schulman, *More Than Real: A History of the Imagination in South India* (Harvard University Press, 2012), 65.

35 Ibid.

36 Ibid., 66.

37 Bhavabhuti, *Rama's Last Act*, translated by Sheldon Pollock (New York University Press and JJC Foundation, 2007), 222.

38 Ibid., 87, 93.

39 Ibid., 97.

40 Ibid.

41 Ibid., 99.

42 Ibid., 105.

43 Ibid., 107.

44 Ibid., 363.

45 Ibid., 377.

46 Ibid., 381.

47 Ibid., 385.

48 Ibid., 389.

49 Ibid.

50 Martin Heidegger, *Basic Questions of Philosophy*, translated by Richard Rojcewicz and Andre Schuwer (Indiana University Press, 1994), 141.

51 Ibid., 144.

52 Ibid.

53 Ibid., 146, emphasis in the original.

54 Ibid., 137.

26

THE TRANSITION

The rise and fall of sympathy: Renaissance stirrings

For the West, *elios* proves to be lacking the generosity and expansiveness of a Sanskrit term like *karuna*. It takes a while for the West to settle on the right word that would have the same elasticity and sense of inclusion. The word that ever-so slowly emerges to meet this demand is the Greek term *sympatheia*, but how this word became the West's "go-to" concept for fellow-feeling is the result of a rather tangled history. It grows out of a series of Greek words with the "sun" prefix that signifies "suffering together." These words include *sunalgein* ("feel pain with"), *sunakthesthai* (to feel pain or grieve with family or friends), *sumpatheia* (medical term for physical interrelatedness), and finally *sumpathaheia* (without the medical connotation and becoming something of synonym for pity).[1]

Sympathy makes a very brief and inconspicuous appearance in Plato when he is attempting to explain why when we see someone yawn, we have a tendency to yawn back. Later Plato will begin to talk about a world soul in which all things are in sympathy. This concept will be taken up by the Stoics and Neo-Platonists like Plotinus. The word goes underground for much of the Middle Ages replaced with the Latin *compassio* (the "com" prefix is equivalent to the Greek "sun" meaning "together" and "passio," the equivalent of "patheia" or "feeling"). It is thanks to the Renaissance and the work of figures like Marsilio Ficino, Giovanni Pico della Mirandola, and Heinrich Cornelius Agrippa von Nettesheim that *sympatheia* returns to Western consciousness. It is they who pick up the thread of Plato, Galen, and Plotinus in order to talk about the nature of influence, attraction, and harmony throughout the macro and micro spheres. This will lead to the popular notion of "sympathetic vibration" where the unique phenomenon found in the tuning of stringed instruments becomes a metaphor for a larger apprehension of an unseen connectivity throughout the universe. A sympathetic vibration, in its direct musical application, is the result of two strings being tuned at the unison. At such a moment, if one string is plucked, the other will respond to the same vibration without being the result of direct human touch. It is as though the second string was responding to the vibration of the first. Now, thanks to the modern-day science of acoustics, we know that such an isochronous affair is due to the energy released by sound waves traveling in the air; but, for Renaissance thinkers, this was believed to be the result of the secret force of "sympathy" that operates throughout the universe and binds all things together. From this "sympathetic vibration" we move to "sympathetic resonance," and finally, "universal sympathy." It is at this point that the term sympathy has conquered the European continent. The word finally makes its way across the channel and into the English language around 1567 when a series of books from the continent are translated. The first of these foreign salvos comes from Matteo Bandello's *Certaine Tragicall Discourses*, translated by Geoffrey Fenton. Here the word *sympatheia* is used to describe a sense of accord with another, this new-fangled term proves to be wonderfully amenable and can be applied to a relative, lover, friend, or complete stranger.

Shakespeare and sympathy: "feeling-with" the bard

What exactly do we feel when we feel for a Shakespearean hero? Is it the same way we feel for the heroes of our contemporary stage? We certainly try to fold such Shakespearean characters into our modern conception of instant relatability and yet they somehow seem to elude this moment-to-moment identification that we've come to expect. We have to remind ourselves that these Shakespearean creations were not constructed just to elicit our total emotional investment. Like the sighting of a dolphin that suddenly appears and then disappears beneath the surface of the sea, these fictive figures of Shakespeare reveal themselves to us and then recede again. They often hide behind their status, social function, or gender; keeping their secret selves in reserve. It is little wonder why the central question of *Hamlet* is "Who's there?" or why Kent's injunction of Lear to "See better" is at the heart of viewing any Shakespearean character. We might as well say to one of Shakespeare's creations what Sir Toby says to Sir Andrew, "Wherefore are these things hid? Wherefore have these gifts a curtain before 'em? … What dost thou mean? Is it a world to hide virtues in?" In these moments of Shakespearean hiding, the characters display their extraordinary distance and difference as: king, courtier, commoner, usurper, jester, friar, father, mother, daughter, son, lover, rival, and outsider. But then in certain key moments—when they are threatened, about to die, or fall in love—they show themselves as actually not that far from us. It is here, that our sympathy emerges for these characters. We are aware of their fundamental distance and difference from us as king or commoner; yet we are able to find, within our own lives, a human corollary to what they are experiencing; how an aspect from our life might rhyme with theirs. This is the moment of Shakespearean sympathy, the moment we find our commonality with humanity. It is the moment when Richard II talks of death, the great leveler of all, and tells us,

> Cover your heads, and mock not flesh and blood
> With solemn reverence, throw away respect,
> Tradition, form, and ceremonious duty;
> For you have but mistook me all this while:
> I live with bread like you, feel want,
> Taste grief, need friends—subjected thus,
> How can you say to me, I am a king?[2]

Richard's profound difference dissolves into a momentary glimmer of universality. It is the same for the outsiders like Shylock who famously tells us:

> Hath not a Jew hands, organs, dimensions, senses, affections, passions?— fed with the same food, hurt with the same weapons, subject to the same diseases, healed by the same means, warmed and cooled by the same winter and summer as Christian is? If you prick us, do we not bleed? If you tickle us do we not laugh? If you poison us, do we not die? And if you wrong us, shall we not revenge?[3]

In Shakespeare we can not only sympathize with a person but also with their worldview, as is the case of Hermione in *Winter's Tale* who holds honor above all else:

> For life, I prize it
> As I weigh grief, which I would spare; for honor,
> Tis a derivative from me to mine,
> And only that I stand for.[4]

We can also sympathize for a character, like Falstaff, who maintains a much more adversarial relationship to honor:

> What is honor? A word. What is in that word honor?
> Air—a trim reckoning! Who hath it? He that died
> Wednesday. Doth he feel it? No. Doth he hear it? No. 'Tis
> insensible then? Yea, to the dead. But will it not live
> with the living? No. Why? Detraction will not suffer it.
> Therefore I'll none of it.[5]

We can relate to both sides of the argument, since many of us have been moved, at one time or another, between both points of view. Here sympathy is a kind of agreement between the audience and the character. To feel sympathy is to say, "Yes, I too have felt that" or "imagined feeling it." Sympathy is a "feeling-with" or "alongside-of another." A character's feeling is recognizable through my memory of my own similar sensation. In this way, the feeling of characters and their audiences fit together like the joining of two individual pieces of a jigsaw puzzle.

Sympathy can be an extreme feeling in the spectator as that of Miranda who witnesses, from the safety of the shore, the destruction of a ship in *The Tempest*. Here she tells Prospero, her father:

> Oh I have suffered
> With those that I saw suffer! A brave vessel
> (Who had no doubt some noble creature in her)
> Dashed all to pieces! O, the cry did knock
> Against my very heart! Poor souls, they perished!
> Had I been any God of power, I would
> Have sunk the sea within the earth or ere
> It should the good ship so have swallowed and
> The fraught in souls within her.[6]

This is quite a different response from Ariel (an island spirit) still not accustomed to the sympathetic ways of her human masters, she describes Ferdinand who survived the shipwreck in the following, detached fashion:

> The King's son have I landed by himself,
> Whom I left cooling of the air with sighs
> In an odd angle of the isle, and sitting,
> His arms in a sad knot.[7]

This description sounds almost alien–like in its inability to read Ferdinand's "sighs" as lamentable groans and his "sad knot" as the fetal position of a traumatized and grief-stricken survivor. In many ways, Ariel's entire journey is one toward acquiring a human sense of sympathy; of recognizing the feelings of others as feelings she too may someday experience. We see this education in action when, as she is departing, she suddenly stops and, seemingly out of the blue, asks Prospero, with childlike curiosity,

ARIEL
Do you love me, Master? No?

PROSPERO
Dearly, my delicate Ariel.[8]

Note, the extraordinary, tentative, "No?" of Ariel. It suggests an emotional intelligence still unsure of itself. But by the end of the play Ariel, through watching the interactions of all these humans, has acquired a sense of sympathy as astute and abiding as Miranda's. Ariel's emotive maturation mirrors the audience, who also takes its time learning the rigorous rules of Shakespearean sympathy as characters and play unfold. It is a process. Listen to Ariel's final, emotionally masterful description of the shipwrecked court that she has led to Prospero's cell:

ARIEL

… The King,
His brother, and yours abide all three distracted,
And the remainder mourning over them,
Brimful of sorrow and dismay; but chiefly
Him that you termed, sir, the good old Lord
Gonzalo
His tears run down his beard like winter's drops
From eaves of reeds. Your charm so strongly
works 'em
That if you now beheld them, your affections
Would become tender.

PROSPERO

Dost thou think so, spirit?

ARIEL

Mine would, sir, were I human.

PROSPERO

And mine shall.
Hast thou, which art but air, a touch, a feeling
Of the afflictions, and shall not myself,
One of their own kind, that relish all as sharply,
Passion as they, be kindler moved than thou art?
Though with their high wrongs I am struck to th'
quick, yet with my nobler reason 'gainst my fury
Do I take part. The rarer action is
In virtue than in vengeance. They being penitent,
The sole drift of my purpose doth extend
Not a frown further.[9]

Here, the student becomes the teacher, proving it is time to release her from her bond. A brief scene of reconciliation ensues between Prospero and the shipwrecked survivors, all is almost mended. But Shakespeare, ever the realist, maintains one important discordant note: Caliban, who was forced to be a slave. It is he who refuses the closure of forgiveness. Prospero acknowledges this as his failing. He bequeaths the island to Caliban and then releases Ariel back to the elements. Having done all this, with great dispatch, he turns to us, the audience, and asks that we "Draw near." But this request is unnecessary since we are now, all of us, drawn as near as one can humanly be into the final moments of the play. What began as a disparate assembly of strangers whose only sense of mutuality was that they were all sitting (or standing) in the same direction, has transformed into a unified audience with a sudden and profound sense of *communatus*. The differences between courtier and commoner have shifted ever so slightly and a new social relation has been momentarily engendered. This is the power of Shakespearean sympathy. Both actors and audience have been brought together into a harmonious whole; of feeling-with or alongside one another. Each individual is aware that they are vibrating with the same sympathetic resonance—a feeling so profound that the Renaissance believed it held the very heavens together.

From the Renaissance to the Romantics

By the eighteenth century we find that the concept of sympathy has made itself at home in the fields of medicine, philosophy, and the arts. Europe, at the moment, is caught between calling itself the "age of sentiment" and the "age of enlightenment." A representative figure of the times like Diderot has a foot planted firmly in each realm; giving us both the encyclopedia and popular melodramas for the French stage. "Reason" grabs the spotlight only to be subsequently trounced by "Romanticism." Goethe, who anticipates the Romantics, gives them their rallying cry when he has his Faust proclaim, "Feeling is all, all is feeling." Later, when Goethe sees this expression taken to its furthest extreme, he will recoil and proclaim, "Romanticism equals illness; Classicism equals health" and with this pronouncement he beats a hasty retreat to Weimar where he devotes the rest of his life to recreating dramas based on models from antiquity. But by then, it is too late.

Romanticism would reign supreme, reaching its apotheosis with the works of Wagner. Such a pronouncement would come as a shock to "Magi of Bayreuth," he thought his work was escaping the shackles of Romanticism and heralding the advent of a new aesthetic movement. In reality, his achievement is that of a Romantic maximalist; or, if you will, Romanticism on steroids. If there is anything truly revolutionary about Wagner and the art of the new, it would be his impact on the rethinking of the experience that happens inside the opera house. It is here that Wagner quite literally sets the stage for twentieth- and twenty-first-century audiences. The first thing Wagner institutes is the disappearance of the orchestra from the audience's view. Where the orchestra once stood between the audience and the stage, now it is relegated to a pit beneath the forward-thrusting playing space, safely out of sight and therefore out of mind. Now music seems to exist as something elemental, like weather, rather than merely man-made. The experience of music goes from an awareness of the "actual" conditions of music-making, to one of culture's first forays into the realm of the "virtual." Once the means of music's production are hidden, music takes on an almost occult-like status. This is further heightened by the darkening of the auditorium once the opera begins. Thanks to the recent electrification of Europe, Wagner is able to confer further focus to his work. Now the audience, like the orchestra, disappears. The spectator is plunged into darkness, losing his sense of being a part of a larger group, or any group at all. It is as though he were alone, his attention irrevocably drawn toward the hypnotic glow of the illuminated stage. This revolutionary "erasure" of the audience and the heightening of the individual's singular relation to the event will, subsequently, become commonplace with all future opera houses, theaters, and cinemas. It is a part of Wagner's notion of *Gesamtkunstwerk* (total art experience), which he believed gave equal weight to all the arts in the making of his operas. Again, this is somewhat wishful thinking, since, even with these revolutions within the auditorium, it is Wagner's music, made manifest by Wagner's orchestra, that reigns supreme. It is through this orchestra that:

> the basis of infinite, universally common feeling, from which the individual feeling of the particular artist can blossom to the greatest fullness: it dissolves to a certain extent the static, motionless basis of the scene of reality into a liquid-soft, flexible, impressionable, ethereal surface, the immeasurable ground of which is the sea of feeling itself.[10]

Nietzsche, once Wagner's greatest supporter and later his even greater detractor, warns us that Wagner's instruments can persuade even the intestines of others, bewitch the marrow of the spine. Nietzsche goes on to accuse Wagner of black magic, calling it the music of Circe.[11] Here music metastasizes to mood. Adorno equates Wagner's music to the spell of an opium dream.[12] Heidegger will dismiss the music as nothing more than "the reign of affect."[13] It is Heidegger, lecturing on Wagner during World War II, who warns his students: "it is the conception and esti-mation of Art in terms of the unalloyed state of feeling and growing barbarianization of the affective state to the point where it becomes sheer bubbling and boiling of feeling abandoned of itself."[14] Heidegger continues to acknowledge the import-ance of "feeling" in his philosophy but finds something not quite right with the way Wagner deploys it in his operas. Heidegger concedes that some might find "such arousal of frenzied feeling and unchaining of 'affects'" as a kind of "rescue of 'life,' especially in view of the growing impoverishment and deterioration of existence occasioned by industry, technology, and finance in connection with the enervation and depletion of the constructive forces of knowledge and tradition."[15] But Heidegger ultimately finds that the excuse of a diminished age is simply not enough to warrant Wagner's "sheer bubbling and boiling of feeling abandoned to itself." Such an approach cannot substitute for a solidly grounded and articulated position. In short, what Heidegger finds lacking is what only great poetry and thought can ground. This is something that Wagner's music, no matter how stirring, simply cannot do. "The absolute," Heidegger concludes, "is experienced as sheer indeterminacy, total dissolution into sheer feeling, a hovering that gradually sinks into nothingness."[16]

But Wagner's fundamental changes in the nature of an artistic event and the resulting experience of the audience mark the beginning of the end of sympathy ("feeling with") and the ascendancy of a new concept which will ultimately go by the name of empathy ("feeling in"). The search for this alternative synonym is due, in part, to the ever-increasing intensity of feelings aroused by the works of late Romantics like Wagner and the transition into the early expressionist movement. Critics begin to search for a new word to capture this extreme sensation that such encounters provoke. Art critic Robert Vischer will first coin the word *Einfühlung* (feeling in) and psychologist Theodor Lipps will be one of the first to successfully use the term outside of the rarified world of aesthetics. This concept of *Einfühlung* will be given further respectability by the American psychologist Edward Titchener who translates the word into "empathy."[17] The new term alludes to Ancient Greeks but actually captures a very modern turning point in the development of our sense of fellow-feeling. And so, after several centuries, we move from sympathy's "feeling with" to the beginnings of empathy's "feeling in." Let us briefly examine this subtle but significant shift in culture that results from what, at first, seems like a rather simple change in nomenclature.

From "feeling with" to "feeling in": the birth of empathy

Titchener's "empathy" takes the Greek prefix "em" and adds it to the now familiar "pathos." The ensuing meaning of such a co-mingling is somewhat murky. The resulting word suggests both a person who could be in a state of pathos or has pathos inside of them. The standard etymological compromise has been to think of empathy as meaning "in passion" or "in feeling." Neither definition quite captures *Einfühlung*'s intimation of "feeling in." It seems rather pedantic to make a distinction between the simple word order of "feeling in" over "in feeling"; but, in this case, they become opposite ends of a telescope. What Vischer and Lipps were after with *Einfühlung* was the creation of a word that could conjure a kind of mental leap. The moment when the spectator imaginatively places them-selves inside an artwork or another human being and feels what that object or person feels. Empathy prides itself on being more direct. There is a one to one equivalence in the act of empathy, "I" feel "your" pain; with sympathy, your pain rhymes with my memory of pain. A distinction remains between your feeling and my feeling of your feeling. Sympathy seems to happen alongside another's sensations; whereas, empathy is more of an entering and blending. Finally, in the act of empathy, the perceiving self, momentarily, disappears and is subsumed by the feeling of the other.

Empathy can be found when we encounter an art work (Vischer's initial usage of *Einfühlung*) or with relating to another individual (Lipps' extrapolation of Vischer's original concept). An example, along the lines of Vischer would be: I project myself into an abstract painting, I become one with its explosion of color and having done so, I feel what the painter felt in the midst of creation. Lipps takes this dynamic and applies to the experiencing of another's state of being. So, when watching an acrobat, we become the acrobat. The thrill of her leap becomes our thrill; her terror of losing balance, our terror.

The stages of this emotional alchemy can vary from theorist to theorist; but, in most examples, we find a threefold process for the empathetic act. First, there is some form of projection where we imaginatively place ourselves into another's state of being. Second, from this new experiential vantage point we are able to internalize the other's state, thereby making it our own. Third, having done all this, we momentarily lose our sense of self; what was two, now is one. In many ways, empathy is the perfect child of its times, reflecting the ultimate ascent of the "feeling individual." And marking the true beginning of the moderns.

Notes

1 See Eric Schliesser's *Sympathy: A History* (Oxford University Press, 2015) for a wonderfully detailed look at the evolution of this concept.

2 William Shakespeare, *Richard II*, edited by Charles R. Forker (Arden Shakespeare, Third Edition, 2002), 328 (III.2).

3 William Shakespeare, *The Merchant of Venice*, edited by John Drakakis (Arden Shakespeare, Third Edition), 284.

4 William Shakespeare, *The Winter's Tale*, edited by J.H.P. Pafford (Arden Shakespeare, Second Edition, 1966), 60 (III.2).

5 William Shakespeare, *Henry IV, Part I*, edited by David Scott Kasdan (Arden Shakespeare, Third Edition, 2002), 312.

6 William Shakespeare, *The Tempest*, edited by Frank Kermode (Arden Shakespeare, Second Edition, 1958), 9 (I.2).

7 Ibid., 24 (I.2).

8 Ibid., 96 (IV.1).

9 Ibid., 113 (V.1).

10 Martin Heidegger, *Nietzsche Volume One: The Will to Power as Art*, translated by David Farrell Krell (Harper and Row, 1969), 86.

11 For a better understanding of Nietzsche's complicated relationship with Wagner see *The Case Against Wagner*, which can be found in *The Basic Writings of Nietzsche*, edited by Peter Gay (Modern Library, 2000).

12 For Adorno's trenchant critique of Wagner see Theodore Adorno, *In Search of Wagner*, translated by Rodney Livingstone (Verso, 2009).

13 Martin Heidegger, *Nietzsche Volume One*, 88.

14 Ibid.

15 Ibid.

16 Ibid., 87.

17 For more about the origins of the concept of empathy see Remy Debes, *From Einfühlung to Empathy: Sympathy in Early Phenomenology and Psychology* in *Sympathy: A History*, edited by Eric Schliesser (Oxford, 2015) 286–323.

27

THE MODERNS

Let us take a moment to look at Hofmannsthal and Strauss' *Elektra*, one such work that marks a movement where empathy begins to supersede sympathy. This work falls between the advent of late Romanticism which is best typified by the works of Wagner and the rise of what would become the expressionist movement (what we could call a kind of metastasized Romanticism). It is during this very transition that we find both the coining of the word empathy and its first aesthetic uses.

"How could I not hear the music? It's coming from me": Strauss and Hofmannsthal's *Elektra*

In 1903 Hugo von Hofmannsthal, the soon-to-be-librettist for Richard Strauss, would pen the epoch-defining short story *The Lord Chandos Letter*[1] where the main character confesses to a paralyzing unaccountable emptiness. This sudden and inexplicable emptiness of Hofmannsthal captured the *fin de siècle* feel that had struck the heart of the Austro-Hungarian Empire. Much of Europe itself seemed plunged into a strange state of exhaustion, made all the stranger by the fact that a new century had just arrived. But this otherwise momentous turning of time seemed to only puzzle rather than galvanize Hofmannsthal's generation. The grand events of the nineteenth century with its Napoleonic Wars and Industrial Revolutions had given way to the rise and solidification of the bourgeois. Along with this came a newfound stasis and a vague sense that there were no more grand endeavors to undertake. And so, we find a generation atrophying in the slumbering, somnambulant peace bequeathed to them by their grandfathers. It was Nietzsche that called it a diminished age, devoid of all vigor and critique. Freud had another newfangled term for the times: repressed. Diminished or repressed, Hofmannsthal's generation would ultimately do just about anything to feel again.

It is this desire that sends Hofmannsthal, like Hölderlin and Nietzsche before him, back to the Greeks in search of some primal inspiration. Ancient Greece had always been something of an antidote for those moments when the German Spirit seemed to slacken. The result of this return to the Aegeans would be Hofmannsthal's proto-expressionist adaptation of Sophocles' *Electra*. It became a huge success thanks to the direction of Max Reinhardt and the powerful performance of his lead actress Gertrud Eysoldt. Richard Strauss, the composer who was also in search of a similar sort of vitality in music, had been inspired by Reinhardt and Eysoldt's previous collaboration on *Salome*. This would become the source material for Strauss' first opera. Eysoldt prefigured the hypnotic primal potency of Nijinsky who created equal shock waves four years later with Stravinsky's *Rite of Spring*. Both of these performers seemed to be channeling some powerful pagan force from the past that both scandalized and revivified the bourgeois audiences of Europe. When Strauss saw Eysoldt's performance in *Electra*, he knew he was in the presence of his next opera.

Strauss, often called "the Barnum of German music," comes of age under the large shadow cast by Wagner's music. This upstart composer would spend his entire career attempting to escape the gravitational pull of Bayreuth. He ultimately had little patience for Wagner's grand philosophy of music and was far more interested in its basic mechanics. This "mechanics" allows for tonality to give way to what Schoenberg would call the emancipation of dissonance. Schoenberg reminds us that dissonance is really just remote consonance.[2] It is furthest from the fundamental tone and therefore more difficult to grasp by the ear, making it harder for the ear to assimilate. If consonance is ultimately more restful and euphonious, the intriguing byproduct of dissonance is its ability to achieve extreme expressiveness with an extraordinary brevity of means. The result is a rich chromaticism that lends itself to the expression of moods and pictures. Strauss' early programmatic work (often referred to as tone paintings) capitalizes on this coloristic virtuosity, bringing such stories as *Don Juan*, *Don Quixote*, *Till Eulenspiegel* to vivid life. These works, according to Adorno, were the prototype of what would become the Hollywood film score; where every cinematic moment is simultaneously captured in music, relieving the viewing audience of any possible ambiguity when it came to what they should feel. This music felt for you. Critic Robin Holloway will call Strauss,

> a wizard, a conjuror, a puppet master, a charlatan even … He is the greatest master there has ever been of the means of music; and his vehicle is the most highly-developed machine yet produced by musical culture—the turn of the century orchestra at its highest pitch of efficiency and pride.[3]

Strauss would, with *Elektra*, assemble the largest orchestra that the modern opera house had ever known, even out-marshaling Wagner in its instrumental demands. All for the daughter of the dead king Agamemnon. But why such immense orchestral resources for a character whose station in life is now no better than that of a stray dog? Or, to paraphrase Shakespeare, "What's Elektra to him, or he to Elektra?"

For Hofmannsthal, Elektra represented a re-paganized Hamlet, one that spoke to a whole generation of melancholy-like princes who were kept in check by an ever-growing bourgeois bureaucracy; uncertain of what to think or feel, let alone do. In this respect the circumstances of Hamlet and Elektra mirror one another, they know something is terribly rotten but lack the means to take action or persuade those around them "to take arms against a sea of troubles" and simply "end them." Where the two part company is in terms of their respective resolution. Elektra, being the good pagan that she is, never for a moment doubts what must be done. This unrelenting singularity of purpose is what is so appealing to all those turn-of-the-century Hamlets like Hofmannsthal. It is this Greek singularity of purpose that our German poet longs to discover; to become what Elektra calls "an accomplisher."

And so Elektra conjures up a time past, as well as an intimation of Hofmannsthal's present tense world. Much has been made of this temporal rhyme; how *Elektra* mirrors the case studies found in Breuer and Freud, whose second edition of *Studies in Hysteria* was reissued the year before the premier of *Elektra*. It is there we learn that hysteria (from the Greek word for uterus) is

> the effect and residue of excitations which have acted upon the nervous system as traumas ... a considerable part of the "sum of excitation" of this trauma is transformed into purely somatic symptoms. It is this characteristic of hysteria which has so long stood in the way of its being recognized as a psychical disorder.[4]

The symptoms of hysteria make up a veritable dictionary of disturbances, running the gamut from abasia to zoopsia. Freud describes the onset of a hysterical attack by his patient Fraulein Elisabeth Von R. in the following fashion:

> To the accompaniment of an increasing clouding of consciousness, there followed hysterical symptoms: hallucinations, pains, spasms, and long declaratory speeches. Finally, these were succeeded by the emergence in a hallucinatory form of an experience from the past which made it possible to explain her initial mood and what had determined the symptoms of her present attack.[5]

This account could easily be confused as a review of the singer Annie Krull who was the original Elektra in the 1909 Dresden premiere. Here we have Elektra, incapable of moving beyond the traumatic death of her father Agamemnon, reliving the tale to every onlooker and interlocutor she finds. She screams, rends her clothes, acts out, behaves like a wild animal, all as a result of her father's tragic end. And so, with the advent of both play and opera, Elektra joins the ranks of Breuer and Freud's Fraulein Anna O., Frau Emmy Von N., Miss Lucy R., Katharina, Fraulein Elisabeth Von R., and an ever-growing number of women throughout the Austro-Hungarian Empire who manifest hysterical tendencies.

One could say the "hysteric" captivates this period. In France the neurologist Jean-Martin Charcot (nicknamed the Napoleon of neuroses) became an overnight sensation with his Friday demonstrations of hysterical women of the Salpêtrière asylum. From the 5,000 inmates, Charcot would select the most promising cases of hysteria and put them on display in a specially built clinical gallery. These demonstrations drew physicians from all over Europe, including the young and very impressionable Sigmund Freud, as well as laymen, journalists, and even curious society figures. Charcot's Tuesday and Friday lectures were organized down to the smallest detail, delivered in a miniature theater replete with stage lighting and a parade of patients who could easily pass as performers of some grotesque pantomime.[6] Listening to Charcot himself, it is sometimes difficult to tell if we are inside a scientific lecture hall or just outside a carnival tent. Here is a typical preamble form Charcot to his fellow clinicians:

> No sign will treat you to the interior spectacle, for there is now no painter able to give even its sad shadow. I bring you, living (and preserved through the years by sovereign science) a Woman of bygone days. Some naive and original madness, an ecstasy of gold—I know not what!—that she calls her hair, folds with the grace of cloth around a face illuminated by the bloody nudity of her lips.[7]

And then the "show" would begin, the hysteric was presented, followed by a parade of paroxysms: epileptic, cataleptic, and even ecstatic. Charcot breaks these attacks into four distinct phases.

There is the "epileptoid attack," a mimicking of an epileptic fit; the "clownish phase," characterized by mad contortions and illogical movements; "attitudes passionelles," where the patient strikes a sequence of suspended poses suggesting a gallery of tormented personages; and finally, a protracted "delirium," where the agonies of the body now find their way into the wild, violent words of the patient who begins to rant and rave until forcibly silenced.

What is happening here? What is behind this sudden phenomenon? We now know that most of these tragic cases were due to the trauma of rape and incest, a brutal reality that the nineteenth- and early twentieth-century medical community found not only impossible to believe, but equally difficult to outright accuse. After all, they worried, who would suspect such "respectable" fathers, uncles, and brothers to do such terrible things to their daughters, nieces, and sisters? This ultimately forced the medical community to say the conditions of these women were the result of hereditary madness, or worse, that these women were making these stories up (Freud's default argument will ultimately become the Elektra complex). This is the secret root of this historical phenomenon but it does not quite explain the late nineteenth-century and early twentieth-century fascination with its manifestation.

To begin to make sense of this, it is instructive to return to Nietzsche and his critique of the times. A critique that finds its most dramatic argument in *The Birth of Tragedy* where he attempts to reconnect readers with the Dionysian impulse that is often blocked by its Apollonian counterpart. This quasi-Romantic call for a return to the Dionysian is clearly heard by Hofmannsthal, Strauss, and Freud. It is what draws such large audiences to the lecture halls of Charcot and the opera houses where *Elektra* plays. It is the thin red thread of Romanticism that still runs through the culture, looking to emotion as the antidote to an age where control and reason seem to be once again gaining the upper hand and stifling natural human expression. And so, the hysteric, in this light, is channeling something fundamentally Dionysian, becoming a kind of early twentieth-century Bacchae. In this respect these women and their disturbances are not just symptoms but also symbols of a radical revolt against the repressive constraints of their age. It is a violent "no" during a time of otherwise unquestioning consent. Such a process of vicarious identification also helps us to understand how empathy begins to supplant sympathy. Here an audience can "inhabit" the radical behavior of a hysteric, enabling them to vicariously "act out" against societal norms and give expression to their own repressed anxieties just as it will with the rise of such expressionist artworks like Munch's *The Scream*. Nietzsche would note his was not a great age of passion, "it heats itself up continuously, because it feels it is not warm—basically it is freezing."[8] Here a "frozen" generation can emphatically "heat itself up" by imaginatively entering inside the contortions of a hysteric, the swirling pigments of Munch, or the relentless play of dissonance in Strauss.

It is important to note that Hofmannsthal and Strauss' Elektra is not just a hysteric but also something of a hypnotist. This may sound strange, especially since it is hypnotism that was used on hysterical patients and not the other way around. But it seems Elektra has a gift for inducing a hypnoid state in almost all of her interlocutors, whether that is the chorus, Chrysothemis, Klytaemnestra, Orestes, or even, by the end, the audience itself. It is as though she can locate the internalized hysteric in all of us. Everyone who comes into contact with Elektra finds themselves, at some point, under her spell and undergoing what Breuer and Freud would call the need for a kind of cathartic release. It is here that Hofmannsthal's Libretto parts company with its Sophoclean source.

Let us begin, by examining how Hofmannsthal's Chrysothemis deviates from Sophocles' original depiction. Sophocles' Chrysothemis wastes no time and confronts her sister's inability to change her ways, she argues that she hates her oppressors as much as Electra but there is nothing that either of them can do about it since neither have power. Chrysothemis is a pragmatist, she offers the adage, "in rough waters, lower your sail" and sees no point in risking her life when no real damage can be done to those they are against.[9] Ultimately her speech is a perfect example of what the Greeks called an *agon logon*, or battle of wits. This was the Greeks' preferred dramatic mode of interaction. They savored a well-articulated rhetorical argument. Here Chrysothemis places herself under the sign of realpolitik. Her opening salvo is for a pragmatism over Electra's idealism which has gotten her nothing but the life of an outcast. There is only one moment of humanity, of a glimpse toward interiority. It happens when Chrysothemis confesses that she suffers as well. This could be true, or it could be a rhetorical tactic to make her

seem human in the eyes of her sister. Hofmannsthal's Chrysothemis is far less resolute and ultimately more comfortable talking about her own suffering. She speaks
of her inability to dwell in darkness, of having a fire in her breast that drives her
incessantly from room to room. When she sits, her legs cannot stop shaking.[10] This is
a very different Chrysothemis from the Sophocles. The scene is no longer an argument over the efficacy of an oppositional stance when the populace has consented.
Now the scene has moved from the realm of the political to the very personal, the
familial. This is not an argument between ideological points of views but between
sisters. In this way, the play could be construed as a bourgeois family drama gussied
up in Greek garb.

Sophocles, on the other hand, has little patience for the personal, his eye remains
firmly fixed on ramification of his character's actions. His Klytaemnestra shows
no signs of external remorse and revels in her seemingly implacable argument. As
far as Clytemnestra is concerned she was merely the vessel for justice to right the
wrong of Agamemnon who butchered their innocent daughter. She insists that if
Iphigenia were brought back from Hades, she would come to her mother's defense.[11]
Compare this to Hofmannsthal's guilt-ridden Klytaemnestra who could just as
well be speaking, in hushed tones, over tea in her well-appointed receiving room
or while reclining on the ever-so comfortable couch found in Sigmund Freud's
consulting chambers. This Klytaemnestra is preoccupied with a strange, indefin-
able sensation of unease that persists just on the periphery of her days and nights,
beckoning her to end it all. And yet she continues to live, perfectly happy, perfectly
healthy.[12] With this speech, we have moved from the political, past the personal, and
into the depths of the psychological. From here Klytaemnestra's aria shifts to Freud's
other early preoccupation: the dark dream life of the bourgeoisie. Klytaemnestra,
it would seem is besieged, nightly, with the most unsettling of dreams. There she
sees the very marrow of her bones melting away; waking brings no reprieve, only
a low-level dread that follows her throughout the day like some vengeful ghost.[13]

In all these key encounters, Hofmannsthal continually transmogrifies what was
a highly sophisticated *agon logon* in Sophocles into moments more in keeping with
Breuer and Freud's theory of hypnoid states. It is in such moments (when the subject is hypnotized, daydreaming, or in Klytaemnestra's case: sleep deprived) that
ideas of a very intense nature may emerge; thoughts and images that have been
otherwise cut off from the rest of the contents of consciousness (i.e., repressed)
reveal themselves. The above examples would be classified as a dispositional hypnoid
state and can grow out of daydreams, which are common even in healthy people
and to which, according to Breuer and Freud, needlepoint and similar occupations
render women especially prone. There is no "needlepoint" for our Elektra, but that
does not stop her from her own pathogenic visions, like the reoccurring invocation
of the day of reckoning for her dearly departed father. In these flights of fancy she
envisions a heaven that will rain down blood, creating a red deluge to wash away
the wrongs of the world.[14] Again, let us note that there is no such pathological
explosion from Sophocles' Electra, who remains more a proud and resolute political
dissident than hysteric. It is only toward the end of the work that Sophocles turns

the tables on our relationship with Electra, casting doubt on her state of mind and her rhetoric of revenge. Hofmannsthal seems disinterested in such a reversal of our opinion and rather revels in all aspects of Elektra's emblematic pathology.

And so, Hofmannsthal proffers up a variety of tormented souls for us to experience: the grieving daughter, the guilty mother, and the disaffected sister. Here scenes are no longer debates, but a series of opportunities to encounter extreme emotions. The audience become "emotional tourists" using empathy to enter into exotic states of mind, experiencing emotions that they themselves might be suppressing. Want to experience the death drive? Spend some time with Elektra and her mother. Hofmannsthal creates the opening for Strauss music to cast its spell and transport us into these mental locals. Music becomes mood; performer and spectator are merged.

All of this will culminate in a new rethinking of Aristotle's infamous *katharsis*. We have Freud's uncle-in-law, Jacob Bernays, to thank for this renewed interest in Aristotle's most disputed dramatic concept, which he tackles in a 1854 paper entitled "Aristotle on the Effect of Tragedy." Here, Bernays reminds us of the two basic and somewhat contradictory meanings of *katharsis*. The oldest meaning being that of a "lustration," suggesting the absolving of guilt by means of a priestly intervention; or, a "purgation," which conjures up images of the alleviation of an illness by medical means. In Bernays' hands, *katharsis* becomes a kind of emotional emetic or psychic laxative for those suffering from an excessive inclination toward pity and fear. Such an emotional pressure, according to Bernays' reading of Aristotle, is dangerous and in need of periodic release. This release is best affected through the spectacle of tragedy, which arouses these very feelings of pity and fear and enables them to flow out of the spectator during the viewing of tragedy until, by the end, the spectators find themselves purged. The final result is a sense of much-needed psychic relief. Greek scholar Jonathan Barnes notes that this is a significant shift in the thinking of *katharsis*, moving it from an earlier notion of "moral improvement" to a new concept of "emotional relief." A trajectory that takes *katharsis* "from the pulpit to the psychiatrist's couch."[15]

Breuer would link *katharsis* with work done with patients in hypnoid states where they were able to share their otherwise repressed trauma. Freud, who was less successful with hypnosis, would ultimately associate *katharsis* with Breuer's "talking cure." The term was actually coined by Breuer's famous patient Anna O. (Bertha Pappenheim). It was Ms. Pappenheim who noted that she felt a great psychic relief when she was able to recover the seeds of her trauma and put it into words. It should be noted that both *katharsis* and the "talking cure" in psychoanalysis have taken something of a beating with later revelations that patients like Ms. Pappenheim experienced severe relapses after their initial treatment and required even more medical assistance and, in many cases, institutionalization.

Where Bernays' rethinking of katharsis may have ultimately run aground in psychoanalysis, it has become the very foundation for much of modern theater, where the audience's *katharsis* now must vicariously rhyme with that of the character. This, for many audiences and critics, has become the sole criteria for the success or failure of the dramatic event. The central, defining question becoming: "Did I feel what the main character felt?" Or, put more bluntly: "Did I cry in the end?" If not, the event is now judged as somehow lacking. We find such a moment where character and audience meld in Elektra's final dance. It is here, after the deaths of Klytaemnestra and Aegisthus, that Elektra finds her *kathartic* release from mourning. A final climatic moment ensues where Elektra dances a wild dance of indescribable intensity. She sings another verse, dances a few more steps of mad triumph, and then dies.[16] Arnold Whittall describes these last moments:

> It might almost be a peculiarly Expressionist kind of happy ending, were it not for the brutal juxtaposition of the very last bar. Does the 'gesture' matter more than the fact that these chords are E flat minor and C major? By no means: Strauss has chosen a profoundly convincing way of ending the opera with specifically dark and bright elements in equally brutal guise. He thereby sets the seal on one of the most sustained demonstrations to date of music's ability to represent extreme emotions through an extravagantly rich and yet formidably coherent structure.[17]

It is indeed difficult to remain immune to the clash of Strauss' E flat minor and C major, they strike one directly in one's solar plexus (the very place where the Greeks thought our *thumos* existed) and for a moment we and Elektra rhyme. *Katharsis* becomes the moment of maximal empathy, almost orgiastic in nature. In this case, we feel ourselves inside a long-lost pagan vitality that sparks our very being. All other aspects of Sophocles' great drama are relegated to the background so that nothing can stop our emphatic reconnection with Elektra. Sophocles' work invites us to be slowly won over to Electra's side, only to find ourselves, much to our own horror, suddenly questioning our own sympathy in the last frightening moments of the play when Electra glories in the bloodshed. In this moment of Sophocles we return to ourselves, wondering where is the line that separates justice from blood lust, politics from pathology. No such questioning happens in the climatic rush of Hofmannsthal and Strauss' *Elektra*. Everything in their adaptation leads to this moment of intense feeling, as though coming in contact with this might reanimate an entire, otherwise deadened generation; a generation that is moments away from rousing its somnambulant self and heading sheep-like into the slaughter of World War I. One is tempted to think that Hofmannsthal is anticipating Freud's theory of the death drive, when in actuality, it would seem that the goal of Hofmannsthal's generation was more simply to feel at all cost, to become the "accomplisher." It was all the Hamlet-like questioning that had stopped the flow of accomplishment. *Elektra* sings to Hofmannsthal's generation, "Feel first and save one's thinking for another day."

We have reached the epitome of empathy. The dawning of a new age. Where the injunction for the modern individual is: Feel. Or perhaps, more to the point: Let your feelings be your new passport to life. The world and all its contents are there to be imaginatively inhabited. The modern individual knows no boundaries, boldly projecting oneself into all manner of things. One's feelings become the gateway to new experiences. It is now the mark of every cultivated bourgeoisie. A new kind of emotional consumerism or is it vampirism? Now the new improved modern individual "feels" their way through their days with an infinite variety of emphatic options: music, books, theater, film, opera, other people, why the list is endless.

Herr Bertolt Brecht begs to differ

If Aristotle comes of age during a time when Athenian culture is suspicious of emotion, than Brecht's situation is the exact polar opposite. There he is, cigar in hand, walking down the pre-war streets of Berlin; everywhere he turns he finds a variation of Goethe's dictum: "All is feeling, feeling is all." It envelops him: at the movies, on billboards, over the radio, across the front page of newspapers, and now in the political arena. The little man with the funny mustache is stirring things up, appealing to Germany's darkest feelings. The secret zeitgeist seems to whisper in every Berliner's ear: feel first; think later. Brecht, being the contrarian he is, rejects such a way of being. For Brecht it is empathy that has become the opium of the masses. And so begins his 30-year war with such emotions. How much longer, Brecht wonders, shall our souls leave our ungainly bodies to invade those dreamlike figures up there on stage. Why can we not wean ourselves from wanting to share in their ecstasies? As a result, according to Brecht, we still slink into Oedipus or Othello. This process becomes the theater of empathy. Brecht astutely sees this as a comparatively new phenomenon that breaks from the complex and ever-shifting works of the past, works that demanded more from an audience than just an emotional response.

Empathy, Brecht comes to believe, often limits the spectator's worldview to only what the central character understands. The problem with such a dramatic approach is that the world is always bigger and more complex than what any given character may feel.[18] This is key to Brecht. Our worldview should never be circumscribed in such a fashion that it stops us from seeing "the bigger picture." The real issue is not what brought the character to tears, but how could the situation be rectified to spare future generations such grief? Brecht was fond of noting that the source of tears (its root causes) often disappear like meat into a cleverly prepared sauce. This is not to say that all tears are banned in Brecht's theater. Brecht attempts to make a distinction between tears, sorrow, and lamenting. Tears are an understandable and necessary release. Sorrow, on the other hand, is an oceanic feeling that drowns all thought, this is why thought is hostile to sorrow. Brecht believes that at least lamenting in sounds, or words—is a great liberation. In such cases, the sufferer is beginning to produce something. He or she has begun a process where sorrow begins to merge with observation. We, the audience, must cultivate this true art of observation. Brecht uses the example of our response to a sister crying for her brother who is going to join the Peasant War since he is a peasant; we should feel for sister's loss but also be critical of the brother allowing himself to be used by warmongers. What Brecht is looking for is a manner of playing where the emotion does not "upstage" our seeing the problem. Brecht believes that if such emotional identification is blocked then an audience can begin to view a character's behavior and actions more critically.

His search for a theater of the future begins with a thorough examination of past, looking for lost models. Brecht begins to find what he is looking for in the paintings of Bruegel, the plays of Shakespeare, and the theater of the East. It is the ancient theater of China that first makes a significant mark on Brecht's overall theatrical praxis. This interest begins in the mid–1930s when Brecht attends a series of lectures, demonstrations, and performances by the actor/director Mei Lan-fang of *Kuei-fei tsui-chiu* (The Drunken Beauty) and *Da yu sha jia* (The Fisherman's Revenge). These encounters would lead to a series of notes that would be later published under the title "Verfremdungseffekt in Chinese Acting." Brecht was particularly taken with what he characterized as the "coldness" of the Chinese performance style, which seemed to reject the portrayal of feelings. Passion was present, but without becoming overheated. Emotion was more a sign than an actual experience. Everything was played economically thanks to the performer distancing himself from the character.[19] Brecht is intrigued by this shift in emphasis in Chinese theater; he believes that the Chinese actor focuses on the outward manifestations of the emotion, rather than the emotion itself. This blocks the potential for "emotional infection" and opens up a new relationship with the audience. Now, rather than just spectators, they have become collaborators in the emotion. The audience is engaged in a kind of emotional detective work, they must fill in what is missing in a given actor's suggestion of behavior. This filling in comes from a more considered point of view, a very different response from the empathy we might feel when the emotion is fully represented. Such "collaboration" can also lead to a certain kind of pleasure that is independent to what the characters might be feeling in a given scene. A pleasure that is derived from being engaged in such a creative discovery process. In such instances, the audience can enjoy moving from a passive spectator to a more engaged collaborator; moving from causal "looking" to active "seeing."

Such an undertaking allows scenes to escape their usual descent into emotionalism, which short-circuits an audience's ability for critical thinking. Take for instance a story where a young girl must leave home for a job to help her family, a scene usually played for as much bathos as possible. The de-emphasis of emotion, according to Brecht, allows the audience space to consider other aspects of the given situation.

How this perfectly everyday event is actually rather remarkable, and demanding of our further scrutiny, eliciting such questions as: Is the daughter of the family able to do this on her own? Has her family prepared her? Why can't families hold onto their children longer? Have children, in this world, become a burden? Is this true of every family? Has it been like this since the beginning of time? Is this a biological reality or economic necessity? Here we find ourselves in the very roots of what Brecht's *Verfremdungseffekt* is supposed to engender: a veritable "Big Bang" that creates an immediate universe of questions. It is these questions, rather than an emotional connection, that he uses to draw us deeper into the mystery of the play, especially if it is a play or situation we thought we knew. Brecht wants to transform every story into a kind of mystery, not necessarily turning it into a "who-done-it" but rather, more like a "why-was-it-done-this-way." By connecting us to this sort of question, Brecht activates our great penchant for solving puzzles. This is why Brecht insist that such a shift in relating to a story can indeed be both enlightening and pleasurable at the same time. Let us now, ever so briefly, look at how these theories were applied to Brecht's actual theatrical practice.

Brecht in action: *Antigone* as anti-*Elektra*

Brecht develops many of his major theories over the period of his exile, from 1933 to 1947. During this 14-year period he saw his work sporadically and, by his estimation, rather poorly realized by other theater practitioners. Upon his arrival back to a post-war Europe, he had immediate plans to revive versions of *Galileo* and *Mother Courage* but the first project he was able to get off the ground was a hastily conceived adaptation of Sophocles' *Antigone* for an old colleague, Hans Curjel, who ran a German-speaking theater in Zurich. The work provided a much-needed vehicle to reintroduce Brecht's wife Helene Weigel to German audiences and also allowed him to explore many of the theories he had been developing during the time of his exile. In this respect, *Antigone* is more than a production, it is Brecht's first theatrical-philosophical statement to his new audience, the first salvo in his ongoing battle to fully eradicate any last vestiges of what he called "The theatre of Goring." This "theatre" speaks to the hypertrophy of emotionalism that Brecht believed clouded one's cognitive capabilities. Brecht tells us that *Antigone* was chosen not as a pretext for conjuring up the spirit of antiquity. The impulse rested in a certain topicality but even more importantly it raised some interesting formal issues. Issues that Brecht believed would begin a reconstruction of the aesthetic ruins of post-war German theater. For Brecht, Greek tragedy utilized certain innate forms of *Verfremdungseffekt* that he could exploit, thereby beginning to convert his audiences toward his ends. *Antigone* became a new type of performance for an ancient play.

Like, Hofmannsthal and Strauss, Brecht chose an ancient play that would speak to his modern-day audience. The Hofmannsthal/Strauss *Elektra* was for an audience on the cusp of World War I, longing for some kind of unarticulated call to action, which ultimately culminated in the unnecessary bloodshed of Europe; the audience of Brecht's *Antigone* was just recovering from the devastation of World War II and struggling with how, after all this devastation, to move forward. One can immediately see the corollaries between *Antigone* and post-war Germany. Brecht makes this readily apparent by writing a prologue that takes place in the Berlin of 1945 where two sisters meet in an air raid shelter mirroring the clandestine meeting between Antigone and Ismene that opens Sophocles' drama. In Brecht's new prologue, the brother of the two German sisters is a deserter from the army and has been hanged for his actions. The one sister wants to cut their hanged brother down, the other does not know what to do. So begins Brecht's *Antigone*. He acknowledges that the character of Antigone has clear parallels with the German resistance fighters who fought bravely against the Nazis; but Brecht is more interested by the role of force and in the collapse of a head of state; in other words, it is Creon who interests Brecht, and how that story mirrors the fall of Hitler. His ultimate goal for the play was to show how enterprises that need too much violence readily fail. Brecht draws our attention to the unfurling of Creon's actions that can be experienced in an objective manner precisely because the old play was historically so remote that identification with this figure was next to impossible. And so, thanks to the wide historical gap between the play and Brecht's times, one could short-circuit the demon of identification (empathy). Here, in Brecht's dramatic equation, historical distance = objectivity. This objectivity is further enhanced by the setting where actors are always in plain sight, sitting openly on the stage and only adopt the attitudes of their characters when they entered the clearly delineated playing space. Brecht wants to insure that the audience does not believe that they have been transported to the scene of the action; but rather feel as though they have been invited to witness the delivery of an ancient poem.[20]

Perhaps the most intriguing *Verfremdungseffekt* of Brecht's *Antigone* is in his use of the poet Hölderlin's translation. It was Caspar Neher, Brecht's lifelong friend and set designer, who first suggested Hölderlin as the basis for a new production of the play. Brecht was intrigued by the fact that the work was relatively obscure and, upon closer scrutiny, much deeper and radical in its use of language than any other existing German translation. For those who may not be familiar with Hölderlin's translations of *Antigone* or *Oedipus Rex*, both works are indeed notoriously idiosyncratic in their bringing Sophocles' Greek into the German language. Legend has it that Goethe and Schiller assembled a group of actors to read aloud one of Hölderlin's translations. The company, allegedly, could not finish the reading because they were doubled over in laughter. What exactly did they find so amusing about Hölderlin's work? Most likely it was the strange and unnecessarily difficult syntax which produced such lines as "O common sisterly Ismene's head" or seemingly hermetic utterances along the lines of "Sister, sister, you have made that word red to me."[21]

Why such tortured/cryptic language? Is this the product of a bad translation? The beginning signs of Hölderlin's mental disintegration? He was, indeed, institutionalized shortly after penning these translations. The rest of his life was spent in a cell in a tower, with a specialized muzzle forever compromising his ability to speak or scream. Part of the translation's marvelous strangeness stems from Hölderlin being one of the first translators who is more interested in recasting the German language in order to bring it closer to the constructions of the Greeks, rather than forcing the Ancient Greek to conform to the logic of German syntax. The result of such an undertaking leads to an otherworldly rendering of *Antigone*. One could argue that in an attempt to get at the text's primordial roots, Hölderlin inadvertently produces what feels like the first modernist text. Critic George Steiner notes that Hölderlin's

Antigona carries to extremity the radicalization of lexical and syntactic means, the shift from sequential-logical conventions and from the external reference of ordinary discourse to an internalized coherence of metaphor and image clusters, which make of Hölderlin's late work a primary source of modernism.[22]

He goes onto call the text paratactic, discontinuous, elided, and forever fragmented. In other words, a fascinating precursor to modernist poetry. Steiner suggests that if one did not know better, they might easily mistake a fragment of Hölderlin's translation for the work of Mallarme. But this strange, broken syntax also points beyond Mallarme and anticipates the impulses of the Holocaust survivor and poet Paul Celan who believed that, after World War II it was not only the German cities that lay in ruins, but the German language itself.[23] Through Celan, we can begin to understand Brecht's fascination with Hölderlin's broken diction. What we see is that Brecht's interest moves beyond a fetish for formalism and speaks to his own concerns to what has happen to the German language post-Hitler. For Brecht, the use of Hölderlin both acknowledges the broken nature of the post-war German language and simultaneously creates a further *Verfremdungseffekt*. Language itself becomes a way of creating a critical distance between audience, character, and story.

Yet, even after all this attention given toward a new kind of theater for a German audience, the production did little to stir the audiences or critics. It received a mere five performances with one matinee. Critics would acknowledge the updated Prelude and epic touches such as the actors showing rather than feeling their roles but remained perplexed by the language of the adaptation and the shift from the familiar reading of *Antigone* as the individual against the state. Brecht would have to wait for his production of *Mother Courage* in 1948 to have the profound impact on audiences that he had hoped. Yet, even here, the audience could not achieve the requisite distance Brecht demanded of them. Brecht had hoped that audiences would leave *Mother Courage* critical of its titular character, but instead they left in tears. Their *Mother Courage* was a heroic survivor as opposed to Brecht's concept of Courage as bereft of understanding her culpability in the deaths of her children. Does such audience reaction immediately invalidate Brecht's theoretical aspirations? Brecht would resign himself to the fact that all of this depends on the growth in self-awareness among the proletariat audience, a historical process still very much in the making. Class issues aside (if such a statement is actually possible) what Brecht is pointing to is the ongoing re-education of the audience that would take time. There is a kind of peasant patience in Brecht's understanding that one does not necessarily undo 2,500 years of theatrical habit with one or two productions; that it is, in short, a further historical process.

Regardless of post-war audiences' initial lukewarm reaction to Brecht's renewed theoretical aspirations, he would continue to de-emphasize empathy in his work with the Berliner Ensemble. In this respect, he was not alone. One can see a similar tendency in much of high modernism, which would dominate the arts for the next

20 years of the twentieth century. We find this hesitancy in modernist literature, music, and visual arts, all of which tend to eschew high emotionalism as the primary means of expression. The idea of art's overreliance of empathy remained somewhat problematic for the surviving modernists of both world wars. Emotion, like language, had been so misused during this time of bloodshed that there is an understandable caution in its fully fledged redeployment. This was not the case when it came to populist art, which maintained a steady continuum that favored all forms of empathy. When high modernism finally cedes to post-modernism, emotions begin to return, but first with quotation marks hovering over any given emotion so that whatever feeling is reintroduced is done so under the ever-watchful eye of irony. It will take the final decade of the century for high art to fully reconcile itself to the realm of straightforward emotions.

Notes

1 See Hugo Von Hofmannsthal, *The Lord Chandos Letter and Other Stories*, translated by Joel Rotenberg (New York Review of Books, 2005).
2 For more on Arnold Schoenberg's theory of tonal and atonal music see his *Theory of Harmony*, translated by Roy E. Cocter (University of California Press, 2010).
3 Robin Holloway, *The Orchestration of Elektra: A Critical Interpretation* in *Richard Strauss' Elektra: Cambridge Opera Handbook*, edited by Derrick Puffett (Cambridge University Press, 1989), 147.
4 Josef Breuer and Sigmund Freud, *Studies in Hysteria*, translated and edited by James Strachey (Basic Books, 2000), 86.
5 Ibid., 177.
6 See Georges Didi-Huberman, *The Invention of Hysteria: Charcot and the Photographic Iconography of the Salpetriere*, translated by Alisa Hartz (MIT Press, 2004), 175–259.
7 Ibid., 237.
8 Martin Heidegger, *Nietzsche Volume One*, 47.
9 Sophocles *Electra*, translated by Anne Carson, in *The Complete Sophocles Vol. 2*, edited by Peter Burian and Alan Shapiro (Oxford University Press, 2010), 243–244.
10 Richard Strauss and Hugo Von Hofmannsthal, *Salome/Electra: English National Guide 37*, edited by Nicolar John (Overature, 2011), 96.
11 Sophocles, *Electra*, 251–252.
12 Strauss and Hofmannsthal, *Salome/Electra*, 101–102.
13 Ibid.
14 Ibid., 92–93.
15 Jacob Bernays, *Aristotle on the Effect of Tragedy*, translated by Jennifer Barnes, introduction by Jonathan Barnes, in *Oxford Readings in Ancient Literary Criticism*, edited by Andrew Laird (Oxford, 2006), 158–159.
16 Strauss and Hofmannsthal, *Salome/Electra*, 126.
17 Arnold Whittall, *Dramatic Structure and Tonal Organization* in *Richard Strauss' Elektra: Cambridge Opera* Handbook, edited by Derrick Puffett (Cambridge University Press, 1989), 72–73.
18 See Bertolt Brecht, *Brecht on Theatre*, edited by Marc Siberman, Steve Giles, and Tom Kuhn (Bloomsbury, Third Edition, 2015), particularly 140–148 for Brecht's unique thinking on the issues of empathy in the theater.

19 Although many Chinese theater theorist would disagree with Brecht's assessment of Chinese acting style, this willful misreading on the part of Brecht is instrumental toward the grounding of his own theories on performance practice. See Brecht's *On Chinese Theatre: Verfremdung and Gestus* in *Brecht on Theatre*, 149–157.

20 For a more in-depth understanding of Brecht's production of *Antigone*, see *On The Antigone of Sophocles (1947–8) from Antigone Model Book*, which can be found in Bertolt Brecht's *Brecht on Performance: Messingkauf and Modelbooks*, edited by Tom Kuhn, Steve Giles, and Marc Silberman (Bloomsbury, 2014), 163–180. For a look at Brecht's adaptation of *Antigone* see Bertolt Brecht, *Collected Plays Eight*, translated by David Constantine and edited by Tom Kuhn and David Constantine (Methuen, 2004), 1–51.

21 For a sense of what Hölderlin's translation might actually sound like in English, see *Hölderlin's Sophocles*, translated by David Constantine (Bloodaxe Books, 2001). For a look at Brecht's adaptation of Hölderlin see *Brecht Collected Plays Vol. 8*, edited by Tom Kuhn (Methuen, 2018).

22 George Steiner, *Antigones* (Yale University Press, 1996), 67.

23 For more insight into Celan's post-Holocaust relationship to the German language see Paul Celan, *Selected Poems and Prose of Paul Celan*, translated by John Felstiner (Norton, 2001) and also Celan's *The Meridian, Final Version—Drafts—Materials*, edited by Berhnhard Boschenstein and Heino Schmull, translated by Pierre Joris (Stanford University Press, 2011).

28

AND NOW?

"Just 'cause you feel it, doesn't mean it's there"

And so, even with all our new scientific toys, we still know as much about fellow-feeling as our friends, the Ancient Greeks. Someday soon we may, indeed, locate the seat of fellow-feeling but unpacking how it actually works within us will no doubt continue to challenge our understanding. A marvelous mystery whose solution remains just out of our reach. Regardless of our inability to fully locate and articulate the neurological nature of fellow-feeling, we have become a hypertrophic culture of empathy. Throughout this section, we have seen Western culture veering back and forth between embracing and rejecting the power of emotions. Our current culture's total reliance on empathy as the major mode of communication is perhaps without precedence, never before has technology and the marketplace worked so relentlessly to arouse and maintain this particular human dynamic. Everything we encounter asks for our implicit and immediate emotional response; from our daily news to the ubiquitous advertising that insinuates itself into every facet of our lives. A constant, unstoppable, and insatiable demand is directed upon the most vulnerable part of ourselves: our feelings. We are asked to imaginatively feel for everything from starving children to a person deprived of extra-soft toilet paper.

No wonder many of us are feeling what could be called a kind of "empathy fatigue." The most extreme cases becoming a kind of low grade existential autism (not to be confused with clinically diagnosed autism). Lack of empathy is, as we know, a significant symptom of actual autism. It is interesting to note, in light of our twenty-first-century over-saturation of emotional information, that one of the current reigning theories in the cause of autism is that the subjects are suffering from a hyper-sensitivity to outside stimulus. This theory was put forth by Henry Markram, Tania Rinaldi, and Kamila Markram in a 2007 paper entitled "The Intense World Syndrome—An Alternative Hypothesis for Autism."[1] In this article the Markrams and Rinaldi postulate that autistic subjects actually have the propensity to feel too much. This hyper-responsivity manifests itself in enhanced stress responses that leads the subjects to seek a profound withdrawal from the world around them. Notice, for instance, how autistic individuals will often cover their ears in pain when they hear sounds that seem quite normal to us. This also may account for autistic individuals who refuse to look directly at the people who are engaging with them. Researchers report, across the growing spectrum of autism, that their patients find it painful to look at other people's faces, that eye contact is too intense for them, and that such direct engagement is like hypnosis, ultimately depleting the energy of the subjects. It was Baudrillard who said every age has its own emblematic mental pathology; for the nineteenth century, it was hysteria; for the twentieth, it was schizophrenia. Could our emblematic twenty-first-century psychic malaise become an autism that is, on the one hand, clinical and, on the other hand, more existentially diffuse? Could we, like these autistic subjects, be suffering from a much more minor variation of their hyper-emotional overload? A condition that is forcing us to retreat from our feelings for one another and the world?

In addition to this non-stop bombardment on our emotions, we now find our-selves experiencing these feelings in private as opposed to within social networks or units such as a family, congregation, or community. The news we read, the music we listen to, the movies we watch are now all experienced through the semi-soothing isolation of our computers. Suddenly the words, melodies, and images one encounters are rarely experienced with another by one's side, let alone with any semblance of a group, whether familial or otherwise. Is this sense of dislocation adding to our feeling of empathetic sophistry?

And finally, is this somehow, in part, related to the very use and misunderstanding of the word empathy and its bold lexical promise of an imaginative projection that fuses one with the other?

Even when the word empathy was first coined by Lipps, there were immediate questions about what this new term actually implied. Perhaps one of Lipps' most persuasive and damning critics was the young philosopher Edith Stein who was studying with Edmund Husserl around the time that the word empathy was gaining more and more cultural currency. It would become the topic of her own doctoral dissertation which was straightforwardly titled *On the Problem of Empathy* (1916). It is in these brief 118 pages that Stein systemically takes Lipps and his notion of empathy to task. In point of fact, it only takes the first 16 of those 118 pages for Stein to call Lipps' whole empathetic enterprise into question,

Central to Lipps' thesis of empathy is the dissolution of one's self while empa-thizing with another. This is perhaps the grandest and most appealing part of Lipps' theory: that we, for a moment, during the act of empathy, lose our sense of self and fuse with "the other." We feel what they feel; think what they think; become what they are. It is a beautiful notion and yet Stein believes it is based on a false understanding of what is actually happening when we experience the feelings of others. Stein's basic contention is that a person can grasp the expression of someone's pain from many sides but "in principle, I can never get an 'orientation' where the pain itself is primordially given."[2] Primordiality, for Stein and her fellow phenomenologists, is our "sphere of ownness," meaning what happens directly within us. Therefore, "While I am living in the other's joy, I do not feel primordial joy. It does not issue live from my 'I.'"[3] Stein returns us to Lipps' famous example of becoming one with the movements of an acrobat. Stein is leery of this idea of oneness, explaining:

> I am not one with the acrobat but only "at" him, I do not actually go through his motions but quasi. Lipps also stresses, to be sure, that I do not outwardly go through his motions. But neither is what "inwardly" corresponds to the movement of the body, the experience that "I move," primordial; it is non-primordial for me.[4]

What is primordial is the spectator's sensation of their own movements. Stein gives a simple example of the fallacy at the heart of Lipps' conjecture; say the spectator, who while watching the acrobat, is so overwhelmed, that she drops her program on the floor and bends down to pick it up while her eyes remain fixed on the acrobat up above. If one were truly fused to the acrobat, one would be unaware of the dropping of one's program and subsequently picking it up off the floor. As a result, Stein insists, "What led Lipps astray in his description was the confusion of self-forgetfulness, through which I can surrender myself to any object, with a dissolution of the 'I' in the object. Thus, strictly speaking, empathy is not a feeling of oneness."[5]

The implications of this misunderstanding are worth further teasing out. If what Stein is suggesting is true and we never actually forget ourselves, then when we imaginatively place ourselves inside another's experience, we are never seeing through their eyes—it always remains our eyes, just oriented from the other's vantage point. Stein goes on to point out that not only can we never experience the Other but that we actually suppress the Other's consciousness with our own. Or, put another way, we use our consciousness as a "stand in" for gaining the experience of the Other. In this respect, the empathetic bond is less a sharing and more a colonization of another person's unique perspective.

And so the problem of empathy is several-fold. First, it does not exactly do what it promises; it does not create the possibility for my ego to fuse with another ego, it actually encourages my ego to replace another's ego, allowing me to actually remain in my ego-centered world while thinking I've actually moved beyond this. Second, it re-enforces one's sense of isolation; I am simply mapping my ego over another's ego, never truly getting a sense of others, of a "you" and even more importantly of a "we." This is where a return to the concept of sympathy might be instructive.

Sympathy, by its very nature, reminds us that one can only ever "feel with," or "alongside of." It is humble in its aspirations, it does not presume to "know" another. Sympathy understands that it can only compare a memory of our experience to the experience of another. At best, our fellow-feeling is a kind of rhyming. Just as the words can share the same sound and yet still maintain their own lexical integrity; so too, can people's experiences overlap, while they still maintain their autonomous vantage point. This acknowledges the Other as Other, forging a tentative but realistic "we." Empathy, on the other hand, promises a similar communion; but, at the end of the day, it is the perpetuation of one's "I" over all else, including the Other whose point of view is not shared but colonized. Those who fall under the false spell of empathy often end up lost in a labyrinth of mirrors, reflecting back their own ego projections. There is no true objective social correlative for them. This is further compounded by the isolation in which we now experience much of our culture, sealed off from the world at large, experienced in the privacy of our homes, through our lonely computer screens and headphones, all of which leads to a kind solipsistic vertigo.

This is what makes the theatrical equation still so crucial to the ongoing life of our culture. It reminds us that we are not alone in our thoughts and feelings. One of the extraordinary dynamics of being part of an audience is being reminded that what makes me laugh or cry, can make the Other, seated beside me, do the very same. The two of us can come from completely different backgrounds, have entirely different appetites and proclivities and yet, there we are, both laughing and crying at the same exact thing. In fact, my laughter or tears can be multiplied a thousand times, rhyming with a thousand strangers, all under the same roof, experiencing at the same time the very same feeling. This is not an act of imagination or projection on my part, it is a simple, *brute fact*. This is the power of sympathy, of feeling-with, of returning to a sense of "we." It is the very soil out of which a community can arise. In Sophocles' time 5,000 people wept with the character of Electra as she mourned over the urn that allegedly held the ashes of her dead brother. Now, we are more like Wittgenstein's interlocutor, who holds his own little black box and wonders whether the imagined insect inside bears any resemblance to the imaginings of other fellow possessors of black boxes. How would we know, since we now exist in a technological bubble that isolates each of us from one another. Perhaps it is time to leave the world of Wittgenstein's box and return to the experience of Sophocles' urn.

Notes

1 Henry Markram, Tania Rinaldi, and Kamila Markram, "The Intense World Syndrome—An Alternative Hypothesis for Autism," *Frontiers in Neuroscience*, 1(1), 2007, 77–96.
2 Edith Stein, *On The Problem of Empathy*, translated by Waltraut Stein (ICS Publications, 1989), 7.
3 Ibid., 11.
4 Ibid., 16.
5 Ibid., 17.

29

RECAPITULATION #3: OR TOWARD THE WHY OF THEATER

We have seen, throughout this chapter, theater's complicated history of engaging our hearts and minds. We could argue that the entire history of theater is basically the struggle over which organ to give pride of place. Let us quickly review the high points of this history before turning toward our final thoughts on what all this can tell us about the theater of past and our theater of the present:

1. The journey from *thumos* to *psyche*

We began with an overview of the Ancient Greeks evolving discomfiture with emotion. This history begins with emotion ruling the *thumos* (chest) of Homer's warriors, stirring them to action. It concludes, several centuries later, with emotion becoming subservient to Plato's *psyche* where a more balanced and rational approach to the affairs takes pride of place in the decision-making of Greeks. Sitting between the pure *thumos* of Homer and the *psyche* of Plato are the practices of *es meson protithenai* (to set the course down the middle) where ancient warriors would deliberate the proper path through a combination of emotion and reason. Here emotion retains a crucial place in the persuasion-making practices of the group, with warriors developing such rhetorical strategies as:

a) *Paraiphasis* (persuasion born through familiarity).
b) *Oaristus* (mutual influence arising out of a social life of brotherhood).
c) *Paregoros* (to encourage a sense of comrade-in-arms).

In all three examples there is an engendering of fellow-feeling that would point these warriors toward the proper path of agreed-upon action. A similar dynamic is carried over in the task of theater. This makes a certain sense—both Aeschylus and Sophocles were generals as well as playwrights. They essentially take *es mason protithenai* from the battlefield and place it at the center of theater, harnessing this powerful balancing of emotion and reason to move the Greek *polis*.

2. One step forward: Aristotle's reclamation of emotion

Aristotle, in the wake of Plato's disregard for both emotion and theater, wants to recuperate the role of emotion for the interactions of a democratic polis. Rather than make reason and feeling adversaries, he wants to prove that they actually collaborate to arrive at a unified meaning. He does so by yoking emotion and demonstrative science, explaining how cognition is at the root of every emotion. In this fashion, he shows us that anger comes out of the thought of outrage and how a feeling like fear is the result of the idea of vulnerability. He also reminds us that it is through the appeal of our emotions that ideas are best accepted or rejected. These two rivals are, in actuality, inextricably linked.

3. One step back: Aristotle's theory of *katharsis*

This is Aristotle's much-contested notion of the *telos* of drama, but it hinges on a concept that he never quite fully defines, leading a host of subsequent thinkers to try and understand how Aristotle's equation of emotion (pity + fear = *katharsis*) actually works. We remain haunted by the unanswered questions that this intriguing concept evokes: How is a medical term like *katharsis*, which means to purge, actually related to the watching of a play? Is it another kind of cleansing? If so, is such a cleansing moral or somehow psychically medicinal? If one or the other, how do pity and fear actually factor into arriving at this state? This debate rages on to this very day.

We turn to Heidegger, who was a deep reader of Aristotle, to help us out of this maze of scholarly suppositions. Heidegger puts forth the theory that profound emotions, like fear, often short-circuit our ability to put feeling into words. As a result, these emotions compel us to future articulation in an attempt to understand what we so profoundly felt. Heidegger calls this moment "the need for discourse." This sounds similar to Freud's notion of the "talking cure," except Heidegger is perhaps more realistic; knowing that even a powerful tool like language cannot completely cure us, but rather brings us a little closer to understanding. A profound feeling, like fear, forces us toward finding words to dispel its unsettling effects. One may, need, as the saying goes, 'to talk it out." In this respect, *katharsis* may not dutifully arrive at the end of each play, but happen the very next morning, at the kitchen table, as we attempt to explain to another what has transpired within us. The important takeaway is that powerful emotional states like pity and fear (what Heidegger calls "attunements") move us from one emotional position to another; engendering, along the way, our need for further articulation, often between ourselves and others.

4. *Rasa* or the tasting emotions

We next turned East for an objective correlative to the West's uncomfortable relationship between thought and feeling. This brought us to the shores of Sanskrit drama, which defines the task of theater as the representation of emotional states and shows how, when these emotions (*bhava*) are experienced in their proper way, they can lead to a restoration of harmony in the lives of the audience. This is done through the theory of *rasa* (often translated as flavor) where we are once removed from the character's emotion so that we can experience the experiencing of the emotion (i.e., conscious of emotion as it manifests itself in a given character). The result is a subtle refinement of the Greek dramatic impulse and seems to draw upon a wider array of emotional possibilities than Aristotle's over-reliance on pity and fear. Here we find, in plays like *Rama's Last Act*, the investigation and development of other emotional states. One of the most important being the engendering of wonder in an audience. Although wonder couldn't be further from fear, both create profound sensations within the spectator that often escape language. This returns us to Heidegger's notion of works that engender a "desire for discourse." Here wonder, like fear, becomes such a tool, opening us to the necessity of further articulation and understanding. This alternative dramatic gambit is not restricted to the East. We can find this modality of expression in the West as well; albeit with only a handful of plays, most notably Euripides' *Alcestis* and the late romances of Shakespeare (think *The Winter's Tale*). All of these works point to wonder as being on equal footing with fear when it comes to the profound ways in which theater can move audiences toward new insights and ways of relating to the world at large.

5. The genealogy of fellow-feeling: from pity, through sympathy, and toward empathy

One thing that becomes clear when one begins to examine the history of fellow-feeling is how fluid this concept actually has been. Never static, the concept is constantly on the move. It shifts from the ancient notion of pity, where one feels for those who are less fortunate; to the long European reign of sympathy, where one feels with or alongside another; to our modern form of empathy, where one believes they can imaginatively project themselves into the lives of others, merging with them, and thereby seeing and feeling from their vantage point. It is intriguing to note that we have gone through something of a complete reversal in our relationship with emotion in the arts. Where emotion was once looked upon with suspicion by fifth-century Athenians; it is now, in the guise of empathy, completely accepted as the final arbiter of a work's success or failure. Even with such notable detractors as Bertolt Brecht and Edith Stein, both of whom were critical of empathy from its inception, this relatively young form of fellow-feeling continues to thrive in the new millennium. It would make a certain sense that a world that has retreated more and more from the public sphere and into the cocoon of the private would also move away from a more plural form of fellow-feeling like sympathy and gravitate to a more individualistic approach like empathy. But this shift comes with certain drawbacks that we are beginning to discover. Only recently has a new phase of doubt returned to question the efficacy of empathy.[1] Only time will tell if this emotional disposition will continue to reign supreme, or if some new form of fellow-feeling will come to take its place as we continue to navigate the demands of this new age.

Note

1 See Paul Bloom, *Against Empathy: The Case for Rational Compassion* (Ecco, 2016).

30

FINAL THOUGHTS ON FELLOW-FEELING AND THE MEANING OF THEATER

After witnessing the long march from pity through sympathy to empathy, we are inclined to agree with Aristotle and his Sanskrit counterparts that theater seems to work best when it blends emotion and reason together. When joined, these organs of comprehension form a unique kind of synesthesia where we can collectively feel a thought and think a feeling. The operative word here is "collectively," especially after we have bracketed out our modern penchant for empathy. For when we remove empathy from the theatrical equation, we can once again see clearly how theater has always has been a plural affair. Perhaps the greatest moment of theatrical ek-stasis is the realization that I am part of a much larger whole that is actually a "we" (the audience). And it is this engendering of fellow-feeling that becomes the very why of theater.

Human beings were not built to be alone and although each of us is resolutely singular, life only seems to make sense when it is connected and directed toward others. Theater reminds us of this simple fact. In this respect, theater is perhaps one of the closest intimations to Kant's oxymoron of a Subjective Universal; those rare moments when something profoundly touches us as an individual and yet we know, deep in our marrow, that this somehow touches us all. There is an extraordinary solace and power in such an awareness. One suspects that the very survival of humankind is wrapped up in this. It is a never-ending process; an attempt, across the ages, to resolve the essential tensions that always seem to emerge between such extraordinary opposites as our Self and the Other. Theater, when it is at its best, reminds us of the fundamental plurality of our existence. We are dislodged from our alienated "I" and momentarily returned to our social selves. Our concerns for our existence rhyme with others, and in that rhyming a community can be rediscovered.

It is at this juncture, and in relationship to this issue, that I feel compelled to step out from behind the curtain of this somewhat distanced authorial voice that I have affected and speak directly to the reader from my own personal experience.

I would like, with your indulgence, to share a short anecdote that speaks directly to this particular point. As a matter of fact, it this incident that was perhaps the real impetus for sitting down and writing the book you now hold in your hands. This realization of theater's unique power to engender a community out of an initial gathering of strangers was brought home to me with particular force several years ago when I was the Artistic Director of Classic Stage Company. We were doing a new play entitled *New Jerusalem*, written by the wonderful playwright David Ives. The play concerned itself with the excommunication of the philosopher Baruch Spinoza from the Jewish community of Amsterdam. The first act of the play has Spinoza defending himself before a rabbinical tribunal where things are looking rather grim for our young philosopher. Toward the end of the act Spinoza, rather off-handedly blurts out, "But I can prove the existence of God." The tribunal, is taken aback by the hubris of this statement, but agrees to hear out Spinoza's out-rageous claim; before doing so, however, the tribunal adjourns for a brief break, which coincides with the intermission of the play itself. This turned out to be one of the rare moments in my tenure at CSC where we never lost a single audience member during the break. Everyone returned: believers, atheists, and agnostics alike, all eager to hear this Jewish "kid" prove the existence of God. What followed, night after night, were perhaps the most sublime hours I've ever spent in the theater. The audiences returned, no longer strangers but now joined together in their mad pur-suit to understand. You could hear their shared attentiveness in the very silence that engulfed the room. A quality of silence one almost never hears in the theater these days. Believer, atheist, and agnostic all leaned forward, no one seemed to stir, as if holding their breath for what seemed like the entirety of the play's second act. This silence had the weight and density of a collective kind of listening that comes on those rare occasions when a group confronts an unresolved core issue. It is a silence born out of a communal need to know. And in such moments, we are reminded of the fundamental plurality of our existence.

Now I know what you are thinking, "Yes, yes, this is all very well and good, Brian, but *did Spinoza prove the existence of God?*" Not exactly, or at least not in the way we had hoped. But here's the truly interesting part: *it didn't matter.* What mattered was that we all sat in a room *together* and confronted the very limits of *our* own understanding! We were all humbled by the immensity of the question before us. And the immensity of this question, experienced together, was, in an almost alchemical fashion, transforming a room full of individuated I's into a unified we. The problem before us was not *my* problem, or *their* problem, but *our* problem. We were all brought together by the question, humbled by our shared inability to answer it. Because in theater the question is, oftentimes, much more important than the answer. Because sometimes we need to sit among one another, all in the same space, with an immense question to remind us that we are all in this together. And there, *right there*, in that instant of recognition, a community is born.

This sense of community that is discovered through theater is different from those moments of other social gatherings, say at a political rally or in a house of worship; because when theater really works (which is very rare) it allows us to collectively experience a question just before its answer is articulated by politics or religion. When theater is at its best, we find ourselves, for two hours or so, living within the tension of an unresolved question and discovering our commonality during that very suspension of knowingness. It is a shared experience of being before the immense density of certain fundamental problems that returns us to our basic commonality of *simply not knowing*. In this respect, the why of theater is directly related to all the whys in our lives that refuse pat answers; that demand more of our attention, time, and shared contemplation. In these moments several hundred or so disparate audience members feel as one, even over the destiny of a fictive Other. This returns us to Hamlet's question in regards to the Player King and, by extension, our very selves: What indeed is Hecuba to him or us, and we to Hecuba, that both he and we would weep for her? But weep we do, *even for the fictive beings* of the Ancient Greek tragedians, Shakespeare, or Chekhov.

Take, for example, Chekhov's *Three Sisters*. Here again the CSC audience returned act after act, giving over an unheard-of three and a half hours of their lives to see what would become of these poor unfortunate souls that populate Chekhov's provincial purgatory. By the fourth act, the same deep and attentive silence that I heard in the second act of *New Jerusalem* had returned to the theater. Two hundred audience members were, once again, night after night, breathing as one, all focused on the trajectory of each character on stage. It was as though they had been converted from audience members to recording angels, their job to bear witness to these poor Chekhovian souls who were incapable of changing their fate. We watched the dashing of each character's hope, like the snuffing out of a candle; collectively registering each of these extinguishments, one by one, until we could feel a palpable darkness descending, even though the stage lights told us it was still midday. The question before us was of a slightly different variety than that of *New Jerusalem*; less grand than the one posed by Spinoza, but still equally deep and mysterious. It was the question of what constitutes a life well-lived. And, even more mysterious, what happens when that idea fails to materialize in the way we envisioned it? What then? A question for Chekhov, his characters, oneself, and the person sitting on either side of us. In short, a question that is ultimately addressed to us all.

Again, in such moments, we can find ourselves released from our relativistic mode of empathy and returned to that much older, all embracing form of sympathy. Enabling us to feel "with" rather than "in." That simple, straightforward word, "with" enfolds myself, the fictive other, and an entire audience, all joined by a common concern. This is the power of theater and its gum-stuck machinery comes to life around those burning questions of existence, uniting us in the process as we confront the mysteries that life presents. What does La Fontaine say? "To cry for oneself is human; to cry for another, divine." Theater, this ancient, ancient form, still has the power to confer upon us the momentary possibility of divinity.

INDEX

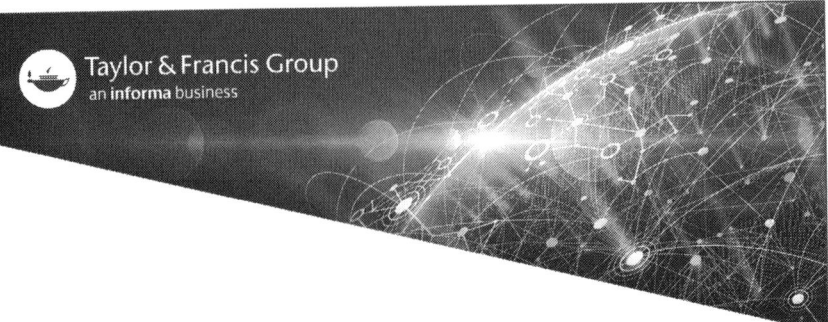
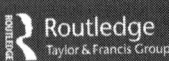
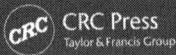